JOINT VENTURE PARTNER SELECTION

Recent Titles from Quorum Books

JOINT VENTURE PARTNER SELECTION

Strategies for Developed Countries

J. MICHAEL GERINGER
Foreword by J. Peter Killing

Q

QUORUM BOOKS
New York • Westport, Connecticut • London

Library of Congress Cataloging-in-Publication Data

Geringer, J. Michael (John Michael)
  Joint venture partner selection : strategies for developed
countries / J. Michael Geringer.
    p.   cm.
  Bibliography: p.
  Includes index.
  ISBN 0–89930–365–X (lib. bdg. : alk. paper)
  1. Joint ventures—United States.   2. Joint ventures.   I. Title.
KF1380.5.G47 1988
346.73'0682—dc19
[347.306682]   88–3107

British Library Cataloguing in Publication Data is available.

Library of Congress Catalog Card Number: 88–3107
ISBN: 0–89930–365–X

First published in 1988 by Quorum Books

Greenwood Press, Inc.
88 Post Road West, Westport, Connecticut 06881

Printed in the United States of America

The paper used in this book complies with the
Permanent Paper Standard issued by the National
Information Standards Organization (Z39.48–1984).

10 9 8 7 6 5 4 3 2 1

To my parents, Raymond and Jo Ann,
and to my wife, Colette Anne Frayne,
for their continued support and inspiration

Contents

Tables

Foreword

This book shines a very bright light on a single, sharply focused question: **How do executives in American firms go about selecting partners for joint ventures in developed countries?** The study is a powerful one because it draws on information collected by Michael Geringer in personal interviews with 101 executives who have been involved in the operation of more than 300 ventures over the past 40 years.

To executives who are skimming this foreword wondering whether or not Geringer's book, which presents the results of an academic study, contains practical, useful advice on the selection of joint venture partners, the answer is yes. I encourage you to read on. To researchers, wondering if Geringer's work has opened the door to new and important questions in an area of increasing academic interest, the answer is also yes. There is a lot of interesting work yet to be done.

Geringer's most lasting contribution is likely to be the very sharp line that he has drawn between the need to identify the skills and resources that a partner can potentially contribute to a joint venture, and the need to assess whether or not there will be effective co-operation between the firms in the venture. He suggests that two fundamental questions be addressed by a firm assessing a potential joint venture partner:

1. Would this partner bring needed skills and resources to the joint venture?
2. Would this partner and my own firm co-operate effectively?

Geringer argues that the first of these questions is always important, and the second will be more or less important depending on how closely the two firms are planning to work together. He reasons that effective co-operation between partners will be more important when environmental uncertainty is high, when the venture involves more rather than fewer functional areas (production, marketing, and so on) and when the partners are planning to share in the management of the venture.

NECESSARY SKILLS AND RESOURCES

This is usually the easier of the two questions for a firm to answer and, according to Geringer, it is usually answered first. He states that a positive response to this question is a "necessary but not sufficient" condition for a good partner choice. When considering whether or not a prospective partner has the required skills and resources, Geringer suggests the following questions:

1. What skills and resources will the joint venture need to be successful?
2. Which of these does your firm already possess?
3. Of the remaining required skills and resources, which could your firm most easily obtain?

The still outstanding skills and resources are those that the firm should look for in a partner. This logic seems sensible and straightforward; the challenge to venturing companies is to accurately assess the needs of the venture and each other's skills.

EFFECTIVE CO-OPERATION

Unless two firms have worked together before, it is usually very difficult to determine in advance how effectively they will be able to co-operate. Firms with no history of collaboration are well advised to begin their relationship with a minor project of some sort, so that they may get to know one another before attempting anything extremely demanding or financially significant. In Chapter 13 Geringer suggests that effective co-operation will be enhanced if

- the partners are of similar size
- the partners share similar objectives for the venture
- the partners have compatible operating policies
- there are a minimum of communication barriers between the firms
- the partners have compatible management teams
- there is a modest level of mutual dependence between the partners
- the partners develop a degree of trust and commitment

Because Geringer did not look at the performance of his ventures (in many cases they were too young for a meaningful assessment), these prescriptions must be taken as conjecture. In fact, they form a good base for future research.

WHAT NEXT?

I believe that the next step for anyone studying joint venture partner selection is to examine the link between the partner selection process, the characteristics of the partners and joint venture performance.

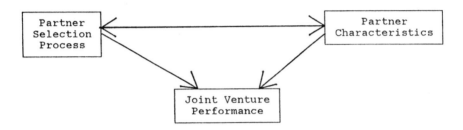

This three way diagram suggests a lot of interesting hypotheses. I shall mention only two of the most fundamental. Geringer emphasizes that the search for joint venture partners is time consuming and expensive. One of the first questions that must be addressed is whether or not firms that spend more time and effort in the search process do in fact end up with what look like, according to Geringer's criteria, more "suitable" partners. The more basic question is whether or not superior joint venture performance really does result when joint ventures are formed between apparently "suitable" partners.

A more complex question was recently posed by a European executive looking for a joint venture partner in the electronics field. The manager explained his situation as follows:

> We cannot find the perfect partner. [This is surely not an unusual occurrence.] One of the final candidates definitely has the required skills, but we have never worked together before and I am not sure if we will be able to work in harmony. The other firm is an old friend, but I am not entirely convinced that their development engineers will prove equal to the task ahead. Do you have any research that would tell us which choice is more likely to be successful?

The easy answer is to tell the executive to keep looking, but in the real world time is scarce, and perfect partners do not exist for every project.

Risks must be taken. The manager cannot wait for us, the academics, to catch up.

Because so many managers are having difficulty creating successful joint ventures, the challenge for researchers is clear. We need to produce solidly based, relevant, descriptions and prescriptions which will help managers as they attempt to create and manage joint ventures more successfully. Mike Geringer's book is a step in the right direction.

J. Peter Killing

Acknowledgments

I have been examining the design and management of joint ventures for over five years now. Developing an understanding of these ventures has only been possible through the assistance and direction of many individuals, who generously contributed their time and energies in helping me to formulate and defend my ideas. Among the people who played the most influential roles in developing and sharpening my thoughts, I wish to thank the following: Professor Richard Moxon, who first exposed me to the concept of interfirm strategies and encouraged me to break new ground on the topic; Professor Charles Summer, a pioneer in the field of strategy, whose exceptional conceptual abilities and leadership acumen helped me see the underlying order in a seemingly disorganized environment; and Professor Don Beard, who always found time in a busy schedule to provide invaluable assistance on issues of strategy and effective research methodology. Without the assistance of these three scholars, this project would not have been possible.

My deepest appreciation is also extended to the following individuals who provided materials, suggestions, and comments on the manuscript at various stages of its development: Tom Roehl, Fred Truitt, Tom Jones, Cecil Bell, Tom Lee, Bill Scott, Jody Fry, Johny Johanssen, Terry Mitchell, Dennis Strong, Hugh Blalock, Kozo Yamamura, and Reza Moinpoir, all of the University of Washington; Dick Osborn, Wayne State University; Jeff Gale, Loyola; John Reynolds, Texas A & M; Bill Tomlinson, University of British Columbia; Peter Killing and Paul Beamish, University of Western Ontario; Jean Louis Schaan, University of Ottawa; Peter Lorange, Wharton School; and Johan Roos, Stockholm School of Economics.

Studies such as this typically require extensive resources and this study has been no exception. I would like to thank the Edna Benson Foundation and Touche-Ross for their assistance in providing the financial resources necessary for this project's completion. Similarly, in recognition of their critical assistance, my thanks go to the libraries and librarians of the University of California, Harvard University, Indiana University, the Library of Congress, the University of Pennsylvania, Southern Methodist University, and the University of Washington; the schools and graduate schools of business at the University of Washington, the University of Western Ontario, and Southern Methodist University. Data collection was facilitated by the generous assistance of the following people, who contributed lodging, friendship, contacts, or other forms of support: Rick Moss, Kevin Hennings, Paula Angel and Randy Jones, Patty and Joe Ketner, Don Gates, Jay Geringer, and Jack and Lucille Frayne. Special thanks are also due to Wanda Hanson, Hazel Seabolt, and Marg Reffle for their assistance in typing the tables, and to Jane Clark for her tireless efforts in helping me overcome administrative hurdles throughout the past five years.

Collection of the research data would not have been possible without the generous assistance of the executives who consented to participate anonymously in this study. They completed questionnaires, supplied archival data, and volunteered precious time for personal interviews and other activities associated with this study. Only through their willingness to openly and candidly discuss their own experiences, both successes and failures, could a book like this be written. This type of assistance and enthusiasm is critical for effectively conducting relevant academic research on managerial issues. To these individuals, I extend my deepest appreciation.

Finally, there are the "special" people who have enabled me to truly enjoy the pursuit of knowledge and new understandings. I would like to thank Kit, whose companionship has been invaluable, and Rick Moss, who has remained a devoted and trusted friend throughout the years. I would also like to thank my family, especially my parents, for their encouragement and support in all of my endeavors. And finally, I would like to thank my wife and friend, Colette Frayne. She, more than anyone else, fully appreciates the many joys and frustrations associated with conducting the research reported in this book.

I

INTRODUCTION, HYPOTHESES, AND METHOD

1

Introduction

COLLABORATION AS A PERVASIVE PHENOMENON

In a world of limited resources, interdependence is the norm. Throughout history, humans have engaged in collaborative efforts of one form or another in an attempt to overcome resource constraints and to manage interdependence. Recognizing the potential benefits which may derive from working together, humans have utilized collaboration in nearly every aspect of their lives, including religion, politics, journalism, education, sports, and warfare. From the Crusades to the Constitution, *The Pentagon Papers* to public schools, baseball to the Balkan Wars, people have collaborated.

Collaborative efforts have been extensive in the business world as well. Many different contractual or organizational forms of collaboration have been employed in business, ranging from options which may require relatively low levels of interaction, such as spot sales and contractual supply agreements, to those entailing complete integration of separate entities, such as mergers.

While it may be said that the potential benefits of collaboration have long been recognized, the potential drawbacks of such activity must also be acknowledged. By definition, collaboration refers not only to "the act of performing work or labor together," but also to "co-operation with the enemy," where "enemy" refers to "a person who hates another, and wishes or tries to injure him."[1] Thus, the decision to collaborate with one or more partners may appear to be a double-edged sword, capable of both aiding and injuring those who combine efforts in a collaborative venture.

This book examines one particular type of collaborative activity which has occurred with some frequency in the business world: namely, the joint venture. The discussion focuses on the criteria that organizations have employed in selecting partners for joint ventures and on several variables that may evidence a relationship with these criteria. As used herein, a joint venture is defined as a discrete entity created by two or more legally distinct organizations (the partners), each of which contributes less than 100 percent of its assets and actively participates, beyond a mere investment role, in the joint venture's decision making.

AGGREGATE LEVEL OF JOINT VENTURE ACTIVITY

Joint ventures represent a relatively small, yet significant, component of world economic activity. Although no comprehensive accounting exists, perusal of figures from several sources can provide an indication of the frequency of joint venture formation. For example, the U.S. Federal Trade Commission recorded 2,287 new joint ventures from 1964 to 1975.[2] The U.S. Commerce Department's Office of Trade and Investment Analysis found that, out of 1,145 reported foreign direct investments made in the United States in 1982, 79 of these were joint ventures.[3] A recent survey conducted for the Conference Board suggested that the majority of Fortune 500 corporations were involved in at least one international joint venture and, further, that the frequency of these projects might be increasing.[4] Over half of the respondents to the latter survey had initiated one or more joint ventures in the preceding five years, and approximately one-third of the respondents also reported that their international joint venture formation rate had risen during this time. Consistent with these findings, researchers extrapolating from data on a sample of 106 American corporations estimated total U.S. experience by the mid–1970s to be approximately 25,000 joint ventures.[5]

The preceding figures provide an indication of the extent of joint venture activity in the United States or engaged in by predominantly U.S.-based organizations. However, these data may not accurately reflect the extent of joint venture activity worldwide. Citing data on ownership patterns of foreign affiliates of multinational corporations, several authors have contended that firms from other nations have historically exhibited a greater proclivity toward the use of joint ventures than have U.S.-based firms.[6] For example, the data in Table 1 show that only 34.0 percent of the foreign affiliates of the sampled U.S.-based corporations were joint ventures, whereas the proportion of Europe-based and Japan-based corporations' foreign affiliates which were joint ventures were 43.6 percent and 89.9 percent, respectively. Therefore, this table suggests not only that joint ventures are relatively common, but also that the worldwide frequency of joint ventures may exceed the level suggested by the U.S.-based data.

Table 1
Foreign Manufacturing Subsidiaries of 391 Multinational Enterprises, Classified by Ownership Patterns

Country and owner-ship patterns	180 U.S.-based enterprises (a)		135 Europe- and U.K.-based enterprises		61 Japan-based enterprises		All 391 enterprises in sample(c)	
	No.	%	No.	%	No.	%	No.	%
IN ALL COUNTRIES								
Total subsidiaries	5727	100.0	4661	100.0	562	100.0	9601	100.0
Wholly owned(b)	3730	65.1	2278	48.9	34	6.0	4907	51.1
Majority-owned	1223	21.4	1320	28.3	74	13.2	2177	22.7
Minority-owned	723	12.6	712	15.3	431	76.7	1537	16.0
Unknown	51	0.9	351	7.5	23	4.1	980	10.2
IN INDUSTRIALIZED COUNTRIES								
Total subsidiaries	3603	100.0	3207	100.0	46	100.0	6060	100.0
Wholly owned	2612	72.5	1788	55.7	6	13.0	3634	60.0
Majority-owned	657	18.2	802	25.0	8	17.4	1260	20.8
Minority-owned	302	8.4	404	12.6	30	65.2	626	10.3
Unknown	32	0.9	213	6.6	2	4.3	540	8.9
IN DEVELOPING COUNTRIES								
Total subsidiaries	2124	100.0	1454	100.0	516	100.0	3541	100.0
Wholly owned	1118	52.6	490	33.7	28	5.4	1273	36.0
Majority-owned	566	26.6	518	35.6	66	12.8	917	25.9
Minority-owned	421	19.8	308	21.2	401	77.7	911	25.7
Unknown	19	0.9	138	9.5	21	4.1	440	12.4

Source: Harvard Multinational Enterprise Project.
(a) Data for U.S.-based enterprises are provisional, as of 1975; others are final, as of 1970.
(b) Subsidiaries of which the immediate parent in the system owns 95 percent or more are classified as wholly owned; 50 percent or more, as majority-owned; 5 to 49 percent as minority-owned.
(c) Includes 15 multinational enterprises based elsewhere than in the United States, Europe and the United Kingdom, or Japan.

Source: Vernon, Raymond, *Storm Over the Multinationals* (Cambridge, Mass: Harvard University Press, 1977), p. 34. Reprinted by permission.

INFLUENCE OF JOINT VENTURES ON INDUSTRY STRUCTURE, CONDUCT, AND PERFORMANCE

Joint ventures are an important phenomenon for study not only because they occur frequently, but also because the presence or potential development of joint ventures may have important effects on the structure, conduct, and performance within and between industries. The work of numerous researchers supports the contention that joint ventures may frequently be utilized by organizations in an effort to manage environmental interdependence and uncertainty through controlling, influencing, or reducing competition and/or influencing suppliers.[7] Although the focus of these prior analyses was primarily restricted to effects within a single nation, many of their conclusions regarding potential anticompetitive effects seem to apply across national borders as well.[8]

In contrast to these findings, however, the work of several proponents has heralded the possible procompetitive effects of joint ventures, including the creation of new competitors and the reduction of the time required to develop and introduce new products and processes.[9]

IMPORTANCE OF PARTNER SELECTION

As previously stated, joint ventures may affect the nature of competition within and between industries. The extent of this effect will depend, in part, on the performance of the joint venture. In this regard, the work of several researchers has suggested that the choice of a partner may be an important variable influencing the joint venture's resulting performance.[10]

Not only may choice of partner influence joint venture performance, but the partner selection process itself has frequently been characterized as fraught with difficulty.[11] Therefore, it seems imperative that the relevant stakeholders, including potential partners, existing and potential competitors, suppliers, customers, and public policy makers, attempt to develop an understanding of the mechanism by which joint venture partners are selected, including identification of the key variables that may influence this process and the anticipated effects such variables may produce.

STATEMENT OF THE PROBLEM

Despite the apparent importance of joint venture partner selection, the literature relevant to this issue is noticeably meager. As will be discussed in Chapter 2, few researchers have directly addressed the topic, and the empirical studies that have been conducted have typically been hindered by methodological problems or by a narrow research focus which limits the general applicability of the results. At present, there is no well-developed conceptual framework outlining the mechanism by which joint venture partners are selected. This can limit the understanding of the process by the relevant stakeholder groups, and thereby hinder efforts to influence the outcome of the process. Our objective in undertaking this research was to enhance the level of understanding of the partner selection process through the collection and interpretation of empirical data regarding joint venture partner selection criteria. Therefore, our research attempted to examine one component of the mechanism by which partners are selected for joint ventures. Specifically, the discussion will examine the selection criteria valences that organizations have employed when selecting joint venture partners, as well as the relationship of several variables from the strategic management literature to these selection criteria valences.

DEFINITION OF KEY VARIABLES

Selection Criteria and Valences

The concept of a "criterion" refers to "a standard of judging; any established law, rule, principle, or fact by which a correct judgment may be formed."[12] Criteria are an essential prerequisite to any decision, including the selection of joint venture partners, although the internal logic and the degree of explicitness of criteria may vary.

A key variable in this study will be one dimension of joint venture partner selection criteria: namely, the valences that organizations assign to the criteria. As used here, the term "valence" refers to relative importance or priority. Knowledge of how organizations evaluate prospective criteria, and assign valences to them, is integral to understanding the selection of partners and requires the identification of the principal variable(s) that may influence the selection criteria valences.

Strategy

To discuss the concept of strategy and its relationship to partner selection criteria and their valences, the meaning of the concept should be clarified. Although no single accepted definition of strategy exists, "strategy is generally viewed as a pattern of important decisions that (1) guides the organization in its relationships with its environment, (2) affects the internal structure and processes of the organization, and (3) centrally affects the organization's performance."[13]

The strategic management literature frequently refers to the existence of three hierarchical levels of strategy—corporate, business, and functional. The distinction between these levels typically centers on the relative comprehensiveness of coverage. In this regard, corporate strategy represents the most comprehensive and overarching construct, and functional strategy represents the least. Kenneth Andrews defined corporate strategy as the decisions regarding "the businesses in which a company will compete," whereas business strategy "is the determination of how a company will compete in a given business and position itself among its competitors."[14] Functional strategy involves the development of "'annual objectives and short-range strategies" and "the implementation or execution of the company's strategic plans."[15] Consistent with these definitions, it is apparent that the decision to consider the joint venture option, and thus to assign selection criteria valences, would be classified as elements of business level strategy-making. Therefore, our use of the term "strategy" will refer to business level strategy.

LIMITATIONS ON THE SCOPE OF STUDY

To restrict our study's scope to manageable proportions, it was necessary to impose several limitations on the population of potentially qualifying joint ventures. The first limitation concerns the nationality of the joint venture's primary target market. It has been suggested that the joint venture process in industrially developed market countries may be different than in industrializing or non-market countries, in terms of motivation for joint venture formation, availability and types of partners, and the typical division of equity, among other factors.[16] Therefore, the study was limited to joint ventures having a primary target market which included, but may not have been restricted to, one or more of the developed countries.[17] The partners to the joint venture may have been from other nations besides the developed countries, however, and the operations of the joint venture may also have been located elsewhere.

Due to resource and language constraints, we restricted the scope of our analysis to organizations, or their subsidiaries, which located both their legal base of incorporation and their primary joint venture partner selection criteria decision making activities in the United States.

In order to control for any variation that might result from the number of partners in a venture, we limited our focus to joint ventures which comprised only two partners, or bilateral joint ventures. In addition, no more than 75 percent of the venture's total initial equity may have been held by either partner. In general, a higher concentration of equity was perceived to reflect a minority investment project, rather than a joint venture and its characteristic give-and-take operational format.

Another requirement for inclusion in this study was that final agreement for the joint venture must have been reached no earlier than January 1, 1979. This arbitrary cutoff date was chosen because it enhanced the likelihood that the person(s) involved in developing the joint venture partner selection criteria would still be employed with the parent organization of the joint venture, and that the desired information on selection criteria would still be "fresh" enough. Because the passage of time tends to compromise both of these points, and because selection criteria are sometimes developed several years before the final joint venture agreement is ultimately concluded, this study did not examine joint ventures consummated before 1979. Joint ventures which were pursued wholly or in part during 1979 or later, but which were not consummated, qualified for inclusion if the interviewees perceived that the selection criteria had been sufficiently developed to have been operational for the organization. An organization which engaged in a qualifying joint venture was considered for inclusion in this study even if the joint venture had subsequently been terminated due to liquidation, sale, or absorption into one or both of the partners' organizations.

In those cases in which both partners from a qualifying joint venture satisfied the above constraints, each of the partner organizations qualified for inclusion in the sample.

ORGANIZATION OF REMAINING CHAPTERS

In this chapter we have introduced the research focus of the study—joint venture partner selection criteria and their relative importance, or valences. We have also presented the rationale for examining this topic, defined the principal terminology that will be used, and discussed limitations on the research scope. Chapter 2 reviews prior literature which has addressed the topic of joint venture partner selection. The third chapter discusses several variables which may bear a relationship to partner selection criteria valences, and the hypothesized relationships that were expected to be observed. The fourth chapter outlines the methodology that was used for data collection and testing of the research hypotheses. The research results and their interpretation are reported in chapters 5 through 11. Chapter 12 presents the conclusions that were derived from the study, Chapter 13 discusses implications of the results, and Chapter 14 evaluates the research method we employed and provides suggestions for future research on the topic of joint venture partner selection.

NOTES

1. *Webster's Deluxe Unabridged Dictionary*, 2d ed. (New York: Simon & Schuster, 1983), pp. 354 and 601, respectively.

2. Sanford V. Berg, Jerome Duncan, and Philip Friedman, *Joint Venture Strategies and Corporate Innovation* (Cambridge, Mass.: Oelgeschlager, Gunn & Hain, 1982), p. 13.

3. U.S. Department of Commerce, International Trade Administration, *Foreign Direct Investment in the United States: 1982 Transactions*, February, 1984, p. 17.

4. Allen R. Janger, *Organization of International Joint Ventures* (New York: The Conference Board, 1980).

5. G. Richard Young and Standish Bradford, Jr., *Joint Ventures: Planning and Action* (New York: Financial Executives Research Foundation, 1977), p. 5.

6. Lawrence G. Franko, *The European Multinationals* (London: Harper & Row, 1976); Joseph La Palombara and Stephen Blank, *Multinational Corporations and National Elites: A Study in Tensions* (New York: The Conference Board, 1977); Raymond Vernon, *Storm over the Multinationals* (Cambridge, Mass.: Harvard University Press, 1977); Neil Hood and Stephen Young, *The Economics of Multinational Enterprise* (New York: Longman, 1979); J. Peter Killing, *Strategies for Joint Venture Success* (New York: Praeger, 1983).

7. Daniel R. Fusfield, "Joint Subsidiaries in the Iron and Steel Industry," *American Economic Review* (May, 1958), pp. 578–87; Michael Bergman, "The Corporate Joint Venture under the Antitrust Laws," *New York University Law Review* 37 (1962), p. 711; Paul Rand Dixon, "Joint Ventures: What Is Their Impact on Competition?" *Antitrust Bulletin* (May–June, 1962), pp. 397–410; Lewis Bernstein, "Joint Ventures in the Light of Recent Antitrust Developments: Anti-Competitive Joint Ventures," *Antitrust Bulletin* (January–April, 1965), pp. 25–29; Walter J. Mead, "The Competitive Significance of Joint Ventures," *Antitrust Bulletin* 12 (Fall, 1967), pp. 819–49; Stanley Boyle, "An Estimate of the Number and Size Distribution of Domestic Joint Subsidiaries," *Antitrust Law and Economic Review* (Spring, 1968), pp. 81–92; J. L. Pate, "Joint Venture Activity, 1960–1968," *Economic Review*, Federal Reserve Bank of Cleveland (1969), pp. 16–23; John W. Wilson, "Market Structure and Interfirm Integration in the Petroleum Industry," *Journal of Economic Issues* (June, 1975), pp. 319–35; David S. Schwartz, "Comments on 'Market-Structure and Interfirm Integration,' " *Journal of Economic Issues* (June, 1975), pp. 337–40; Joseph F. Brodley, "The Legal Status of Joint Ventures under the Antitrust Laws: A Summary Assessment," *Antitrust Bulletin* (Fall, 1976), pp. 453–83; Jeffrey Pfeffer and Phillip Nowak, "Joint Ventures and Interorganizational Interdependence," *Administrative Science Quarterly* (September, 1976), pp. 398–418; William M. Landes, "Harm to Competition: Cartels, Mergers and Joint Ventures" (Summer, 1983), pp. 625–35; Kathryn Rudie Harrigan, "Joint Ventures and Global Strategies," *Columbia Journal of World Business* 19, no. 2 (Summer, 1984), pp. 7–16.

8. John C. Berghoff, "Antitrust Aspects of Joint Ventures," *Antitrust Bulletin* (March–April, 1964), pp. 231–54; Joseph F. Brodley, "Joint Ventures and the Justice Department's Antitrust Guide for International Operations," *Antitrust Bulletin* 24 (Summer, 1979), pp. 337–56; Joseph F. Brodley, "The Legal Status of Joint Ventures under the Antitrust Laws"; Frederick M. Rowe, "Antitrust Aspects of European Acquisitions and Joint Ventures in the United States," *Law and Policy in International Business* 12, no. 2 (1980), pp. 335–68.

9. Jules Bachman, "Joint Ventures and the Antitrust Laws," *New York University Law Review* 40 (1965); Jules Bachman, "Joint Ventures in the Light of Recent Antitrust Developments: Joint Ventures in the Chemical Industry," *Antitrust Bulletin* 10 (January–April, 1965), pp. 7–23; Joseph F. Brodley, "The Legal Status of Joint Ventures under the Antitrust Laws"; Lee Adler and James D. Hlavacek, *Joint Ventures for Product Innovation* (New York: American Management Associations, 1976); James D. Hlavacek, Brian Dovey, and John Biondo, "Tie Small Business Technology to Marketing Power," *Harvard Business Review* (January–February, 1977), pp. 106–16; Berg, Duncan, and Friedman, *Joint Venture Strategies and Corporate Innovation*.

10. Malcolm W. West, Jr., "Thinking Ahead," *Harvard Business Review* (July–August, 1959), pp. 31–32; Charles de Houghton, *Cross-Channel Collaboration* (London: PEP, 1966); James W. C. Tomlinson and M. Thompson, "A Study of Canadian

Joint Ventures in Mexico," working paper, College of Commerce and Business Administration, University of British Columbia, 1977; Stephen M. Hills, "The Search for Joint Venture Partners," in Jeffrey C. Susbauer, ed., *Academy of Management Proceedings* (1978), pp. 277–81; Richard B. Peterson and Justin Y. Shimada, "Sources of Management Problems in Japanese-American Joint Ventures," *Academy of Management Review* (October, 1978), pp. 796–804; John I. Reynolds, *Indian–American Joint Ventures: Business Policy Relationships* (Washington, D.C.: University Press of America, 1979); Ram K. Vepa, *Joint Ventures* (New Delhi: Manohar Publications, 1980); Sanford V. Berg and Philip Friedman, "Corporate Courtship and Successful Joint Ventures," *California Management Review* (Spring, 1980), pp. 35–51; Janger, *Organization of International Joint Ventures*; Philippe Lasserre, "Selecting a Foreign Partner for Technology Transfer," *Long Range Planning* (December, 1984), pp. 43–49; John Walmsley, *Handbook of International Joint Ventures* (London: Graham and Trotman, 1982); Killing, "How to Make a Global Joint Venture Work"; F. Simiar, "Major Causes of Joint-Venture Failures in the Middle East: The Case of Iran," *Management International Review* 23, no. 1 (1983), pp. 58–68; F. Kingston Berlew, "The Joint Venture—A Way into Foreign Markets," *Harvard Business Review* (July–August, 1984), pp. 48–54; Robert J. Radway, *Joint Ventures in Mexico* (New York: American Management Association, 1984); Kathryn Rudie Harrigan, "Coalition Strategies: A Framework for Joint Ventures," working paper, Columbia University, 1984; Harrigan, "Joint Ventures"; Michael E. Porter and Mark B. Fuller, "Coalitions and Global Strategy," in Michael E. Porter, *Competition in Global Industries* (Boston: Harvard Business School Press, 1986), pp. 315–43; Paul W. Beamish, *Multinational Joint Ventures in Developing Countries* (London: Croom Helm, 1988).

11. de Houghton, *Cross-Channel Collaboration*; K. K. Bivens and E. B. Lovell, *Joint Ventures with Foreign Partners* (New York: National Industrial Conference Board, 1966); Reynolds, *Indian-American Joint Ventures*; Killing, "How to Make a Global Joint Venture Work"; Berlew, "The Joint Venture."

12. *Webster's*, p. 432.

13. Donald C. Hambrick, "Operationalizing the Concept of Business-Level Strategy in Research," *Academy of Management Review* 5, no. 4 (1980), p. 567.

14. Kenneth Andrews, *The Concept of Corporate Strategy* (Homewood, Ill.: Richard D. Irwin, 1971), pp. 18–19.

15. John A. Pearce, II, and Richard B. Robinson, Jr., *Strategic Management: Strategy Formulation and Implementation* (Homewood, Ill.: Irwin, 1982), p. 7.

16. Tomlinson and Thompson, "A Study of Canadian Joint Ventures in Mexico"; Stefan H. Robock, Kenneth Simmonds, and Jack Zwick, *International Business and Multinational Enterprises* (Homewood, Ill.: Irwin, 1977); Beamish, *Multinational Joint Ventures*.

17. Consistent with the World Bank, *World Development Report 1984* (New York: Oxford University Press, 1984), p. ix, industrially developed countries with market-based economies include Australia, Austria, Belgium, Canada, Denmark, the Federal Republic of Germany, Finland, France, Iceland, Ireland, Italy, Japan, Luxembourg, The Netherlands, New Zealand, Norway, Spain, Sweden, Switzerland, the United Kingdom, and the United States.

2

Review of Selection Criteria Literature

As pointed out in Chapter 1, the issue of partner selection has received insufficient attention in the literature on joint ventures. In general, prior studies either have been characterized by a total absence of direct reference to partner selection, or the issue has been accorded only one or a few sentences. Even when mentioned, the selection of partners was typically treated as a given.

The review provided in this chapter is intended to highlight the findings of prior research that has examined partner selection criteria, including the potential contributions and limitations of these studies.

ALTERNATIVE APPROACHES EXAMINING PARTNER SELECTION CRITERIA

From analysis of the previous studies that have addressed the issue, it is possible to distinguish three principal approaches used to examine partner selection criteria. These approaches can be categorized as (1) studies which attempt to derive partner selection criteria from stated motivations for forming a joint venture, (2) studies which attempt to derive partner selection criteria from examination of the characteristics of partners ultimately chosen for a joint venture, and (3) studies which directly examine the selection criteria that firms have employed. Each of these approaches will be examined individually.

Approach 1: Derivation from Stated Motivations

The first approach used for examining partner selection criteria typically lists the stated motivations for engaging in a joint venture and then implies that selection criteria can be readily derived therefrom. Although knowledge of an organization's motives for forming a joint venture may provide insights into the selection criteria it employed, the usefulness of this approach may be limited by two potential drawbacks. First, the validity of this approach may be questionable since the stated motivations for entering into a particular joint venture may provide inadequate insight into the decision to select a particular partner. In those cases in which motivations are broadly stated, so that several different organizations have the basic qualifications necessary for achieving the joint venture objectives, knowledge of the dominant motivations for pursuing a joint venture may be of minimal assistance in discerning the rationale for selecting one prospective partner rather than another. For instance, suppose a firm's stated motivation for joint venture formation is to "strengthen its presence in European markets." Knowledge of this motivation provides little guidance into whether the firm will tend to seek a partner who embodies technological capabilities, who has a complementary product line, who has a perceived identity as a European company, who has a strong marketing or distribution system, or who has some other trait or combination of traits. Therefore, knowledge of a firm's motives for forming a joint venture may offer only limited assistance in understanding the selection criteria that were, or will be, employed.

A stronger criticism of this first approach is that there may be an incentive for management to state motivations that are misleading or totally inaccurate. To illustrate, Stanley Boyle noted two major classes of joint venture motives: technical and power.[1] Where the power motive reigns supreme, and where antitrust proscriptions or other factors inhibit the overt pursuit of such objectives, the incentive for reporting secondary or irrelevant motives will be increased. Under these circumstances, it would be difficult or impossible to use stated motivations as the basis for accurately identifying the partner selection criteria employed by an organization.

The considerations outlined above seriously hamper the efficacy of this first approach, which attempts to derive partner selection criteria from the stated motivations for forming a joint venture.

Approach 2: Derivation from Partner Characteristics

A second approach to the identification of partner selection criteria attempts to deduce these criteria through an examination of the characteristics of the selected partners. This approach typically entails the use of secondary data, frequently general in nature and in aggregated form, on organizations currently or previously engaged in joint ventures.[2] These data are then analyzed in an attempt to describe general characteristics of joint venture partners, with the implication that the observed characteristics reflect the selection criteria that were employed.

Deductive reasoning from the traits of joint venture partners may have limited usefulness in attempting to develop a thorough understanding of the assignment of criteria valences and the selection of partners, however. There may be a significant distinction between the outcomes that are ultimately obtained from the partner selection process and the selection criteria that were originally developed and applied by the organization. For instance, sometimes suitable partners are unavailable, or sometimes they are unwilling to participate in a joint venture with the organization. We encountered several instances where organizations reported an inability to conclude a joint venture agreement with their top two or three partner choices. Under these circumstances, relying on characteristics of the partners ultimately participating in a joint venture may result in misleading conclusions regarding the selection criteria valences which were employed.

Another potential drawback of this second approach is that, even if an organization were able to elicit the participation of its top partner choice, a researcher may be unable to discern which characteristics were actively sought or to determine the relative valence of each. Some partner characteristics may "come with the territory" and not be traits on which selection was based, or they may be only tangentially related to the selection decision. Other characteristics may have been more actively sought in a partner, but the relative importance (valence) of one characteristic vis-a-vis another cannot be accurately discerned from analysis of aggregate *ex post* data.

This second approach may provide insights into the joint venture partner selection process through its ability to identify general characteristics or trends of joint ventures and their partners. It may also be attractive to researchers because of the relative ease of accessing the necessary information, particularly via the use of secondary data sources. However, due to the limitations stated above, attempts to deduce criteria valences from data on characteristics of partners ultimately selected can result in misleading conclusions regarding the criteria valences that were employed by organizations when they selected joint venture partners. Therefore, the validity of the results and conclusions obtained from employing this second approach may be questionable.

Approach 3: Direct Examination of Partner Selection Criteria

Recognizing the limitations inherent in the two research approaches described above, the third approach for examining partner selection criteria has entailed the collection of data specifically on the selection criteria developed by organizations. Since it is the method that we employed in our study, the principal previous research efforts utilizing this third approach are reviewed below. After discussing the contributions and limitations of these previous efforts, conclusions regarding the usefulness of this third approach will be presented.

The first example of this third approach is the seminal study conducted by James W. C. Tomlinson.[3] During 1967, Tomlinson interviewed executives from a non-random sample of 49 British firms, collecting information on a total of 71 joint ventures in India and Pakistan. One objective of this study was to examine the criteria employed by the British firms in selecting joint venture partners. Tomlinson found that the selection of a partner generally constituted a distinct and separable decision in the joint venture formation process, which facilitated his research efforts.

Tomlinson examined six categories of selection criteria, which are listed and described in Table 2. Of these categories, favorable past association was cited as being the single most important reason for selecting a particular partner. Although less important than past association, the four selection criteria categories of facilities, resources, partner status, and forced choice were listed as being approximately equal in importance as primary selection criteria. Tomlinson's results suggested that the final selection criteria category, local identity, was seldom a primary criterion for selecting a joint venture partner. In addition to examining the relative importance of potential selection criteria, Tomlinson investigated the possibility of identifying a set of variables which might help predict the selection criteria used for particular joint ventures, specifically for joint ventures in India and Pakistan. Eight groups of variables were examined for possible relationships to partner selection criteria, including:

1. Size and profitability of British parent firms
2. The nature of the business involved
3. British parent firms' attitudes toward control
4. Variables describing various features of the background
5. Motivations for forming a joint venture
6. Reasons for selecting a specific partner
7. Structural characteristics of the joint ventures
8. Internal and external evaluation criteria used

Of these variables, Tomlinson found that parent size, nature of the business (categorized as oil, chemicals, engineering, electricals, vehicles, metals, or tobacco/food), and stated motivation for forming the joint venture exhibited the strongest relationship to the partner selection criteria that were subsequently employed for particular joint ventures.

Tomlinson's study, a truly pioneering effort, has provided several valuable insights into the joint venture partner selection process; however, the generalizability of Tomlinson's results to joint ventures in developed countries may be hindered by several factors. First, his study focused solely on joint ventures by British firms in India and Pakistan, and these joint ventures were almost exclusively oriented toward serving local markets in these two less developed countries. In addition, the accuracy of his data may be limited by the likelihood that some of the interviewees had not been involved in

Table 2
Partner Selection Criteria Categories Measured by Tomlinson

Criterion	Definition
Forced	Cases in which the choice is effectively forced upon the foreign investor whether because of explicit host government direction or indirectly because the associate preempts an exclusive license.
Facilities	Convenience to the foreign partner of local facilities under the control of the associate. Among these would be a site or plant, marketing or distributive facilities, or a strong market position; cases in which the associate was already in the same line of business as that of the proposed joint venture.
Resources	Convenience of local sources of managerial and technical personnel, materials, components, or local capital which can be contributed by the associate.
Status	Status and capability of the associate in dealing with local authorities and public relations. This subset would also include status defined in terms of general financial and business soundness and standing.
Past	Favorable past association with the associate when the latter had been an agent, licensee, major customer, or partner in a previous joint venture. The category includes special cases in which there might have been strong personal contacts between individuals in the foreign and local parent companies, possibly even individuals common to both.
Identity	Cases in which a partner would be chosen chiefly to obtain local identity, often through association with a potential "sleeping partner."

Source: Tomlinson, James W. C., *The Joint Venture Process in International Business: India and Pakistan* (Cambridge, Mass.: MIT Press, 1970), pp. 47–48. Reprinted by permission.

the selection of partners. Since several of the joint ventures had been formed twenty or more years before the interviews were conducted, the prospects for obtaining accurate information regarding partner selection criteria were diminished even if the executives *had* been participants in the selection process. Furthermore, Tomlinson's selection criteria and "nature of business" variables both suffered from a lack of conceptual distinctness, due to their highly aggregated natures and the lack of mutually exclusive categories, thus limiting the practical application of the results.

Research conducted by Tomlinson and M. Thompson examined Canadian firms' joint venture experiences in Mexico.[4] Drawing from interview data, these authors listed five traits that Canadian firms should seek in Mexican joint venture partners: financial status, business compatibility, common goals, ability to negotiate with the government, and compatible ethics. In addition, seven traits sought by Mexican firms in foreign partners were identified: financial resources, technology and experience in its application, international visibility and reputation, commitment to the Mexican joint venture, international experience, management depth, and the ability to communicate with Mexicans.

As with Tomlinson's earlier study, the generalizability of Tomlinson and Thompson's results to developed country joint ventures may be limited somewhat by their geographic focus: joint ventures in Mexico. In addition, their study did not indicate the relative frequency or intensity with which the previously stated traits were sought by either Mexican or Canadian firms, further hindering the applicability of their results for our study.

Another study which focused on partner selection criteria was William E. Renforth's examination of the joint venture process between U.S. multinational corporations and local family or non-family firms in Jamaica and in Trinidad and Tobago.[5] The international division manager in each U.S. parent's home office rated eleven possible criteria according to their relative importance in the selection of foreign joint venture partners. The results showed that the U.S. corporations appeared to have distinct criteria regarding desirable characteristics of partners, with varying levels of importance attributed to each criterion. On the basis of the responses, Renforth divided the selection criteria into three groups: those with strong, mild, or no influence on the selection decision. These results, along with the means and standard deviations for each criterion, are presented in Table 3. Renforth did not, however, document any explicit attempts to identify variables which might influence the relative valence that firms applied to each criterion.

The usefulness of Renforth's results for developed country joint ventures may be constrained by several factors. First, the geographic focus of his sample—two nations in the Caribbean Basin—may pose a significant limitation to generalizability. Another potential drawback was that, apparently, his respondents assigned valences with respect to hypothetical joint ventures, rather than the actual joint ventures that constituted the remainder of the study, which might have introduced some degree of artificiality into the responses. A more serious limitation, however, was that the criteria did not exhibit statistically significant differences in means when evaluated at even a 0.10 level. Therefore, the validity of his classification of criteria into strong, mild, and no influence categories is questionable.

In an examination of foreign direct manufacturing investment in the United States, John D. Daniels also examined investments made by joint ventures.[6] Although the coverage of joint ventures was abbreviated, the results enabled Daniels to conclude that firms seek similarly sized organi-

Table 3
Factors Influencing U.S. Firms' Selection of Partners for Joint Ventures in Jamaica and in Trinidad and Tobago

Factors Strongly Influencing Selection Decision	Mean	Standard Deviation
Obtain Best Management	4.6	0.6
Favorable Image	4.3	0.6
Local Management Talent	4.2	0.7
International Quality Standards	4.2	0.8
Local Financing	4.0	0.7
Factors Mildly Influencing Selection Decision		
Close Relations with Government	3.7	1.1
Reinvest Profits	3.6	0.8
Equity Transfer	3.4	1.1
Secrecy	3.4	1.4
Factors Not Influencing Selection Decision		
Diversified Product Mix	2.8	1.2
Non-Paternalistic	2.6	1.1

Source: Renforth, William E., "A Comparative Study of Joint International Business Ventures with Family Firm or Non-Family Firm Partners: The Caribbean Community Experience." Ph.D. diss., Indiana Univeristy, 1974, p. 90. Reprinted by permission of the Author.

zations as partners. The rationale for this preference was that, by selecting a similarly sized partner, a company, "could be assured that the two firms placed the joint venture in about the same importance. Furthermore, the two firms were then in more nearly equal power positions for bargaining."[7]

In contrast to Daniels' findings, a study by Lee Adler and James D. Hlavacek focused on a non-random sample of joint ventures which were formed almost exclusively between firms considered "large" and "small" relative to each other, and which were oriented toward product innovations.[8] Among their results was the following list of six "typical criteria" used to select partners for such ventures:

1. An established marketing/distribution system in the market to be served
2. A sales force of suitable size, caliber, and image calling on specific customers

3. Technology to improve on or complement one's own current technology base
4. The kind of personnel needed
5. A given minimum available financial resource
6. Relative company size

Adler and Hlavacek's work provided several insights into the joint venture partner selection process, particularly for ventures undertaken to enhance product innovation. However, the potential contribution of their work toward improved understanding of partner selection criteria, particularly for developed country joint ventures, is constrained by several factors. First, the "typical criteria" were merely listed; no information was presented in regard to the relative frequency or importance attached to each one, nor was any indication given of how these criteria might vary from those used for joint ventures not oriented toward product innovations. The sample was also strongly biased in its composition: Fourteen of the nineteen sample joint ventures were dispersed among only three 2-digit SIC codes, and nine of the ventures involved the chemical products industry. Another potential limitation was that only current joint venture general managers were interviewed. These managers may not have been intimately involved in the partner selection process and thus may have lacked the requisite knowledge regarding the selection criteria that were employed. Therefore, the generalizability and possibly the accuracy of Adler and Hlavacek's results are suspect.

SUMMARY AND CONCLUSIONS REGARDING PRIOR RESEARCH

To reiterate, there has been only limited prior research on the topic of joint venture partner selection criteria. In general, results of past research have been unable to provide substantial assistance toward increased understanding of partner selection criteria and their valences, particularly for developed country joint ventures. Most of the studies which have explicitly addressed the issue suffer from potentially serious methodological shortcomings, or they embody a narrow or biased geographic or industrial focus, thereby limiting the applicability of their results. There has been only limited success in identifying the selection criteria valences that firms utilize or in identifying the critical variables that might help explain why or how criteria valences can be expected to vary.

However, past studies suggest several important considerations. First, specific criteria *do* seem to be employed in the selection of prospective joint venture partners. In addition, although memory decay may pose certain constraints, it appears that data regarding these criteria can be collected in an *ex post* manner from individuals who were intimately involved in the partner selection process. Prior studies also suggest that criteria valences may exhibit variation between industries, between firms within a single industry, and even between specific joint ventures of the same firm. Therefore, it may be possible not only to identify variables associated with variations in criteria valences, but also to examine the nature of the relationship between these variables and the criteria valences. To the extent this is possible, the ability of the relevant stakeholders to understand and influence the partner selection process may be significantly enhanced.

Examination of prior studies also suggests the potential for distinguishing two broad categories of partner selection criteria, namely, "task related" and "partner related." The concept of task-related selection criteria refers to those variables, both tangible and intangible, human and nonhuman, that are related to an investment project's viability regardless of whether the chosen investment medium entails shared ownership and decision making. Examples of these variables include patents, financing, trademarks, technically skilled personnel, and marketing and distribution systems.

The concept of partner-related selection criteria, on the other hand, refers to those variables, both tangible and intangible, human and nonhuman, that are relevant only if the chosen investment medium entails shared ownership and decision making. In contrast to task-related criteria, these criteria are operational only if the investment includes the active participation of two or more partners. Partner-related criteria may include such variables as national or corporate culture of a partner, compatibility of and trust between partners' top managers, and the size or corporate structure of a partner.

Although it was not directly addressed in prior studies, there seems to be some support for the distinction between task-related and partner-related selection criteria. For example, Tomlinson identified favorable past association between prospective partners as the single most important selection criterion mentioned by his respondents.[9] As opposed to his other, more task-related criteria categories, such as facilities and resources, favorable past association seems to qualify as a partner-related criterion, and an important one, as well. Similarly, Tomlinson and Thompson reported the importance of compatible ethics, an apparent partner-related criterion, when selecting a joint venture partner.[10]

As the above examples indicate, the identification of, and distinction between, the concepts of task-related and partner-related categories of selection criteria are believed to have usefulness in enhancing understanding of the mechanism by which joint venture partners are selected. Therefore, Chapter 3 will be devoted to the examination of task-related and partner-related categories of partner selection criteria and of several variables which may bear a relationship to these concepts.

NOTES

1. Stanley Boyle, "The Joint Subsidiary: An Economic Appraisal," *Antitrust Bulletin* (May–June, 1960), pp. 303–18.

2. For instance, see F. N. Burton and F. H. Saelens, "Partner Choice and Linkage Characteristics of International Joint Ventures in Japan: An Exploratory Analysis of the Inorganic Chemicals Sector," *Management International Review* 22, no. 2 (1982), pp. 20–29.

3. James W. C. Tomlinson, *The Joint Venture Process in International Business: India and Pakistan* (Cambridge, Mass.: MIT Press, 1970).

4. James W. C. Tomlinson and M. Thompson, "A Study of Canadian Joint Ventures in Mexico," working paper, College of Commerce and Business Administration, University of British Columbia, 1977.

5. William E. Renforth, "A Comparative Study of Joint International Business Ventures with Family Firm or Non-Family Firm Partners: The Caribbean Community Experience," Ph.D. diss., Graduate School of Business, Indiana University, 1974.

6. John D. Daniels, *Recent Foreign Direct Manufacturing Investment in the United States* (New York: Praeger, 1971).

7. Ibid., p. 60.

8. Lee Adler and James D. Hlavacek, *Joint Ventures for Product Innovation* (New York: American Management Associations, 1976). See also James D. Hlavacek and Victor A. Thompson, "The Joint-Venture Approach to Technology Utilization," *IEEE Transactions on Engineering Management* (1976), pp. 35–41.

9. Tomlinson, *The Joint Venture Process.*

10. Tomlinson and Thompson, "A Study of Canadian Joint Ventures in Mexico."

3

Research Hypotheses

Chapter 2 identified, and distinguished between, the concepts of task-related and partner-related categories of partner selection criteria. This chapter will outline several concepts from the strategic management literature which may have some usefulness in conceptualizing the mechanism by which task-related and partner-related selection criteria valences are assigned, as well as the hypothesized relationship between these strategy concepts and the partner selection criteria valences.

TASK-RELATED CRITERIA: LITERATURE AND HYPOTHESES

This section addresses the concept of task-related partner selection criteria as well as the relationship between selected variables from the strategy literature and the valences that organizations assign to these criteria.

Strategy and the Decision to Form a Joint Venture

It has been maintained that the fundamental orientation of managers is toward the acquisition of sufficient resources to permit strategic objectives to be obtained.[1] It has also been asserted that organizational decision making tends to be very rational, or at least "intendedly rational."[2] As will be discussed in the following section on partner-related criteria, the joint venture form of organization entails additional costs attributable to the need for shared decision making and the coordination of partners.[3] Therefore, although nonrational factors may influence the decision making process,[4] it is assumed that an organization typically will attempt to form a joint venture only if the perceived additional benefits outweigh the expected additional costs of utilizing the joint venture option.[5] Numerous studies have suggested that these additional benefits will accrue from the selection of partners who can supply complementary skills or capabilities which are expected to help the organization attain its strategic objectives.[6] Prospective partners can complement an organization on a variety of different dimensions. Therefore, the notion of merely seeking a partner with complementary capabilities provides relatively little guidance regarding the specific capabilities that an organization expects or desires a potential partner to provide, or the tradeoffs a firm is likely to make between alternative complementary skills or resources. However, an examination of the strategy formulation process, particularly the role of critical success factors in that process, may help to distinguish the specific capabilities that will be more actively sought in a partner.

Critical Success Factors

Essential to understanding the strategy formulation process is an understanding of the concept of critical success factors (CSFs).[7] As used in this study, critical success factors may be broadly conceptualized as those few key areas of activity in which favorable results are absolutely necessary in order for strategic goals to be obtained.[8] To qualify as a CSF, an activity must be both necessary and potentially difficult to achieve.[9] These factors may vary by industry and by company, and they may even change over time. Yet, because CSFs can have a significant effect on an organization's performance, and therefore on the attainment of corporate objectives, managers must endeavor to identify them. Consistent with this, Charles W. Hofer and Dan Schendel have asserted that critical success factors are well-known to the existing competitors in an industry, although they may not be as evident to others, including potential new entrants.[10]

In contrast to Hofer and Schendel's assertion, it has been claimed that accurate identification of the CSFs confronting an organization may entail significant difficulties.[11] Nevertheless, the critical issue for this study is the managers' perceptions regarding CSFs and the organization's position relative to them. The rationale for this assertion is that, "following the arguments of Weick (1969), it is generally accepted that the perceptions of environmental and internal characteristics (rather than the 'objective' characteristics of the environment) are the important properties to consider in the strategy formulation process."[12]

Managers' evaluations of the relevant CSFs and the organization's position vis-a-vis these factors provide the foundation for an organization's competitive strategy.[13] Consistent with the strategy literature, if an organization has decided to enter a particular business, it can be assumed that the management of the organization will attempt to formulate and implement a strategy that will promote the attainment of corporate objectives. Therefore, an organization's decision to pursue formation of a joint venture, and thereby assume the additional costs entailed by interorganizational coordination, should reflect management's perception that one or more partners can be selected who will enhance the organization's position vis-a-vis the CSFs, thereby enhancing prospects for attaining organizational objectives. The assignment of valences to selection criteria should reflect the relative importance to the organization of the various contributions a partner is expected to make to the venture's relative competitive position.

Research Hypotheses: Task-Related Criteria

Following this line of reasoning, it is expected that managerial perceptions of CSFs and the organization's position vis-a-vis these factors will bear a strong relationship to the partner selection criteria valences that are employed. This conclusion permits the assertion of several hypotheses. Before stating these hypotheses, however, the relevant variables are defined as follows:

CSF IMPORTANCE refers to managerial perceptions of the importance of a potential critical success factor to the joint venture's performance.

COMPETITIVE POSITION refers to managerial perceptions of their organization's competitive position vis-a-vis the requirements dictated by a potential critical success factor.

DIFFICULTY OF INTERNAL DEVELOPMENT refers to managerial perceptions of the difficulty associated with future intraorganizational efforts to achieve or maintain a tenable competitive position vis-a-vis the CSFs.

TASK-RELATED CRITERIA VALENCE refers to the relative valence attributed by management to the selection criteria associated with a particular potential CSF.

Measurement of each of these variables was based on their perceived value at the time the partner was being selected and the joint venture was being formed.

The first hypothesis can now be stated as follows:

Hypothesis 1: CSF IMPORTANCE will be positively correlated with TASK-RELATED CRITERIA VALENCE.

This hypothesis asserts that an increase in perceived importance of a potential critical success factor to joint venture performance will be correlated with an increased valence being attributed to the selection criteria associated with that factor. For example, as the perceived importance of a well-established distribution system (a potential CSF) to a joint venture's performance increases, it is expected that the valence associated with the criterion of finding a partner with access to a well-established distribution system will exhibit an increased value.

Support for this hypothesis may be found in the work of William H. Davidson, who maintained that

> selection of a local partner is a critical decision in joint venture formation. In the most general terms, the global firm requires a partner whose strengths meet the primary needs of the venture. If marketing and distribution are the principal requirements, the ideal local partner will be an experienced and established distributor of related products. If relations with the home government is critical, a local partner with close ties to the government is needed.[14]

The above statement supports Hypothesis 1 in predicting that a positive correlation between CSF IMPORTANCE and TASK-RELATED CRITERIA VALENCE will be observed. However, this first hypothesis fails to take into account the relationship between criteria valences and the organization's capabilities vis-a-vis the CSFs. The expected nature of the latter relationship can be stated as follows:

Hypothesis 2: COMPETITIVE POSITION will be negatively correlated with TASK-RELATED CRITERIA VALENCE.

The second hypothesis asserts that a greater perceived competitive position vis-a-vis the requirements dictated by a potential CSF will be correlated with a relatively lower valence on criteria related to that factor. Using the previous example, as managerial perceptions increase regarding their organization's relative competitive position on access to a well-developed distribution system, it is expected that the reported valence associated with selection of a partner with such access will exhibit a decrease in value.

Although a negative correlation between the variables in Hypothesis 2 is expected to be observed, this relationship is not expected to be obtained for every case. The second hypothesis addresses the expected relationship between the existing competitive position of the organization vis-a-vis the CSFs, but it fails to account for the dynamic component of the relationship between criteria valences and CSFs, such as the perceived difficulty associated with future intraorganizational efforts to achieve or maintain a tenable competitive position vis-a-vis the CSFs. The expected nature of this latter relationship can be stated as follows:

Hypothesis 3: DIFFICULTY OF INTERNAL DEVELOPMENT
will be positively correlated with TASK-RELATED CRITERIA
VALENCE.

This hypothesis asserts that a greater perceived difficulty associated with future intraorganizational efforts to achieve or maintain a tenable competitive position vis-a-vis a CSF will be correlated with a relatively higher valence on partner selection criteria related to that factor. Again using the distribution system example, as the perceived difficulty of future intraorganizational efforts to develop access to a well-developed distribution system increases, it is expected that the reported valence associated with selection of a partner with such access will exhibit an increase in value.

PARTNER-RELATED CRITERIA: LITERATURE AND HYPOTHESES

The preceding section addressed the issue of organizations seeking joint venture partners who can contribute complementary task-related resources to the venture and thereby increase the organization's capability for achieving strategic objectives.

However, the potential benefits derived from interorganizational cooperation, such as a joint venture, are accompanied by costs attributable to the existence of a partner. General systems theory maintains that each element of a system is dependent on the others to some degree.[15] Therefore, the use of a joint venture form of investment introduces an additional element—the partner—into the organization's decision making environment. The presence of a partner introduces new stresses, due to the need to coordinate the resources and activities of interdependent partner organizations.[16] Because of the presumed long-term nature of the relationship[17] and the partners' continuing participation in decision making, the joint venture relationship may be characterized as one that entails continuous bargaining.[18] The presence of this interdependence means exchanges between partners are uncertain and potentially unstable.[19]

A central goal of management is to manage uncertainty in an organization's environment, including the sources of organizational interdependence.[20] Since uncertainty may be defined in terms of information deficiency,[21] a critical task in managing organizational uncertainty and interdependence is the collection and processing of information about different components of the organization and how these components are functioning.[22] This task is especially critical during task execution.[23]

Effective interorganizational communication is essential for coordinated responses of partners.[24] If an organization is slow in acquiring and processing information, and acting thereupon, then it confronts the risk of preemption

by the swifter actions of a rival. Organizational characteristics of the partners, including language, culture, strategy, structure, and size, *inter alia*,
may influence the efficiency and effectiveness of information transfers, thus
affecting risk.[25]

Organizations may attempt to manage uncertainty by seeking partners
that evidence certain characteristics that are believed to be related to the
enhancement of positive, or the reduction of negative, repercussions associated with the coordination of interorganizational activities. It is suggested that firms seeking to manage interorganizational communications,
and the uncertainties arising therefrom, will attempt to select partners evidencing compatibility on partner-related dimensions of selection criteria.
In general, it is expected that the partners perceived as the most compatible
will be those that are similar on partner-related selection criteria dimensions.
For instance, Thomas C. MacAvoy, vice-chairman of Corning, suggested
that joint ventures are more likely to be successful when both partners are
comparable in sophistication and size because, "Then they are likely to have
similar values and control systems, similar tolerance for losses, and appetite
for risk."[26] As the goals, size, culture, and other partner-related dimensions
of joint venture parents diverge, dysfunctional strains and misunderstandings are more likely to occur.[27]

The relative need for interacting with a partner and, thus, for seeking a
partner that embodies specific "partner-related" characteristics, is expected
to differ with different tasks.[28] At least three distinct dimensions of the joint
venture task environment were expected to be correlated with the extent
of inter-partner interactions, and thus with criteria valences for partner-
related selection criteria, including perceived uncertainty characterizing the
joint venture's task environment, diversity of line functions expected to be
engaged in by the joint venture, and the extent of shared control sought in
the joint venture. The remainder of this section will be devoted to addressing
these three dimensions and the hypotheses associated with them.

Perceived Task Environment Uncertainty

As suggested, it is asserted that partner-related criteria will tend to assume
greater importance, or exhibit higher valences, when the joint venture is
expected to require more extensive interaction between the partners. One
variable that is expected to influence the extent of interaction is the degree
of uncertainty perceived by managers as characterizing the joint venture's
task environment. Given that managers are rational, or intendedly rational,
they attempt to plan future resource deployments.[29] Uncertainty, conceptualized as an information gap, is the nemesis of planning.[30] The presence
of uncertainty means decision makers do not have complete information,
and the prospect of unanticipated changes exists. As the perceived level of
uncertainty escalates, decision makers increasingly confront situations in

which the information relevant to a decision is unavailable, and the outcomes of a decision may not be able to be assessed with the desired degree of accuracy.[31] With declining ability to anticipate future changes accurately, planning becomes a more tenuous activity. Instead, the organization must continually learn to re-adapt, rather than rely on past practices and procedures.[32] Plans must be reviewed, and possibly revised, on a more frequent basis. This means that, as the uncertainty of the task environment increases, the amount of information that must be collected and processed by decision makers also tends to increase.[33] For cooperative projects such as joint ventures, interorganizational communication is essential for the transmission of the necessary information.[34]

The previously outlined logic is supported by several studies which suggested that, in highly complex and uncertain environments, effective organizations tend to be characterized by greater levels of participation within or between groups.[35] Conflicts between parents can cripple the efficiency and effectiveness of interorganizational transmission of information, thereby threatening the joint venture's performance.[36] Furthermore, the characteristics of a partner may influence the nature of partner interactions and, thus, the efficiency and effectiveness of information transfers between partners.[37] For instance, organizations with different strategic objectives may interpret their task environments differently, resulting in a differential ability to interpret one another's estimates possibly leading to conflict and problems. As a result, partner-related criteria may represent an important consideration when selecting joint venture partners, particularly when the joint venture's task environment is characterized by relatively high levels of perceived uncertainty.

Before stating a hypothesis regarding the relationship between the perceived task environment uncertainty and the partner-related selection criteria variables, these variables must be defined. Therefore:

PERCEIVED TASK ENVIRONMENT UNCERTAINTY was defined as managerial perceptions, at the time the partner was being selected and the joint venture was being formed, of the level of uncertainty embodied in the proposed joint venture's task environment.

PARTNER-RELATED CRITERIA VALENCE referred to the relative valence attributed by management to partner-related selection criteria, as evaluated at the time the partner was being selected and the joint venture was being formed.

Based on these definitions and on the preceding discussion, the following hypothesis can be asserted:

*Hypothesis 4: PERCEIVED TASK ENVIRONMENT
UNCERTAINTY will be positively correlated with PARTNER-
RELATED CRITERIA VALENCES.*

This hypothesis asserts that an increase in the perceived level of uncertainty in the joint venture's task environment will be correlated with increased valences being assigned to partner-related selection criteria categories.

Diversity of Line Functions

Organizations may be conceptualized as being composed of sets of groups organized around differentiated tasks.[38] These groups are interdependent to varying degrees (e.g., the output of one group may be the input for another group), and they must share scarce resources. Each differentiated group interacts with a specialized subenvironment which requires different goals, values, and skills.[39] In order for strategic goals to be achieved, organizations must integrate the divergent goals and activities of these differentiated groups.[40] In joint ventures, integration requires effective communication and joint problem solving activity not only between the differentiated groups but also between the parent organizations. This interaction is a potential source of uncertainty that must be managed.[41]

As mentioned, partner-related selection criteria are expected to assume greater importance (reflected in the higher valences assigned to them) when higher levels of interaction are anticipated between joint venture partners. The level of inter-partner interaction necessary for effective integration of the joint venture's activities is expected to be correlated with the level of diversity in the joint venture's decision making environment.[42] This diversity is expected to be partially a function of the number of different line functions the joint venture was originally expected to embody. Therefore, we expected increased diversity of line functions to be correlated with increased interaction between partners.[43]

DIVERSITY OF LINE FUNCTIONS was defined as the number of different line functions (e.g., extraction, basic or applied research and development, manufacturing or processing of raw materials or components, manufacturing or assembly of finished goods, marketing, distribution, and post-sales service) which, at the time the partner was being selected, the joint venture was expected to embody.

Our fifth research hypothesis can now be stated as follows:

Hypothesis 5: DIVERSITY OF LINE FUNCTIONS will be positively correlated with PARTNER-RELATED CRITERIA VALENCES.

This hypothesis asserts that an increase in the number of line functions expected to be incorporated in the joint venture's activities will be correlated with an increase in the valence being attributed to partner-related selection criteria categories. For example, if a joint venture was expected to engage not only in marketing, but also in applied research and development, production of components, assembly of finished goods, and post-sales service, then greater emphasis would be placed on partner-related selection criteria than would be the case if the joint venture was expected to involve only the marketing function.

Extent of Shared Control

A potential limitation of Hypothesis 5 is that it ignores the issue of control within joint ventures and the relationship of control to the selection criteria valences. As discussed earlier, we proposed that partner-related criteria would tend to exhibit higher valences when a greater amount of interaction between partners was expected to be necessary. Correspondingly, we felt that a greater need for partner interaction vis-a-vis a particular joint venture activity will occur when decision making control over that activity is shared, instead of being allocated to one partner or the other. Therefore, we proposed that the extent to which a firm expects to share joint venture decision making control with its partner will be correlated with the valences it assigns to partner-related selection criteria categories.

> EXTENT OF SHARED CONTROL referred to the relative degree to which control over a specific joint venture activity was expected, at the time the partner was being selected and the joint venture was being formed, to be shared by the two partners, rather than being allocated principally to one partner or the other.

On the basis of this definition and on the discussion that preceded it, the following hypothesis can be asserted:

Hypothesis 6: EXTENT OF SHARED CONTROL will be positively correlated with PARTNER-RELATED CRITERIA VALENCES.

This hypothesis states that expectations of more equally shared control over a specific joint venture activity would be correlated with higher valences on partner-related criteria than would be the case if control was expected to be unequally divided between the partners. Support for this hypothesis may be found in the work of J. Peter Killing, who maintained that, "The more 'shared' the management of the venture promises to be, the more difficult it will be to manage."[44]

This section's discussion and hypotheses regarding partner-related selection criteria suggest that, through judicious selection of a partner, it may be possible to mitigate the managerial difficulties frequently encountered in the joint venture.

CHAPTER SUMMARY

This chapter discussed several concepts from the strategy literature which were expected to bear a relationship to task-related and partner-related selection criteria valences, as well as the hypothesized nature of these relationships. The next chapter describes the methodology that was used to collect and analyze the research data necessary to test these hypotheses.

NOTES

1. E. Yuchtman and S. E. Seashore, "A System Resource Approach to Organizational Effectiveness," *American Sociological Review* 32 (1967), pp. 891–903.

2. For a discussion of the rational decision making model, see M. Weber, "Bureaucracy," in H. Gerth and C. Mills, eds., *From Max Weber* (New York: Oxford University Press, 1947); and W. Edwards, "Behavioral Decision Theory," *Annual Review of Psychology* (1961), pp. 473–98. For a discussion of intendedly rational models of decision making, see James March and Herbert Simon, *Organizations* (New York: Wiley, 1958); James D. Thompson, *Organizations in Action* (New York: McGraw-Hill, 1967); and Karl E. Weick, *The Social Psychology of Organizing*, 2d ed. (Menlo Park, Calif: Addison-Wesley, 1979).

3. Michael Aiken and Jerald Hage, "Organizational Interdependence and Intra-Organizational Structure," *American Sociological Review* (December, 1968), pp. 912–30; Steffan Gullander, "Joint Ventures and Corporate Strategy," *Columbia Journal of World Business* (Spring, 1976), pp. 104–14; G. Richard Young and Standish Bradford, Jr., *Joint Ventures: Planning and Action* (New York: Financial Executives Research Foundation, 1977); Sanford V. Berg and Philip Friedman, "Corporate Courtship and Successful Joint Ventures," *California Management Review* (Spring, 1980), pp. 35–51; Kathryn Rudie Harrigan, "Integrating Parent and Child: Successful Joint Ventures," working paper, Columbia University, 1984; Richard W. Moxon and J. Michael Geringer, "Multinational Ventures in the Commercial Aircraft Industry," *Columbia Journal of World Business* 20, no. 2 (Summer, 1985), pp. 55–62.

4. M. D. Cohen, J. G. March, and J. P. Olson, "A Garbage Can Model of Organizational Choice," *Administrative Science Quarterly* 17 (1972), pp. 1–25; Raymond E. Miles and Charles C. Snow, *Organizational Strategy, Structure, and Process* (New York: McGraw-Hill, 1978).

5. Aiken and Hage, "Organizational Interdependence"; Paul W. Beamish, *Multinational Joint Ventures in Developing Countries* (London: Croom Helm, 1988).

6. Business International, *Pros and Cons of Joint Ventures Abroad* (New York: Business International, 1964); Aiken and Hage, "Organizational Interdependence"; Lawrence G. Franko, "The Art of Choosing an American Joint Venture Partner," in Michael Z. Brooke and H. Lee Remmers, eds., *The Multinational Company in Europe: Some Key Problems* (London: Longman Group Ltd., 1972), pp. 65–76; Lee Adler and James D. Hlavacek, *Joint Ventures for Product Innovation* (New York: American Management Association, 1976); Gullander, "Joint Ventures and Corporate Strategy"; J. Peter Killing, "How to Make a Global Joint Venture Work," *Harvard Business Review* (May–June, 1982), pp. 120–27; Moxon and Geringer, "Multinational Ventures."

7. Critical success factors are sometimes referred to as "key success factors."

8. For a similar definition, see John F. Rockart, "The Changing Role of the Information Systems Executive: A Critical Success Factors Perspective," *Sloan Management Review* (Fall, 1982), p. 4.

9. George S. Day, *Strategic Marketing Planning: The Pursuit of Competitive Advantage* (St. Paul, Minn.: West Publishing, 1984), pp. 55–58.

10. Charles W. Hofer and Dan Schendel, *Strategy Formulation: Analytical Concepts* (St. Paul, Minn.: West Publishing, 1978), p. 77.

11. Joel K. Leidecker and Albert V. Bruno, "Identifying and Using Critical Success Factors," *Long Range Planning* 17, no. 1 (1984), p. 24.

12. Carl R. Anderson and Frank T. Paine, "Managerial Perceptions and Strategic Behavior," *Academy of Management Journal* (December, 1975), p. 813.

13. Michael E. Porter, *Competitive Strategy* (New York: Free Press, 1980).

14. William H. Davidson, "Participation Policies," in William H. Davidson, ed., *Global Strategic Management* (New York: John Wiley, 1982), p. 46.

15. Kenneth Boulding, "General Systems Theory—The Skeleton of a Science," *Management Science* 2 (1956), pp. 197–208; Ludwig von Bertalanffy, "General Systems Theory—A Critical Review," *General Systems* 7 (1962), pp. 1–20.

16. Aiken and Hage, "Organizational Interdependence"; Gullander, "Joint Ventures and Corporate Strategy"; Young and Bradford, *Joint Ventures*; Berg and Friedman, "Corporate Courtship"; Jack K. Ito and Richard B. Peterson, "Effects of Task Difficulty and Interunit Interdependence on Information Processing Systems," *Academy of Management Journal* (March, 1986), pp. 139–48; Moxon and Geringer, "Multinational Ventures."

17. Stephen M. Hills, "The Search for Joint Venture Partners," in Jeffrey C. Susbauer, ed., *Academy of Management Proceedings* (San Francisco: Academy of Management, 1978), pp. 277–81.

18. R. M. Cyert and J. G. March, *A Behavioral Theory of the Firm* (Englewood Cliffs, N.J.: Prentice-Hall, 1963).

19. Aiken and Hage, "Organizational Interdependence"; Jeffrey Pfeffer and G. R. Salancik, *The External Control of Organizations* (New York: Harper and Row, 1978).

20. Thompson, *Organizations in Action*; Weick, *The Social Psychology of Organizations*.

21. Jay Galbraith, *Designing Complex Organizations* (Reading, Mass.: Addison-Wesley, 1973).

22. G. Zaltman, R. Duncan, and J. Holbek, *Innovation and Organizations* (New York: Wiley, 1973).

23. Galbraith, *Designing Complex Organizations*.

24. Oliver E. Williamson, "A Dynamic Theory of Interfirm Behavior," *Quarterly Journal of Economics* (November, 1965), pp. 579–607.

25. Thompson, *Organizations in Action*; Young and Bradford, *Joint Ventures*; Killing, "How to Make a Global Joint Venture Work"; Beamish, *Multinational Joint Ventures*.

26. "Are Foreign Partners Good for U.S. Companies?" *Business Week* (May 28, 1984), pp. 58–60.

27. Edward B. Roberts, "New Ventures for Corporate Growth," *Harvard Business Review* (July–August, 1980), pp. 134–42.

28. Galbraith, *Designing Complex Organizations*.

29. Weber, "Bureaucracy"; Edwards, "Behavioral Decision Theory."

30. Galbraith, *Designing Complex Organizations*.

31. Thompson, *Organizations in Action*; Robert B. Duncan, "Characteristics of Organizational Environments and Perceived Environmental Uncertainty," *Administrative Science Quarterly* (1972), pp. 313–27.

32. Duncan, "Characteristics of Organizational Environments."

33. Galbraith, *Designing Complex Organizations*.

34. Williamson, "A Dynamic Theory"; Thompson, *Organizations in Action*.

35. Thomas Burns and Gerald M. Stalker, *The Management of Innovation* (London: Tavistock, 1961); Warren G. Bennis, *Changing Organizations* (New York: McGraw-Hill, 1966); Paul Lawrence and Jay W. Lorsch, *Organization and Environment* (Boston: Graduate School of Business, Harvard University, 1967); Richard N. Osborn and James G. Hunt, "Environment and Organizational Effectiveness, *Administrative Science Quarterly* 19 (1974), pp. 231–46; Michael L. Tushman, "Technical Communication in Research and Development Laboratories: An Exploratory Study of Their Impact on Organization Structure," *Academy of Management Journal* 22 (1979), pp. 672–93; Richard L. Daft and Karl E. Weick, "Toward a Model of Organizations as Interpretive Systems," *Academy of Management Review* (1984), pp. 284–95.

36. Beamish, *Multinational Joint Ventures*.

37. Killing, "How to Make a Global Joint Venture Work"; Beamish, *Multinational Joint Ventures*.

38. Lawrence and Lorsch, *Organization and Environment*; Michael L. Tushman and David A. Nadler, "Information Processing as an Integrating Concept in Organization Design," *Academy of Management Review* (July, 1978), pp. 613–24.

39. Richard L. Daft, *Organization Theory and Design* (St. Paul, Minn.: West Publishing, 1983).

40. Lawrence and Lorsch, *Organization and Environment*; A. Van de Ven, A. Delbecq, and R. Koenig, "Determinants of Coordination Modes within Organizations," *American Sociological Review* 41 (1976), pp. 322–38; Daft, *Organization Theory and Design*.

41. Thompson, *Organizations in Action*.

42. Lawrence and Lorsch, *Organization and Environment*; Duncan, "Characteristics of Organizational Environments"; Steven M. Shortell, "The Role of Environment in a Configurational Theory of Organizations," *Human Relations* 30 (1977), pp. 275–302.

43. Lawrence and Lorsch, *Organization and Environment*; Duncan, "Characteristics of Organizational Environments."

44. Killing, "How to Make a Global Joint Venture Work," p. 19.

4

Research Methodology

Once we determined our research objectives, defined our variables, and stated our hypotheses, we confronted the problem of selecting a research design that would permit the hypotheses to be tested. This chapter discusses the method we employed to collect the data used to test the hypotheses developed in Chapter 3.

DATA REQUIREMENTS AND COLLECTION APPROACH

In selecting a data collection approach, it was necessary to give careful consideration to the study's data requirements. Because of severe limitations of existing data bases, the option of relying on secondary data sources was rejected as inadequate. Hypothesis testing required perceptual data from managers who were intimately involved in the partner selection process. This information was not available from preexisting secondary sources.

The nature of the research topic, which did not permit manipulation of the research variables without the potential introduction of artificiality via use of hypothetical joint ventures, dictated employment of an *ex post facto* design. Therefore, two principal methods were available for eliciting the necessary data from respondents: mail questionnaires and interviews. Collection of the data exclusively through use of mail questionnaires was rejected for several reasons. Because of the limited prior research on partner selection, particularly for developed country joint ventures, the precise identity of the critical variables and the relationships among them was not evident a priori. Therefore, access to qualitative as well as quantitative data was desired to avoid spurious or misleading conclusions. A study based on mail questionnaires is typically constrained in its ability to provide extensive breadth and depth of qualitative, as well as quantitative, data.[1] Therefore, using mail questionnaires as the sole source of data was suspect.

Use of a mail questionnaire, particularly one of sufficient length to collect all of the necessary data, was also hampered by the typically low response rates associated with such instruments.[2] For instance, of the 61 test sample firms contacted by James W. C. Tomlinson, only 2 firms returned fully completed joint venture questionnaires.[3] Although this example may represent the extreme, response rates of less than 30 percent are quite common.[4]

Even more critical than the rate of response, however, is the composition of the sample obtained therefrom. Managers with a particular interest in the research topic are more likely to return mail questionnaires than are those who are less interested. This suggests that mail surveys evidencing low response rates will almost invariably exhibit significant bias in ways directly related to the research objectives, which can compromise the data and their generalizability.[5] Because of these limitations, exclusive reliance on mail questionnaires was rejected.

In contrast to mail questionnaires, interviews tend to be an effective means of enlisting participant cooperation.[6] A research project can be presented to prospective participants more effectively through face-to-face contact than with letters—an approach which also mitigates the problem of nonresponse. In addition, interviews typically provide richer data than do mail questionnaires.[7] Interviews may not only focus on respondent attitudes toward very specific issues, but also enable a researcher to construct a relatively complete, well-organized, and realistic picture of the research subject. Resource limitations typically dictate a smaller number of cases able to be accessed via interviews than through the use of mail questionnaires. However, absolute sample size is less critical than the quality of the data and the depth of understanding that can be generated from a detailed review of the subtle and interrelated processes operating within a relatively few whole systems. Therefore, generalizability may be enhanced by employing a relatively limited interview sample rather than using results from a mail questionnaire-based sample of larger absolute size. In addition, in-person interviews tend to enhance the development of trust and rapport between the interviewer and the respondent, increasing the prospects for probing sensitive topics. Therefore, due to the data requirements and the relative advantages listed above, face-to-face interviews were our primary data collection device.

The interviews were supplemented with data collected from a self-administered questionnaire distributed to each participant prior to the interview. Employing interviews and questionnaires simultaneously proved synergistic, combining the individual strengths and reducing the respective weaknesses associated with each approach, thereby enhancing the construct validity and the statistical conclusion validity of the results that were obtained. For instance, participation rates for prior interview-based studies addressing analogous topics averaged 80 percent or more, enhancing data generalizability compared to the exclusively mail questionnaire-based re-search.[8] In addition, distribution of the questionnaire prior to the interviews required respondents to focus on a large number of specific factors and to indicate their attitudes very precisely by assigning numerical values. This was more difficult to do in the interview environment without damaging the "flow" of the interview. The questionnaire also helped overcome mem-ory decay and enhance the data's thoroughness by permitting respondents to consult records or other colleagues for additional information.

The use of open-ended questions in the interviews provided the qualitative data which further mitigated prospects for reporting spurious or misleading conclusions, a critical consideration when there may be a significant like-lihood of noise due to extraneous variables. The interviews helped to high-light the critical variables, processes, and interactions relevant to the research problem. We were able to probe the respondents in greater depth if a particular response was not fully understood. This interaction would not have been possible in an exclusively questionnaire-based study.

GENERATION OF THE SAMPLING FRAME

The sampling frame is the set of joint ventures that has a chance to be included in the research sample, given the sampling approach that is utilized. The research sample, and the data obtained therefrom, can be representative only of the population included in the sampling frame. Therefore, the cor-respondence between the sampling frame and the population which we were attempting to describe was important.

An inherent problem confronted when developing a sampling frame of joint ventures is that no preexisting, comprehensive roster of joint ventures exists. A number of sources *do* report the existence of joint ventures, al-though the data vary greatly in their breadth and depth. Conducting a systematic and complete review of all the possible information sources would have been an extremely time-consuming task, one certainly beyond the feasible scope of this study. Therefore, after extensive review of the available data sources, evaluating each on both thoroughness and ease of access, it was decided to rely on the following five sources: the journal *Mergers and Acquisitions*; *The Wall Street Journal Index*; Predicasts' *F&S Index of Corporate Change*; the Cambridge Corporation's *Yearbook on Corporate Mergers, Joint Ventures and Corporate Policy*; and the U.S. Department of Commerce's International Trade Administration publications entitled *Foreign Direct Investment in the United States*.

Using these sources, a listing was obtained for all joint ventures reported as formed or attempted between January 1, 1979, and March 1, 1985. After culling multiple listings, this list was subjected to an initial screening to eliminate nonqualifying joint ventures, using date of joint venture forma-tion, number and nationality of partners, and primary target markets as screening criteria. From this initial screening, a roster of 1,018 listings of U.S.-based corporations involved in attempted or actual bilateral joint ventures, each having a primary target market that included one or more developed country, was obtained. It was assumed that this roster of joint ventures sufficiently approximated the universe of qualifying joint ventures in such a manner that no significant systematic bias was introduced via the sampling frame's composition.

Resource and logistical considerations dictated a restriction in the geographical scope of the sample, due to the emphasis on face-to-face interviews as the primary data collection approach and the geographical dispersion of the organizations involved in the joint ventures. Therefore, it was decided that the research sample would comprise organizations from a convenience sample of five geographical clusters: central California (the San Francisco Bay metropolitan areas); southern California (the Los Angeles and San Diego metropolitan areas); Texas (the Dallas–Fort Worth and Houston metropolitan areas); the Great Lakes (the Indianapolis, Chicago, and Milwaukee metropolitan areas); and the East Coast (the Washington, D.C., Philadelphia, and Wilmington, Delaware, metropolitan areas). Therefore, after the initial screening, it was necessary to determine whether the remaining organizations, all U.S.-based, were located within the five geographical sampling clusters and, if so, what their contact addresses were. This required a thorough, and very time-consuming, search of several directories of corporations and their affiliates, as well as corporate annual reports.[9] After screening on geographical location, 547 qualifying joint ventures, involving over 400 different companies, remained. This constituted approximately 53.7 percent of the 1,018 qualifying joint venture listings obtained in the initial screening.

SELECTION OF A SAMPLE

Once the sampling frame was developed, it was necessary to determine a sampling method consistent with our research objectives. In this regard, it must be recognized that we were not interested in the characteristics of the sample per se. Rather, the reason for collecting data about the sample was to obtain conclusions about the entire population of related joint ventures. To enhance the generalizability of the results, a sampling method ensuring representativeness had to be employed. Therefore, the research sample was selected using simple random sampling without replacement. Random sampling enhances generalizations from the sample results to the sampling frame population because it cancels out the effect of any systematic error and any potential bias that might result from extrinsic variables related to the research variables. Although random selection does not necessarily guarantee representativeness of the sample vis-a-vis the sampling frame population,[10] it ensures that sampling error is only random in its occurrence

Table 4
Participation Characteristics of Research Sample

```
Number of companies contacted                    120

Number of companies which did
   not qualify for the study                   - 11

Number of qualifying companies
   which were contacted                         109    (100.0%)

Number of companies which no
   longer existed                             -  5    (  4.6%)

Number of companies which were
   unable or unwilling to
   participate                                - 10    (  9.2%)

Number of companies participating              94    ( 86.2%)

Number of companies participating
   but not supplying complete data            -  4    (  3.7%)

Number of companies which
   supplied complete data                       90    (82.6%)
                                              ====
```

Participation rate = 90 / 109 = 82.6%

instead of containing systematic bias.[11] Thus, random sampling helped control numerous potential influencing variables without the researcher's having to even be aware of those variables' existence.

SAMPLE SIZE

A sample of from 55 to 60 joint ventures was sought, since a sample of this size would permit the use of selected univariate and multivariate statistical tools for data analysis while simultaneously ensuring that, given the expected diversity of the sample population, a sufficient level of qualitative data could be obtained to satisfy the research objectives.

The participation rate was conservatively estimated to be 50 percent of the organizations contacted. Therefore, 120 organizations (21.9 percent) were randomly selected from the 547 sampling frame listings. The final composition of the sample is shown in Table 4. Of the 120 organizations contacted, 11 of these (9.2 percent) did not qualify because they did not satisfy the joint venture requirement (e.g., they were licensing agreements or agreements to cooperate via a non–joint venture format) or they had more than two partners. The level of nonqualifying ventures highlights the limitations of existing sources of joint venture listings.

Of the 109 qualifying joint venture listings, 5 of the organizations (4.2 percent) no longer existed, and 10 (8.3 percent) refused or were unable to participate. In addition, 4 organizations (3.3 percent) participated in only a portion of the study and did not supply sufficient information for inclusion in the data analysis efforts. Therefore, the study achieved an 82.6-percent participation rate (90 out of 109 qualifying organizations). This relatively high level of participation is expected to enhance the external validity and statistical conclusion validity of the results and conclusions that are reported in the following chapters.

MEASURES EMPLOYED

All of the variables represented *ex post* measures of managerial perceptions as of the time the partner was being selected and the joint venture was being formed.

For the variables CRITICAL SUCCESS FACTOR, COMPETITIVE POSITION, DIFFICULTY OF INTERNAL DEVELOPMENT, PERCEIVED TASK ENVIRONMENT UNCERTAINTY, EXTENT OF SHARED CONTROL, TASK-RELATED CRITERIA VALENCE, and PARTNER-RELATED CRITERIA VALENCE, all questions were closed ended, and variables were measured at the ordinal level using five-point Likert-type scales. (In contrast, the DIVERSITY OF LINE FUNCTIONS variable was measured at a nominal level.) The use of closed categories permitted responses to be ordered reliably on a single continuum, a task which cannot be fulfilled unless a set of permissible ordered answers is specified in the question. Asking identical questions of all respondents also helped to ensure consistent measurement.

Ordinal classification of perceptions seemed a more realistic task for the respondents than using interval or ratio levels of measurement. In addition, given the limited available time of senior level executives, readily understood and completed Likert-type scales appeared to be a much more feasible means of measurement than the potentially more precise, but more complex and time-consuming, interval approximating scales such as the Thurstone-type scales.[12]

Greater precision in the data, as obtained through the use of a larger number of response categories along a continuum, was a desired objective of the research. However, it was expected that there would be a limit to the degree of discrimination that the respondents would be able to exercise in giving ordered ratings. For this reason, the questionnaire was restricted to five-point scales. More numerous categories simply produce unreliable "noise" rather than greater precision in the data. Five-point scales were not expected to exceed the respondents' ability to discriminate the relative intensity of their perceptions, and comments by executives participating in the pretest sample strongly supported this decision.

Questions from the self-administered questionnaire are presented in Appendix A. In addition, the interviews incorporated a broad range of questions, primarily open ended in their format, regarding various facets of the joint ventures and of partner selection. As discussed earlier, the use of open-ended questions enhanced collection of qualitative data. Unconstrained by specific, predetermined response categories, the open-ended questions permitted the study of selected issues in detail and depth, complementing the data obtained via closed-ended questions and thereby contributing to a better overall comprehension of the partner selection phenomenon.

PRETESTING

Prior to contacting the sample firms, the format and content of the interviews and self-administered questionnaires were subjected to pretesting using doctoral students and faculty members from several U.S. and Canadian universities. Pretesting was also conducted using nine middle and upper level executives from a nonrandom sample of six Seattle-area companies which had been, or currently were, involved in joint ventures.

Pretesting provided an opportunity not only to test the appropriateness and viability of the proposed collection format, but also to solicit comments on the questions' phrasing, usefulness, and ease of response. Respondents provided several insightful suggestions regarding both the content and the process of the data collection approach. Modifications to the research methodology were then implemented and retested before contacts with the sample population were initiated.

CONTACTING THE RESEARCH SAMPLE

A central issue was determining who would be contacted in the sample organizations. Since the information being sought was specialized in nature, the participants had to be the organizational members most knowledgeable about the topic. Prior research and the pretest results suggested that, on the average, from one to three key executives from each firm had been intimately involved throughout the process of identifying, evaluating, and selecting partners for a particular joint venture, and these would have access to the requisite information.[13] Typically, these key executives were located in the upper or upper middle levels of a firm's hierarchy, and they generally occupied line, rather than staff, positions. The proposition of a limited number of key executives per joint venture was further confirmed during data collection.

The combination of a limited population of appropriately qualified respondents and of busy senior executive schedules impeded efforts to obtain multiple respondents. However, pretest results suggested that, particularly for major and nonroutine decisions such as the selection of joint venture partners, there was a relatively high level of consensus among the key executives regarding perceptions of critical success factors, selection criteria valences, and other variables being addressed in this study. Therefore, the critical task was not to determine how many participants to seek within each firm, but to ensure that the individuals participating had truly been among the key executives involved in the partner selection process.

The task of locating key executives was exceedingly difficult due to promotions, transfers, and attrition, as well as variation between firms and between joint ventures of the same firm regarding delegation of decision making responsibilities. Therefore, initial contact was made through a letter of introduction which was sent to the executive in charge of the operating division engaged in the sample joint venture. If this executive could not be identified, the letter was addressed to the president or chief executive officer of the organization. The introductory letter briefly outlined the proposed research and solicited the firm's participation. Confidentiality of responses was emphasized, as was the opportunity for participants to receive the study's results before public dissemination.

Approximately seven to ten days after the introductory letters were mailed, the letters' recipients were telephoned regarding scheduling of interviews. Especially for larger firms, it frequently required a half dozen or more calls and telephone transfers before the key executives could be identified and individually contacted.

Although locating the key executives was often an arduous task, once they had been contacted, they almost unanimously expressed a willingness to participate. It was apparent that partner selection was generally perceived to be an important issue to them and their firms, and that joint venture formation was often accompanied by extensive uncertainty and a large investment of time and other resources. The prospect of receiving information that might assist them in that task proved, in many cases, to be a strong motivator for participation.

Once they had consented to participate, interviewees were sent a brief confirmation letter which thanked them for their willingness to participate. A self-administered questionnaire was included to provide an indication of the study's focus and to collect supporting data. It was requested that the completed questionnaire be brought to the interview, thereby permitting more efficient use of time by eliminating the need to ask these questions in the interview.

INTERVIEW FORM AND CONTENT

The semistructured interviews utilized a core of structured questions from which it was possible to branch off to explore specific topics in greater depth. Since each case had its own idiosyncracies, it was necessary to devise a flexible approach enabling some points to be developed and others bypassed, as circumstances dictated. Often, the context of the interview itself helped explain a question or robbed it of meaning for an interviewee.

The use of a semistructured approach enhanced the respondents' percep-tions that the interview was relatively open and unstructured, though still embracing a definite focus, thus encouraging cooperation and the estab-lishment of rapport. It allowed collection of standardized information from all respondents, while still permitting responses which could reveal unex-pected details and relationships which enhanced the understanding of joint venture partner selection.

We conducted the interviews either in the respondents' offices or at some other location chosen by them. After completing the introductions, we briefly restated the study's objectives and the expected use of the information that was collected, and we emphasized the voluntary and confidential nature of the respondents' participation. The participants were asked if they had completed the self-administered questionnaire and whether they had any problems answering the questions.[14] After collecting the questionnaire, we asked several straightforward questions concerning the background of the organization, the joint venture, and the respondent. Designed for ease of response, these questions were intended to be a means of "breaking the ice" and encouraging rapport between the researcher and the participant.

The interviews proceeded by requesting the respondent to describe, in some detail, the chronological flow of the joint venture formation process from the time the idea of the investment was first raised within the orga-nization until either the joint venture agreement was signed or negotiations were terminated. If an issue was not addressed, or if greater depth was sought regarding a particular topic, breaks in the discussion were utilized to probe for additional information. Responses to the questionnaire were frequently used as the basis for further questions probing the partner se-lection decision.

The problem of memory decay has frequently hindered *ex post* studies such as this one. As the time that has lapsed since the activity increases, the probability of its being reported accurately decreases, although the decay tends to be less prominent for significant events such as the partner selection decision.[15] In general, the respondents stated that the details of the partner selection process were especially vivid due to the importance of the selection decision to their firms and to their own careers. In addition, we attempted to mitigate potential problems associated with memory decay by focusing on joint ventures formed or attempted no more than six years prior to the interview. Extensive use was made of contextual cues to stimulate associ-ations and thereby enhance the respondents' recall process. The self-ad-ministered questionnaire provided an opportunity to reflect on the selection process before entering the interview, and it provided the respondents with an opportunity to utilize other information sources, if necessary, to refresh their memory on specific aspects of the selection decision. In addition, sequencing questions to correlate with the chronological sequencing of the joint venture formation process, and encouraging respondents to refer to their records if they were unsure about a specific point, further stimulated the respondents' recall by providing contextual cues. As a result, it was perceived that potential problems related to memory decay were substantially reduced.

Due to the many demands on senior executives' time, only one hour of interview time was initially requested for data collection efforts. This time constraint imposed certain limitations on the breadth and depth of the information that could be collected. Through careful design of the interviews and the use of self-administered questionnaires, pretests showed that an hour was a sufficient length of time to collect the necessary data. However, once the interviews commenced, most of the executives stated that the research topic was of substantial interest to them, and they tended to extend the discussion beyond the requested hour-long session in order to provide a more complete description of their experiences in selecting partners and forming joint ventures. Therefore, total interview time per organization ranged from 45 minutes to 5 hours in length, with an average of approximately 1–1/2 hours per executive.

SIZE AND COMPOSITION OF INTERVIEW SAMPLE

A total of 101 executives was interviewed. The composition of the research sample is illustrated in Table 5. As shown, 67 interviews involved one respondent discussing one qualifying joint venture; another 7 interviews involved one respondent discussing two qualifying joint ventures. In 9 cases, from 2 to 4 executives from the same organization were interviewed, either individually or together, regarding their experiences with one qualifying joint venture. Four other interviews involving one respondent discussing one qualifying joint venture were excluded from our quantitative analyses and hypothesis testing efforts because it was not possible to obtain sufficient data since the self-administered questionnaires were not returned, despite follow-up letters. Finally, in two of the interviews conducted, the respondent discussed a venture that did not qualify for the research sample.

STATISTICAL ANALYSIS OF DATA

All statistical analysis was conducted using Version 2 of the SPSS-X statistical package.[16] The general procedures employed included frequencies, cross-tabulations (bivariate correlations), partial correlations, and factor analysis. Each of these procedures was applied to the original data set. In addition, to enhance the reliability of the results that were obtained, these procedures were conducted using data for which the "missing values" were recoded to appropriate values. A discussion of the specific procedures employed in data analysis, as well as the rationale for their use, is included in Appendix B.

Table 5
Composition of Research Sample

	Number of Executives	Number of JVs
Number of qualifying interviews involving one executive discussing one JV	67	67
Number of qualifying interviews involving one executive discussing two JVs	7	14
Number of qualifying interviews involving more than one executive discussing one JV	21	9
Totals for qualifying interviews	95	90
Number of interviews involving nonqualifying JVs	2	2
Number of interviews involving qualifying JVs but excluded due to incomplete data	4	4
Totals for nonqualifying interviews	6	6
Totals for research study	101	96

CHAPTER SUMMARY

This chapter discussed the research method employed for collecting the data necessary to test the hypotheses developed in Chapter 3. Chapter 5 presents the results of the statistical analysis of the data on partner selection criteria. Chapters 6 through 8 provide the results for the task-related variables, and Chapters 9 through 11 present similar discussions for the partner-related variables.

NOTES

1. C. William Emory, *Business Research Methods* (Homewood, Ill.: Irwin, 1980).
2. W. W. Daniel, "Nonresponse in Sociological Surveys: A Review of Some Methods for Handling the Problem," *Sociological Methods and Research* (February, 1975), pp. 291–307; Duane F. Alwin, "Making Errors in Surveys," *Sociological Methods and Research* (November, 1977), pp. 131–50.
3. James W. C. Tomlinson, *The Joint Venture Process in International Business: India and Pakistan* (Cambridge, Mass.: MIT Press, 1970).
4. Floyd J. Fowler, Jr., *Survey Research Methods* (Beverly Hills, Calif.: Sage, 1984).

5. Emory, *Business Research Methods*; Fowler, *Survey Research Methods*.

6. Fowler, *Survey Research Methods*.

7. Fred N. Kerlinger, *Foundations of Behavioral Research*, 2d ed. (New York: Holt, Rinehart & Winston, 1973).

8. Tomlinson, *The Joint Venture Process*; William E. Renforth, "A Comparative Study of Joint International Business Ventures with Family Firm or Non-Family Firm Partners: The Caribbean Community Experience," Ph.D. diss., Graduate School of Business, Indiana University, 1974; Paul W. Beamish, "Joint Venture Performance in Developing Countries," Ph.D. diss., University of Western Ontario, 1984.

9. *Directory of Corporate Affiliations 1985* (Wilmette, Ill.: National Register Publishing Co., 1985); Dun and Bradstreet, Inc., *Million Dollar Directory 1984* (Parsippany, N.J.: Dun and Bradstreet, 1984); *Standard & Poor's Register of Corporations, Directors and Executives* (New York: Standard & Poor's, 1985).

10. David Nachmias and Chava Nachmias, *Research Methods in the Social Sciences* (New York: St. Martin's Press, 1976).

11. Fowler, *Survey Research Methods*.

12. Emory, *Business Research Methods*.

13. Tomlinson, *The Joint Venture Process*; Stephen M. Hills, "The Search for Joint Venture Partners," in Jeffrey C. Susbauer, ed., *Academy of Management Proceedings* (San Francisco: Academy of Management, 1978), pp. 277–81; Allen R. Janger, *Organization of International Joint Ventures* (New York: The Conference Board, 1980).

14. In a few instances, insufficient lead time prevented us from mailing a questionnaire to the respondent. Under these circumstances, we incorporated some of the questionnaire topics into the interview and provided the respondent with the questionnaire and a self-addressed, stamped envelope for its return.

15. Fowler, *Survey Research Methods*.

16. See Marija J. Norusis, *SPSS-X Advanced Statistics Guide* (New York: McGraw-Hill, 1985); and Marija J. Norusis, *SPSS-X Introductory Statistics Guide* (New York: McGraw-Hill, 1983).

II

RESULTS FOR PARTNER SELECTION CRITERIA VARIABLE

5

Partner Selection Criteria Variable

This chapter presents the findings regarding the partner selection criteria (PSC) variable. The categories of PSC that were examined, as well as the identification of which were labelled task-related and which were labelled partner-related selection criteria, will be discussed. Analytical results, including frequencies, means, standard deviations, and relative rankings of the partner selection criteria categories will also be presented. In addition, since several PSC categories overlapped conceptually, the efforts made to obtain statistically distinct selection criteria categories via use of factor analysis will be reviewed.

PARTNER SELECTION CRITERIA CATEGORIES

Based on a review of prior studies of joint venture partner selection as well as on responses from pretest interviews, 27 categories of partner selection criteria were included in the questionnaire. These categories, listed by their SPSS-X variable label, are presented in Table 6. Of the 27 categories examined, 14 were directly associated with the categories used for the critical success factor, competitive position, and difficulty of internal development variables. These 14 categories, which will be referred to as the task-related partner selection criteria, are identified in Table 6 with an asterisk (*). An additional 6 categories, identified as partner-related PSC, are identified in Table 6 with an ampersand (&). The remaining 7 selection criteria were not directly associated with either task-related or partner-related variables. Therefore, these 7 categories were included only in analyses involving PSC categories in toto, not those analyses confined to task-related or partner-related selection criteria categories.

Table 6
Variable Labels and Descriptions for Partner Selection Criteria Categories

```
Variable
 Label              Description of Category

*PSCGOVT$    Enables JV to qualify for subsidies or credits
 PSCSLAVE    Can provide low cost labor to the JV
*PSCREGUL    Helps comply with government requirements/pressure
 PSCRM       Has access to raw materials or components
*PSC$        Will provide financing/capital to the JV
*PSCEES      Can supply technically skilled personnel to JV
*PSCMGMT     Can supply general managers to the JV
&PSCNEARU    Is close to respondent firm, geographically
*PSCPATNT    Possesses needed licenses, patents, know-how, etc.
*PSCSITE     Controls favorable location (e.g., for mfg.)
 PSCPLANT    Possesses needed manufacturing or R&D facilities
*PSCMKTG     Has access to marketing or distribution systems
*PSCSERV     Has access to post-sales service network
*PSCTRDMK    Has valuable trademark or reputation
*PSCLOCAL    Enhances perceived local/national identity of JV
&PSCCOMIT    Has a strong commitment to the JV
&PSCFREND    Top management of both firms is compatible
*PSCLOWC     Will enable the JV to produce at lowest cost
*PSCRAPID    Permits faster entry into the target market
 PSCNOMKT    Has knowledge of target market's economy & customs
 PSCXPORT    Can enhance the JV's export opportunities
 PSCACCES    Improves access for respondent company's products
&PSCLIKEU    Has similar national or corporate culture
&PSCSIZE     Is similar in size or corporate structure
&PSCPRIOR    Had satisfactory prior assoc'n with respondent firm
*PSCGSALE    Enhances JV's ability to make sales to government
 PSCUFILL    Has related products, helps fill JV's product line
```

```
* = task-related partner selection criteria category
& = partner-related partner selection criteria category
```

PARTNER SELECTION CRITERIA DESCRIPTIVE STATISTICS

The statistical means, standard deviations, and frequencies obtained for each of the 27 partner selection criteria categories are presented in Table 7 for both the original and the recoded samples.[1] The variables are listed in descending order, based upon the magnitude of their respective statistical mean from the nonrecoded data. The results, including the magnitude and relative ordering of the means, appear to be relatively stable across the two samples.

Analysis of Table 7 provides several insights into the selection criteria results. First, the two categories evidencing the largest average values, PSCCOMIT and PSCFREND, are both classified as partner-related selection criteria. Thus, it appears that the study's respondents tended to perceive at least some partner-related criteria as important considerations in the selection of partners. The most important partner-related selection criteria were PSCCOMIT and PSCFREND; PSCLIKEU also had some potential

Table 7
Descriptive Statistics for Partner Selection Criteria Categories

Variable Label	Unrecoded Data			Recoded Data		
	Mean	Std. Dev.	(n)	Mean	Std. Dev.	(n)
PSCCOMIT	3.24	0.676	90	3.24	0.676	90
PSCFREND	3.11	0.841	90	3.11	0.841	90
PSCRAPID	2.92	1.047	89	2.89	1.086	90
PSCEES	2.71	1.068	89	2.68	1.100	90
PSCNOMKT	2.59	1.427	87	2.50	1.478	90
PSCTRDMK	2.55	0.977	89	2.52	1.008	90
PSC$	2.53	1.163	90	2.53	1.163	90
PSCACCES	2.22	1.225	81	2.00	1.341	90
PSCMGMT	2.21	1.050	89	2.19	1.069	90
PSCPATNT	2.17	1.316	89	2.14	1.329	90
PSCMKTG	2.10	1.367	83	1.93	1.428	90
PSCLOCAL	2.08	1.533	88	2.03	1.547	90
PSCPLANT	2.05	1.422	78	1.78	1.497	90
PSCLOWC	2.03	1.005	87	1.97	1.054	90
PSCXPORT	1.89	1.400	73	1.53	1.463	90
PSCLIKEU	1.81	1.226	90	1.81	1.226	90
PSCSIZE	1.56	1.066	89	1.54	1.072	90
PSCPRIOR	1.49	1.274	90	1.49	1.274	90
PSCUFILL	1.47	1.284	87	1.42	1.289	90
PSCREGUL	1.33	1.266	88	1.30	1.267	90
PSCRM	1.33	1.293	84	1.24	1.292	90
PSCSITE	1.19	1.311	83	1.10	1.299	90
PSCSERV	1.14	1.028	80	1.01	1.033	90
PSCGSALE	0.97	1.298	77	0.83	1.247	90
PSCNEARU	0.49	0.917	86	0.47	0.902	90
PSCGOVT$	0.47	0.975	87	0.46	0.962	90
PSCSLAVE	0.33	0.876	89	0.32	0.872	90

The range of possible integer values for partner selection criteria categories is 0 to 4. The maximum number of cases is 90.

significance. It is also interesting to note the relatively low level of importance accorded to selection of a partner with which a firm has had favorable prior association (i.e., PSCPRIOR). This result seems to be in sharp contrast to the research of James W. C. Tomlinson, who found that this dimension represented British firms' highest priority when selecting partners for joint ventures in India and Pakistan.[2]

The results presented in Table 7 also suggest that a prospective partner's influence vis-a-vis government policies was often accorded relatively low importance in the selection decision. The three categories intended to capture dimensions of government influence (i.e., PSCGOVT$, PSCGSALE, and PSCREGUL) had average values of 0.471, 0.974, and 1.330, respectively, for the original sample and lower means for the recoded data. These three categories' statistical means each ranked 20th or lower, out of 27 categories, for both of the samples. The ability of a prospective partner to access government financing or other subsidies (i.e., PSCGOVT$) apparently was not perceived as a particularly important selection criterion. For the nonrecoded data, its average value was significantly less than seven other categories (PSCCOMIT, PSCFREND, PSCRAPID, PSCEES, PSCNOMKT, PSCTRDMK, and PSC$) at a 0.05 level, and less than an additional five categories (PSCACCES, PSCMGMT, PSCPATNT, PSCMKTG, and PSCLOCAL) when evaluated at a 0.10 level for the un-recoded data. It is noteworthy that the PSC$ category had a substantially higher mean than the PSCGOVT$ category. This suggests that, although financing was often an important consideration in partner selection, managers evidenced a strong preference for partners providing nongovernmental sources of financing.

Two final observations can be made from the data in Table 7. First, managers generally placed little emphasis on selection of a partner with access to low-cost labor (i.e., PSCSLAVE). Fully one-half of the selection criteria categories evidenced values significantly greater than the low-cost labor dimension, when evaluated at a 0.05 level. This result may reflect the relatively high wage levels characteristic of the developed countries as a whole. It may also reflect participating managers' tendency to seek partners with skilled management and labor, which would further decrease the relative importance of low-cost labor as a selection criterion.

The second observation concerns the low relative importance attributed to finding a partner in close geographical proximity to the respondent's firm (i.e., PSCNEARU). The average importance managers assigned to this criterion was significantly lower than 14 other criteria, when measured at a 0.10 level. This finding may be explained partly by the large proportion of sample joint ventures which did not have the United States as their principal market focus, or which involved non-U.S. firms seeking a joint venture where the United States would be a primary market focus. Under both of these scenarios, managers commented that selection of a partner evidencing close geographical proximity was seldom an important consideration.

FACTOR ANALYSIS OF PARTNER SELECTION CRITERIA CATEGORIES

Because of potential conceptual overlap among the 27 PSC categories used on the questionnaire, it was decided to identify a smaller number of distinct, nonoverlapping partner selection criteria for the sample data. The most appropriate means of accomplishing this task involved the employment of factor analysis, a commonly employed technique used to derive statistically nonoverlapping, or orthogonal, dimensions from sample data which may not evidence such distinctness.

The specific method used for conducting the factor analysis procedures is discussed in Appendix B. The results of the factor analysis of the PSC categories are shown in Table 8.[3] The analysis produced nine interpretable factors which explained a total of 72.2 percent of the observed variance. The remainder of this section will discuss the interpretation of each of these factors.

Factor 1: Knowledge of Local Market, Not Technology

The first factor evidenced high positive loadings on the following six selection criteria categories: improved access for your firm's products (PSCACCES); ability to enhance the local or national identity of the joint venture (PSCLOCAL); knowledge of the local market economy or customs (PSCNOMKT); access to marketing and/or distribution systems (PSCMKTG); enhancement of the joint venture's ability to export its output (PSCXPORT); and, to a lesser extent, the ability to satisfy government regulations or pressures (PSCREGUL). This factor also had high negative loadings on two other selection criteria categories: access to technically skilled employees (PSCEES) and on possession of patents, licenses, or other technological know-how (PSCPATNT). This first factor was therefore interpreted to be a criterion related to the desirability of selecting a partner that evidenced intimate access to and knowledge of the local market, rather than more technology related capabilities.

Factor 2: Similar Firm with Local Government Influence

This factor had high positive loadings on three selection criteria categories: access to government subsidies (PSCGOVT$), ability to enhance joint venture efforts to sell to the government (PSCGSALE), and ability to satisfy government regulations or pressure (PSCREGUL), as well as lower positive loadings on the criteria of similar national or corporate culture (PSCLIKEU) and on ability to enhance the local or national identity of the joint venture (PSCLOCAL). Therefore, this factor was interpreted as the desirability of selecting a culturally similar partner with the potential to enhance the joint venture's position vis-a-vis government policies, particularly those of the local government.

Factor 3: Compatible Partner

This factor had high positive loadings on four of the partner-related selection criteria categories: compatible top management (PSCFREND), strong commitment to the joint venture (PSCCOMIT), similar organizational size or structure (PSCSIZE), and similar national or corporate culture (PSCLIKEU). It was interpreted that this third factor reflects the perceived desirability of selecting a partner that evidenced compatibility on the partner-related dimensions of selection criteria.

Table 8
Rotated Factors for Partner Selection Criteria Categories

PARTNER SELECTION CRITERIA CATEGORY	FACTOR 1 Knowledge of Local Market, Not Technology	FACTOR 2 Similar Firm With Local Government Influence	FACTOR 3 Compatible Partner	FACTOR 4 Low Cost Production
PSCGOVTS	.17	.84*	.07	.02
PSCSLAVE	-.12	-.14	.08	.70*
PSCREGUL	.30*	.69*	.28	-.11
PSCRM	.04	-.02	.04	.52*
PSCS	.15	.16	.09	.10
PSCEES	-.68*	.08	-.16	.20
PSCMGMT	.28	-.02	-.01	.15
PSCNEARU	-.21	-.01	-.08	.12
PSCPATNT	-.56*	-.23	-.16	-.09
PSCSITE	.04	.03	-.09	.14
PSCPLANT	-.14	.12	-.26	.21
PSCMKTG	.62*	.04	.13	-.30
PSCSERV	.10	.08	.06	-.03
PSCTRDMK	.06	-.01	-.02	-.24
PSCLOCAL	.72*	.31*	.22	-.08
PSCCOMIT	.12	-.07	.84*	.00
PSCFREND	.14	.12	.85*	.12
PSCLOWC	-.13	-.02	.00	.72*
PSCRAPID	.19	.02	.17	.36*
PSCNOMKT	.71*	.27	.10	-.10
PSCXPORT	.54*	.10	-.02	.18
PSCACCES	.80*	.10	-.09	-.01
PSCLIKEU	.25	.42*	.44*	.01
PSCSIZE	.01	.29	.47*	-.16
PSCPRIOR	-.01	-.25	.26	-.34*
PSCGSALE	.06	.81*	-.12	-.06
PSCUFILL	-.13	.16	.06	-.01
EIGENVALUE	5.39	2.45	2.42	2.02
PCT. OF VAR.	20.0	9.1	9.0	7.5
CUM. PCT.	20.0	29.0	38.0	45.5

* factor loading $\geq$ 0.30

Table 8 (continued)

FACTOR 5	FACTOR 6	FACTOR 7	FACTOR 8	FACTOR 9
		Strategically		Similar
	Sales and	Critical		Respected Firm
Shared	Service	Manufacturing	Opportunistic	Controlling
Development	Experience	Capabilities	Neighbor	Inputs
.10	-.01	.03	-.15	-.04
.02	-.19	.09	.33*	-.04
-.08	-.05	-.15	.11	.21
.01	.12	.08	-.25	.63*
.73*	.07	-.06	-.31*	-.02
.08	.37*	-.12	-.01	.07
.07	.53*	.52*	-.21	.16
.08	.05	.10	.77*	-.02
.25	-.11	-.21	.06	.14
-.17	-.00	.87*	.11	-.03
.42*	-.06	.47*	.12	.03
.27	.36*	.13	-.01	.03
.07	.87*	-.04	.13	.11
.00	.11	.02	.00	.75*
-.16	.15	.07	-.29	.17
.02	.21	-.04	-.09	-.24
.02	-.05	-.05	.04	.18
.07	.10	.13	-.03	-.12
-.28	.35*	-.10	.44*	-.16
-.09	.36*	.05	-.03	.01
.15	-.04	-.34*	-.45*	.22
.19	.02	-.32*	-.06	.16
.12	.02	-.10	.37*	.44*
.18	-.27	-.13	-.05	.39*
.44*	-.27	.43*	-.02	.22
.21	.17	.09	.06	-.05
.75*	.10	-.12	.34*	.02
1.79	1.59	1.48	1.30	1.04
6.6	5.9	5.5	4.8	3.9
52.1	58.0	63.5	68.3	72.2

Factor 4: Low-Cost Production

The fourth factor included high positive loadings on four selection criteria categories: ability to facilitate low costs for the joint venture (PSCLOWC), access to low-cost employees (PSCSLAVE), access to raw materials or components (PSCRM), and, to a lesser extent, enhancement of rapid market entry (PSCRAPID). In addition, the criterion of favorable prior association (PSCPRIOR) received a relatively small negative loading. Based on these results, Factor 4 was interpreted as a reflection of managers' desire for selecting a partner that would facilitate implementation of low-cost production by the joint venture.

Factor 5: Shared Development

This factor evidenced high positive loadings on four categories of selection criteria: a partner with products or services to fill the joint venture's line (PSCUFILL), access to financing (PSC$), favorable prior association (PSCPRIOR), and possession of R&D or manufacturing facilities (PSCPLANT). Therefore, this factor was interpreted as the perceived desirability of selecting a partner in the same or a similar industry which might be willing to share facilities or expenses, thereby reducing the burden otherwise encountered by the firm if it pursued the project by itself.

Factor 6: Sales and Service Experience

This factor had high positive loadings on two criteria and lower positive loadings on four other criteria categories. The two categories evidencing the highest loadings were access to a post-sale service system (PSCSERV) and possession of experienced management (PSCMGMT). The categories with lower positive loadings were possession of technically skilled employees (PSCEES), knowledge of the target market (PSCNOMKT), access to marketing or distribution systems (PSCMKTG), and ability to facilitate rapid market entry (PSCRAPID). On the basis of these results, this factor was interpreted as the desirability of finding a partner with skilled and experienced personnel, particularly in the areas of marketing, distribution, and post-sales service in the target market.

Factor 7: Strategically Critical Manufacturing Capabilities

This seventh factor had a high positive loading on the criterion of possession of a valuable location (PSCSITE), along with smaller positive loadings on experienced management (PSCMGMT), possession of R&D or manufacturing facilities (PSCPLANT), and favorable prior association (PSCPRIOR). There were also relatively smaller negative loadings on the criteria of improved access for the firm's products (PSCACCES) and ability to enhance the joint venture's exporting prospects (PSCXPORT). The factor was therefore interpreted as reflecting managers' desire to select a prior acquaintance with strategically important managerial and production facilities, primarily for the development of products intended principally for their local or national market.

Factor 8: Opportunistic Neighbor

This factor had a high positive loading on the criterion of a partner located nearby geographically (PSCNEARU) as well as lower positive loadings on four other categories: ability to enhance rapid market entry (PSCRAPID), similarity of national or corporate culture (PSCLIKEU), possession of products or services to fill the joint venture's line (PSCUFILL), and access to low-cost employees (PSCSLAVE). Ability to enhance exporting by the joint venture (PSCXPORT) and access to financing (PSC$) had negative loadings on this factor. The interpretation of this eighth factor was the perceived desire to select a partner that was in close geographical proximity and in a related industry—one that could enhance rapid entry into the target market.

Factor 9: Similar Respected Firm Controlling Inputs

This factor had high positive loadings on the following criteria: the prospective partner's possession of a valuable trademark or reputation (PSCTRDMK), access to raw materials or components (PSCRM), similarity of national or corporate culture (PSCLIKEU), and similarity of organizational size or structure (PSCSIZE). The factor was interpreted as managers' perception of the desirability of selecting a partner similar in culture, size, and reputation which controlled access to needed inputs.

SUMMARY OF PARTNER SELECTION CRITERIA RESULTS

This chapter presented and discussed the results for the partner selection criteria variable. A total of 27 selection criteria categories was examined, including 14 labelled task-related and 6 labelled partner-related PSC categories. Descriptive statistics were presented for each of the 27 categories, including means, standard deviations, and frequencies. These data supported the contention that partner-related selection criteria represented important input in the partner selection decision, with the most important partner-related criteria categories appearing to be PSCCOMIT and PSCFREND. The results also suggested that selection criteria categories related to government influence tended to be perceived as less important in partner selection than were other criteria categories.

Due to the potential for conceptual or statistical overlap among the 27 PSC categories, we employed factor analysis techniques on the unrecoded data to produce a set of distinct, nonoverlapping selection criteria. Factor analysis of the partner selection criteria categories produced the following nine nonoverlapping factors:

1. Knowledge of local market, not technology
2. Similar firm with local government influence
3. Compatible partner
4. Low-cost production
5. Shared development
6. Sales and service experience
7. Strategically critical manufacturing capabilities
8. Opportunistic neighbor
9. Similar respected firm controlling inputs

These nine factors explained over 70 percent of the observed variance in the sample data.

Some or all of the original 27 partner selection criteria categories, as well as the nine factors obtained from them, will be used in Chapters 6 through 8 and Chapters 9 through 11 for analyses of the task-related and the partner-related variables, respectively.

NOTES

1. For a discussion of the recoding scheme utilized, see Appendix B.

2. James W. C. Tomlinson, *The Joint Venture Process in International Business: India and Pakistan* (Cambridge, Mass.: MIT Press, 1970).

3. Efforts to factor analyze the recoded partner selection criteria categories were undertaken, but the varimax rotation failed to converge. This was the only recoded variable category in the study that did not produce rotated factors. In addition, efforts to obtain oblique rotations of the factors for the unrecoded data were undertaken, but the rotations failed to converge.

III

RESULTS FOR TASK–RELATED VARIABLES

TASK-RELATED VARIABLE CATEGORIES

Sixteen task-related categories were obtained for each of the three task-related variables based on responses from pretest interviews and on a review of related studies.[1] These categories are listed and briefly described in Table 9. There were partner selection criteria categories directly associated with fourteen of these task-related categories. These fourteen categories are identified in Table 9 with an asterisk (*).

The task-related variables—critical success factor, competitive position, and difficulty of internal development—bore a close conceptual relationship to each other. This linkage was intentional due to the desire to develop a thorough and well-integrated schema for understanding the allocation of valences to task-related partner selection criteria categories. However, this linkage also raised the potential for intercorrelation among variable categories. For individual variables, the potential problems of intercorrelation were eased via the use of factor analysis, which helped to identify the nonoverlapping dimensions underlying each of the three task-related variables' categories.

However, the presence of moderate intercorrelation between related variable categories (e.g., between CSFREGUL, CPREGUL, and DDREGUL) had the potential for confounding efforts to test the research hypotheses, thus threatening the validity of the results. As discussed in Appendix B, the existence of intercorrelation would make it difficult to determine the relationship between a particular pair of variables (e.g., CSFREGUL with PSCREGUL) due to the possible effects of other moderately correlated variables (e.g., CPREGUL and DDREGUL). As can be seen by the data in Table 10, the associated task-related categories frequently evidenced mod-

Table 9
Variable Labels and Descriptions for Critical Success Factor Categories

Critical Success Factor Variable Label	Competitive Position Variable Label	Difficulty of Internal Development Variable Label	Description of Category
*CSFGOVT$	*CPGOVT$	*DDGOVT$	Gov't subsidies, tax credits & other inducements
*CSFREGUL	*CPREGUL	*DDREGUL	Government pressures, regulatory requirements, etc.
*CSF$	*CP$	*DD$	Access to financial resources
*CSFEES	*CPFEES	*DDEES	Technically skilled employees
*CSFMGMT	*CPMGMT	*DDMGMT	Experienced managerial personnel
*CSFPATNT	*CPPATNT	*DDPATNT	Licenses, patents, or other proprietary knowledge
*CSFSITE	*CPSITE	*DDSITE	Location of joint venture facilities
*CSFMKTG	*CPMKTG	*DDMKTG	Marketing or distribution systems
*CSFSERV	*CPSERV	*DDSERV	Post-sales customer service network
*CSFTRDMK	*CPTRDMK	*DDTRDMK	Trademarks or reputation of parent firm
*CSFLOCAL	*CPLOCAL	*DDLOCAL	Perceived local or national identity of JV
*CSFLOWC	*CPLOWC	*DDLOWC	Low per-unit costs
*CSFRAPID	*CPRAPID	*DDRAPID	Rapid entry into the target market
CSFLOWP	CPLOWP	DDLOWP	Low price to customers
*CSFGSALE	*CPGSALE	*DDGSALE	Sales to government
CSFFULL	CPFULL	DDFULL	Full line of products or services

* = categories used as input in task-related variable
    computations

Table 10
Tau–B Correlations between Associated Task-Related Variable Categories and Partner Selection Criteria Categories

	CPREGUL	DDREGUL	PSCREGUL
CSFREGUL	.03	.35*	.41*
CPREGUL		-.64*	.28*
DDREGUL			.50*

	CP$	DD$	PSC$
CSF$	-.13	.29*	.42*
CP$		-.67*	-.35*
DD$			.51*

	CPGOVT$	DDGOVT$	PSCGOVT$
CSFGOVT$	-.07	.28*	.53*
CPGOVT$		-.59*	-.44*
DDGOVT$			.51*

	CPMGMT	DDMGMT	PSCMGMT
CSFMGMT	.11	.11	.27*
CPMGMT		-.50*	-.15
DDMGMT			.31*

	CPEES	DDEES	PSCEES
CSFEES	.01	.25*	.52
CPEES		-.51*	-.31*
DDEES			.53*

	CPSITE	DDSITE	PSCSITE
CSFSITE	-.01	.23*	.41*
CPSITE		-.63*	-.34*
DDSITE			.22*

	CPLOWC	DDLOWC	PSCLOWC
CSFLOWC	-.10	.44*	.56**
CPLOWC		-.56*	-.09
DDLOWC			.32*

	CPPATNT	DDPATNT	PSCPATNT
CSFPATNT	.27*	-.02	.26*
CPPATNT		-.67*	-.40*
DDPATNT			.55*

	CPTRDMK	DDTRDMK	PSCTRDMK
CSFTRDMK	.13	.17*	.38*
CPTRDMK		-.41*	.03
DDTRDMK			.12

	CPRAPID	DDRAPID	PSCRAPID
CSFRAPID	.12	.15	.62*
CPRAPID		-.53*	.13
DDRAPID			.01

	CPGSALE	DDGSALE	PSCGSALE
CSFGSALE	-.14	.51*	.85*
CPGSALE		-.64*	-.15
DDGSALE			.46*

	CPLOCAL	DDLOCAL	PSCLOCAL
CSFLOCAL	-.52*	.58*	.70*
CPLOCAL		-.71*	-.57*
DDLOCAL			.61*

	CPMKTG	DDMKTG	PSCMKTG
CSFMKTG	-.13	.21*	.28*
CPMKTG		-.69*	-.46*
DDMKTG			.55*

	CPSERV	DDSERV	PSCSERV
CSFSERV	.22*	-.05	.53*
CPSERV		-.62*	-.34*
DDSERV			.44*

* reflects $P \leq 0.05$

erate intercorrelations.[2] Therefore, to control for the effects of intercorrelation, the analysis includes discussion of relevant partial correlation coefficients as well as the bivariate correlations of the variable categories and their factors with the associated partner selection criteria categories and their factors.

The discussion of task-related variables begins in Chapter 6 with an analysis of the critical success factor variable. After addressing the issues related to that variable, a similar discussion will be presented for the competitive position variable in Chapter 7 and for the difficulty of internal development variable in Chapter 8.

NOTES

1. A number of sources were used; the principal ones were Michael E. Porter, *Competitive Strategy* (New York: Free Press, 1980); and George A. Steiner, "Strategic Factors in Business Success," (Los Angeles: Graduate School of Business Administration, University of California, Los Angeles, 1968).

2. Similarly, several moderate intercorrelations were present between the factors obtained from the data on the task-related variables' categories.

6

Critical Success Factor Variable

This chapter presents the results for the critical success factor variable. The average (mean) values, standard deviations, and frequencies obtained for each of the critical success factor categories are presented in Table 11 for both the original and the recoded data samples; the variables are listed in descending order based on their average value for the unrecoded data.

Analysis of Table 11 provides several insights into critical success factors. First, access to government financing or subsidies (CSFGOVT$) and ability to make government sales (CSFGSALE) had lower average values than any of the other categories. Six categories (CSFEES, CSFMGMT, CSFTRDMK, CSF$, CSFMKTG, and CSFPATNT) had higher means than CSFGOVT$ at a 0.05 level of significance, and these same categories had higher means than CSFGSALE at a 0.10 level. Thus, participants perceived that government subsidies and government sales were generally less important to the successful performance of their prospective joint ventures than were other task-related categories. It is noteworthy that the CSF$ category was perceived to be significantly more important than the CSFGOVT$ category. This suggests that, although financing was frequently perceived to be a critical factor to a joint venture's success, there was a significant difference in the perceived importance of financing which originated from nongovernmental versus governmental sources.

Perusal of Table 11 also suggests that technological capability was often perceived to be a critical success factor for the joint ventures. The categories that are associated with general technological capability [e.g., technically skilled employees (CSFEES); experienced management (CSFMGMT); trademark or reputation (CSFTRDMK); and patents, licenses, or know-how (CSFPATNT)] generally had higher values than did the categories that were less associated with general technological capability. Although the

Table 11
Descriptive Statistics for Critical Success Factor Categories

	Unrecoded Data			Recoded Data		
Variable Label	Mean	Std. Dev.	(n)	Mean	Std. Dev.	(n)
CSFFEES	3.11	0.903	88	3.04	1.005	90
CSFMGMT	2.89	0.831	88	2.83	0.927	90
CSFTRDMK	2.85	0.865	88	2.79	0.954	90
CSF$	2.79	1.074	88	2.73	1.140	90
CSFMKTG	2.78	1.091	80	2.47	1.351	90
CSFPATNT	2.74	1.227	88	2.68	1.279	90
CSFRAPID	2.32	1.356	90	2.32	1.356	90
CSFLOCAL	1.99	1.418	88	1.94	1.433	90
CSFREGUL	1.99	1.293	83	1.83	1.351	90
CSFLOWP	1.96	1.092	84	1.83	1.164	90
CSFLOWC	1.82	1.186	87	1.76	1.211	90
CSFSERV	1.81	1.274	80	1.61	1.330	90
CSFSITE	1.80	1.263	86	1.72	1.290	90
CSFFULL	1.69	1.211	81	1.52	1.256	90
CSFGSALE	0.73	1.162	81	0.66	1.123	90
CSFGOVT$	0.70	0.929	84	0.66	0.914	90

The range of possible integer values for critical success factor categories is 0 to 4. The maximum number of cases is 90.

difference was not significant in a statistical sense, this distinction was never-theless reinforced by managers' responses during the interviews.

HYPOTHESIS-TESTING EFFORTS

In Chapter 3, a positive correlation was hypothesized between managers' perceptions of the critical success factor and the partner selection criteria valence variables. To test this hypothesis, each of the fourteen critical success factor categories was correlated with its associated partner selection criteria category. The results of these correlations are listed in Table 12. As can be readily discerned from this table, the hypothesized relationship between the critical success factor and the partner selection criteria valence variables was overwhelmingly supported. For both the original and the recoded data, each of the fourteen correlations evidenced a positive relationship significant at the 0.01 level.

As previously discussed, a number of the associated task-related variable categories evidenced moderate to high levels of intercorrelation. Therefore, to effectively test Hypothesis 1, it was necessary to also calculate the partial correlation coefficients. The first- and second-order partial correlation coefficients for the critical success factor categories and their significance levels are presented in Table 13.

The results presented in Table 13 are very consistent with the data in Table 12 regarding the hypothesized relationship between the critical success factor variable categories and their associated task-related partner selection criteria valences. When the effects of both competitive position and difficulty of internal development were controlled for, thirteen of the fourteen critical success factor categories evidenced positive correlations significant at the 0.05 level. The remaining category evidenced a positive correlation signif-icant at the 0.10 level. Therefore, the results of the partial correlation analysis strongly support Hypothesis 1.

FACTOR ANALYSIS OF CRITICAL SUCCESS FACTOR CATEGORIES

Because of potential conceptual overlap between the critical success factor categories, we wanted to obtain statistically distinct categories for this var-iable's data. The most appropriate means of accomplishing this task involved the employment of factor analytic techniques.[1] Factor analysis permits the derivation of orthogonal, or nonoverlapping, dimensions of a variable.

The results of these analyses are shown in Tables 14 and 15 for the original and the recoded data, respectively.[2] The results of these two analyses are similar, supporting the statistical reliability of the factors that were obtained. For both samples, factor analysis produced seven interpretable factors, ex-plaining a total of 78.1 and 73.9 percent, respectively, of the observed

Table 12
Tau-B Correlations between Task-Related Partner Selection Criteria Categories and Critical Success Factor Categories

Critical Success Factor Category	Partner Selection Criteria Category	Tau-B for Unrecoded Data	Tau-B for Recoded Data
CSFREGUL	PSCREGUL	.41**	.36**
CSF$	PSC$	.42**	.50**
CSFGOVT$	PSCGOVT$	.53**	.45**
CSFMGMT	PSCMGMT	.27**	.28**
CSFEES	PSCEES	.52**	.53**
CSFSITE	PSCSITE	.40**	.39**
CSFLOWC	PSCLOWC	.56**	.58**
CSFPATNT	PSCPATNT	.26**	.28**
CSFTRDMK	PSCTRDMK	.38**	.38**
CSFRAPID	PSCRAPID	.62**	.64**
CSFGSALE	PSCGSALE	.85**	.82**
CSFLOCAL	PSCLOCAL	.70**	.73**
CSFMKTG	PSCMKTG	.28**	.42**
CSFSERV	PSCSERV	.53**	.46**

** reflects P $\leq$ 0.01
* reflects P $\leq$ 0.05

Table 13
First- and Second-Order Partial Correlations between Associated Categories
of Critical Success Factors and Partner Selection Criteria Variables

| | UNRECODED DATA | | | | RECODED DATA | |
| | CSF CATEGORY CONTROLLING FOR CP | CSF CATEGORY CONTROLLING FOR DD | CSF CATEGORY CONTROLLING FOR CP & DD | CSF CATEGORY CONTROLLING FOR CP | CSF CATEGORY CONTROLLING FOR DD | CSF CATEGORY CONTROLLING FOR CP & DD |
PSC CATEGORY						
PSCREGUL	.55**	.38**	.37**	.52**	.18*	.23*
PSC$	.44**	.34**	.35**	.51**	.34**	.36**
PSCGOVT$	.51**	.43**	.47**	.57**	.33**	.39**
PSCMGMT	.28**	.23*	.23*	.37**	.27**	.27**
PSCEES	.65**	.56**	.59**	.56**	.38**	.45**
PSCSITE	.23*	.17#	.25*	.46**	.26**	.35**
PSCLOWC	.63**	.56**	.54**	.62**	.49**	.47**
PSCPATNT	.40**	.24*	.26*	.54**	.25**	.28**
PSCTRDMK	.49**	.47**	.47**	.50**	.47**	.47**
PSCRAPID	.56**	.58**	.55**	.67**	.56**	.51**
PSCGSALE	.94**	.91**	.90**	.94**	.83**	.81**
PSCLOCAL	.60**	.54**	.52**	.73**	.49**	.52**
PSCMKTG	.22*	.16#	.17*	.38**	.04	.10
PSCSERV	.49**	.41**	.45**	.72**	.46**	.50**

\# reflects $P \leq 0.10$
* reflects $P \leq 0.05$
** reflects $P \leq 0.01$

Table 14
Rotated Factors for Critical Success Factor Categories: Original Sample

PARTNER SELECTION CRITERIA CATEGORY	FACTOR 1 Experienced Technical Personnel	FACTOR 2 Strong Market Presence	FACTOR 3 Rapid, Self-Financed Market Entry W/Service Orient.	FACTOR 4 Low Cost/ Low Price Position	FACTOR 5 Local Identity and Governmental Policies	FACTOR 6 Favorable Site	FACTOR 7 Governmental Promotion, Not Technology
CSFREGUL	-.30	.10	-.33*	-.18	.68*	-.10	.20
CSF$	.28	.23	-.62*	.15	-.27	-.45*	.20
CSFGOVT$	.20	.05	-.06	-.07	.19	-.05	.80*
CSFMGMT	.82*	.17	.02	-.01	-.01	.32*	.02
CSFEES	.88*	.04	.18	-.06	-.01	-.13	.01
CSFSITE	.10	-.07	-.08	.10	-.00	.90*	.07
CSFLOWC	.01	-.02	.02	.92*	-.09	.12	-.01
CSFPATNT	.40*	.00	-.06	.09	.13	-.24	-.68*
CSFTRDMK	.27	.77*	-.01	.02	.26	-.24	-.09
CSFRAPID	.09	.23	.81*	.10	-.13	-.04	-.04
CSFLOWP	-.06	.06	-.02	.91*	-.03	-.03	.04
CSFFULL	.09	.68*	.17	.18	-.14	.32*	.21
CSFGSALE	.29	-.15	.01	.21	.64*	-.21	.41*
CSFLOCAL	.04	.13	.23	-.14	.81*	.18	-.12
CSFMKTG	-.05	.76*	.21	-.08	.02	-.09	-.02
CSFSERV	.30*	.28	.75*	-.07	.15	-.17	.13*
Eigenvalue	2.96	2.14	1.91	1.67	1.51	1.24	1.07
Pct. of Var.	18.5	13.4	11.9	10.4	9.4	7.8	6.7
Cum. Pct.	18.5	31.9	43.8	54.2	63.6	71.4	78.1

* factor loading $\geq$ 0.30

Table 15
Rotated Factors for Critical Success Factor Categories: Recoded Data

PARTNER SELECTION CRITERIA CATEGORY	FACTOR 1 Local Identity and Governmental Policies	FACTOR 2 Experienced Technical Personnel	FACTOR 3 Strong Market Presence	FACTOR 4 Low Cost/ Low Price Position	FACTOR 5 Rapid, Self-Financed Market Entry W/Service Orient.	FACTOR 6 Government Promotion, Not Technology	FACTOR 7 Favorable Site
CSFREGUL	.70*	-.23	-.18	-.28	.06	.17	-.02
CSF$	.11	.12	.10	.05	.86*	.04	-.03
CSFGOVT$	.70*	-.06	.06	.09	.24	-.19	.22
CSFMGMT	-.00	.86*	.08	-.16	.00	-.02	.18
CSFFEES	-.02	.88*	.05	-.09	.08	.06	-.05
CSFSITE	.04	.14	.05	.15	-.05	-.05	.89*
CSFLOWC	-.16	-.07	-.01	.82*	.03	.13	.15
CSFPATNT	-.17	.00	-.01	.11	-.06	.88*	-.01
CSFTRDMK	.32*	.17	.20	.22	.23	.48*	-.35*
CSFRAPID	-.24	-.06	.46*	.20	-.46*	.24	.16
CSFLOWP	.14	-.19	-.04	.84*	.06	.05	-.01
CSFFULL	-.16	.23	.58*	.28	.21	-.32*	-.12
CSFGSALE	.72*	.25	-.13	.17	-.19	-.19	-.30
CSFLOCAL	.47*	.12	.29	-.27	-.53*	.08	.06
CSFMKTG	.02	-.06	.84*	-.20	.07	.15	.19
CSFSERV	.00	.28	.65*	-.03	-.42	-.09	-.28
Eigenvalue	2.47	2.25	1.81	1.64	1.34	1.17	1.14
Pct. of Var.	15.5	14.0	11.3	10.3	8.4	7.3	7.1
Cum. Pct.	15.5	29.5	40.8	51.1	59.5	66.8	73.9

* Factor loadings $\geq$ 0.30

variance in the two samples. The following discussion provides an interpretation of these factors.

Factor 1: Experienced Technical Personnel

The first factor obtained from the nonrecoded data was principally characterized by very high positive loadings on two categories: possession of
technically skilled employees (CSFEES) and of experienced management
(CSFMGMT). This factor also had lower positive loadings on the categories
of patents, licenses, and other know-how (CSFPATNT) and, to a lesser
extent, on access to post-sale service systems (CSFSERV). This first factor
was therefore interpreted as a critical success factor principally pertaining
to the possession of experienced, technically skilled personnel.

The statistical reliability of this first factor was strongly supported by
results for Factor 2 from the recoded data, which had high positive loadings
on the categories CSFEES and CSFMGMT. Thus, the reliability of a factor
emphasizing experienced technical personnel as a potential critical success
factor seems to be supported.

Factor 2: Strong Market Presence

This factor had high positive loadings on three categories: possession of
a valuable trademark or reputation (CSFTRDMK), access to marketing or
distribution systems (CSFMKTG), and ability to offer a full line of products
or services (CSFFULL). Therefore, this factor was interpreted as the importance to the joint venture of having a strong market presence.

The pattern of loadings for Factor 2 from the original data was similar
to the loadings for Factor 3 from the recoded data. The latter factor evidenced high loadings on CSFMKTG, CSFSERV, CSFFULL, and
CSFRAPID, again supporting an interpretation of the importance of possessing a strong market presence. On the basis of these results, the reliability
of Factor 2 seems to be supported.

Factor 3: Rapid, Self-Financed Market Entry with Service Orientation

This factor had high positive loadings on two categories: rapidity of
market entry (CSFRAPID) and access to a post-sales service system
(CSFSERV). It also had a large negative loading on access to financing
(CSF$). Therefore, Factor 3 was interpreted as the importance of rapid,
self-financed market entry, including access to a post-sales service system.

The reliability of Factor 3 seemed to be supported by the results for Factor
5 from the recoded data. Interestingly, the latter factor evidenced inverted
signs for the principal category loadings, with CSFRAPID and CSFSERV

receiving high negative loadings and CSF$ having a high positive loading. In addition, it had a high negative loading on the importance of the local or national identity of the joint venture (CSFLOCAL). Several respondents explained the presence of this latter category because of the frequent necessity of being perceived as a "local" organization in order to hasten acceptance of the new firm and its products in the marketplace. Particularly where post-sales servicing was perceived as important, identification as a local firm helped to assuage potential customers' fears regarding a new entrant into the market. In addition, since the same categories evidenced high loadings, but with opposite signs for the loadings, the statistical reliability of Factor 3 seemed to be supported.

Factor 4: Low-Cost, Low-Price Position

The fourth factor had high positive loadings on two categories: low per-unit costs (CSFLOWC) and low price to customers (CSFLOWP). Factor 4 from the recoded data also had very high positive loadings on these two categories. Therefore, this factor was interpreted as the importance to joint venture performance of the attainment of a low-cost or low-price position.

Factor 5: Local Identity and Governmental Policies

This factor had high positive loadings on three categories: the joint venture's local or national identity (CSFLOCAL), governmental regulations or pressure (CSFREGUL), and sales to the government (CSFGSALE). Therefore, it was interpreted as the perceived importance of the joint venture's having a local or national identity, especially in terms of the influence of that trait vis-a-vis the impact of governmental policies. This factor seemed to bear some similarity to Factor 7 from the unrecoded data, and Factor 1 from the recoded data appeared to represent a consolidation of these two factors. The latter factor had high positive loadings on the three government-related categories (CSFGSALE, CSFREGUL, and CSFGOVT$) and on CSFLOCAL. Therefore, the results suggest some tentative support for the reliability of a factor pertaining to the relative importance of local identity and a relationship to governmental policies for successful joint venture performance.

Factor 6: Favorable Site

This factor had a very high positive loading on the category of the joint venture's having a favorable location for its facilities (CSFSITE). Both this factor and Factor 7 from the recoded data evidenced a high loading on this category. Therefore, the statistical reliability of this sixth factor seemed to be supported.

Factor 7: Governmental Promotion, Not Technology

The seventh factor had a very high positive loading on the importance of government subsidies (CSFGOVT\$) and a high negative loading on the importance of licenses, patents, or other know-how (CSFPATNT), as well as a lower positive loading on sales to the government (CSFGSALE). Therefore, this factor was interpreted as the importance to the joint venture's performance of government promotional policies, rather than technology.

The results suggested that Factors 5 and 7 from the original data may have been consolidated into a single factor for the recoded data. This latter factor included the three government-related categories (CSFREGUL, CSF-GOVT\$, and CSFGSALE), along with the local or national identity category (CSFLOCAL). Therefore, there seems to be some support for the statistical reliability of a factor related to the importance of government influence.

CORRELATION BETWEEN FACTORS OF CRITICAL SUCCESS FACTOR AND PARTNER SELECTION CRITERIA VARIABLES

No specific hypotheses were developed regarding the relationship between the factors for the critical success factor categories and the factors for the partner selection criteria categories. Nevertheless, the bivariate correlations between these two sets of factors were calculated, and the results were examined in an attempt to uncover additional insights into the partner selection process. This section presents the results of these correlations.

The correlations were calculated using the factor results for the original data. In an effort to informally test the reliability of the results, the factors from the recoded data were also correlated with the partner selection criteria factors, and the results were compared to the correlations for the original data factors. Using the results of factor analysis as input, each of the seven factors for the critical success factor categories from both the original and the recoded data samples was correlated with each of the nine factors for the partner selection criteria categories from the original data. The results are listed in Table 16 for the original and recoded samples, respectively. The following subsections examine each of the factors from the original sample's critical success factor categories and the partner selection criteria factors significantly correlated with each of them. The results from correlations involving the corresponding factors from the recoded data are also discussed within each subsection.[3]

Factor 1: Experienced Technical Personnel

The first factor for the critical success factor variable evidenced three positive and one negative correlations, significant at the 0.05 level, with the

Table 16
Tau–B Correlations between Factors of Critical Success Factor and of Partner Selection Criteria Categories

ORIGINAL DATA

PARTNER SELECTION CRITERIA FACTORS	CSF FACTOR 1 Experienced Technical Personnel	CSF FACTOR 2 Strong Market Presence	CSF FACTOR 3 Rapid, Self-Financed Market Entry With Service Orientation	CSF FACTOR 4 Low Cost/ Low Price Position	CSF FACTOR 5 Local Identity & Government Policies	CSF FACTOR 6 Favorable Site	CSF FACTOR 7 Government Promotion, Not Technology
FACTOR 1 Knowledge of Local Market, Not Technology	0.00	0.06	-0.07	-0.13#	0.26**	0.08	0.04
FACTOR 2 Similar Firm with Local Government Influence	-0.17*	0.01	0.08	0.09	0.45**	-0.05	0.31**
FACTOR 3 Compatible Partner	-0.07	0.02	0.15#	-0.15#	0.07	0.00	0.00
FACTOR 4 Low Cost Production	0.03	-0.02	0.15#	0.33**	0.07	-0.01	-0.05
FACTOR 5 Shared Development	0.28**	-0.04	-0.26**	-0.01	-0.09	-0.09	0.16*
FACTOR 6 Sales & Service Experience	0.22**	0.08	0.32**	0.05	0.10	-0.02	0.20*
FACTOR 7 Strategically Critical Manufacturing Capabilities	0.06	-0.13#	0.02	0.16*	0.01	0.35**	-0.02
FACTOR 8 Opportunistic Neighbor	0.17*	0.08	0.07	-0.08	-0.01	0.05	0.19*
FACTOR 9 Similar Respected Firm Controlling Inputs	-0.10	0.24**	-0.07	0.15#	0.11	0.13	-0.02

reflects $P \leq 0.10$
*   reflects $P \leq 0.05$
** reflects $P \leq 0.01$

Table 16 (continued)

RECODED DATA

PARTNER SELECTION CRITERIA FACTORS	CSF FACTOR 1 Local Identity & Government Policies	CSF FACTOR 2 Experienced Technical Personnel	CSF FACTOR 3 Strong Market Presence	CSF FACTOR 4 Low Cost/ Low Price Position	CSF FACTOR 5 Rapid, Self-Financed Market Entry W/Service Orientation	CSF FACTOR 6 Government Promotion, Not Technology	CSF FACTOR 7 Favorable Site
FACTOR 1 Knowledge of Local Market, Not Technology	0.15*	0.00	0.08	-0.22**	-0.13#	0.18*	0.07
FACTOR 2 Similar Firm with Local Government Influence	0.53**	-0.14#	0.05	0.08	-0.12#	-0.04	-0.05
FACTOR 3 Compatible Partner	0.03	-0.11	0.13	-0.17*	-0.09	-0.02	0.08
FACTOR 4 Low Cost Production	0.01	-0.01	0.08	0.28**	-0.16*	0.00	0.01
FACTOR 5 Shared Development	0.06	0.19*	0.01	0.02	-0.32**	0.04	-0.09
FACTOR 6 Sales & Service Experience	0.14#	0.28**	0.24**	0.11	-0.17*	-0.01	-0.09
FACTOR 7 Strategically Critical Manufacturing Capabilities	0.01	0.11	-0.12#	0.19*	-0.13#	-0.12#	0.29**
FACTOR 8 Opportunistic Neighbor	-0.01	0.15*	0.11	-0.06	0.03	-0.05	0.06
FACTOR 9 Similar Respected Firm Controlling Inputs	0.11	0.02	0.16*	0.15*	-0.09	0.03	-0.06

\# reflects $P \leq 0.10$
* reflects $P \leq 0.05$
** reflects $P \leq 0.01$

selection criteria factors. According to these results, as access to experienced technical personnel increased in perceived importance as a critical success factor, selection of partners with the following characteristics was also perceived to be of increasing importance: ability to help share in development responsibilities (Factor 5), experience in sales and service (Factor 6), and embodiment of the qualities of an opportunistic neighbor (Factor 8). Under these same circumstances, selection of a similar firm with local government influence (Factor 2) was perceived to be of decreasing importance. The results for the recoded sample were similar, except that Factor 2 was significant at the 0.06 level.

These results suggest that, as perceptions of the importance of technically experienced personnel increased, respondents evidenced a predilection for selecting partners with technically oriented capabilities, rather than the ability to influence the government, to enhance development efforts.

Factor 2: Strong Market Presence

The second factor was positively correlated at the 0.01 level with one selection criteria factor: the importance of selecting a similar, highly respected firm which controlled important inputs (Factor 9). This second factor was also negatively correlated at the 0.10 level with the importance of selecting a partner with strategically critical manufacturing capabilities (Factor 7). For the recoded data, both Factor 9 and Factor 6 (sales and service experience) had significant positive correlations at the 0.05 level, and Factor 7 was negatively correlated at the 0.10 level.

These results suggest that, as the perceived importance of a strong market presence increased as a potential critical success factor, election of partners with the ability to enhance the strength of the joint venture's market presence also tended to be perceived as increasing in importance. The results also suggested that, under the above circumstances, selection of a partner with strategically critical manufacturing (as opposed to marketing or post-sales service) capabilities tended to decline in importance.

Factor 3: Rapid, Self-Financed Market Entry with Service Orientation

This third factor had positive correlations with three selection criteria factors at the indicated levels of significance: selection of a partner with sales and service experience (Factor 6, 0.01 level), ability of the partner to enhance low-cost or low-price position (Factor 4, 0.06 level), and compatibility of the partner (Factor 3, 0.06 level). Importance of selecting a partner capable of sharing in the development activities of the joint venture (Factor 5) was negatively correlated at a 0.01 level of significance. For the recoded data, both Factor 4 and Factor 6 were positively correlated at a 0.05 level, and

Factor 5 was negatively correlated at a 0.01 level. Therefore, the results for both samples are consistent.

These results suggest that, as the perceived importance of Factor 3 as a critical success factor increased, respondents tended to place increased emphasis on the selection of a partner that would enhance rapid entry, as might occur through improvement of a low-cost, low-price position, through less problematic interactions due to compatibility of the partner and through the partner's experience and capabilities in sales and service. As the importance of Factor 3 increased, there tended to be a decrease in the perceived importance of selecting a partner to help share in the joint venture's development, via contribution of similar products, R&D or production facilities, and financing.

Factor 4: Low-Cost, Low-Price Position

For the original data, this factor loaded positively on selection of a partner with the ability to enhance low-cost production (Factor 4, 0.01 level), possessing strategically critical manufacturing capabilities (Factor 7, 0.05 level), and with control over important inputs (Factor 9, 0.06 level). For the recoded data, factors 4, 7, and 9 all loaded positively at the 0.05 level, and both Factor 1 (knowledge of local market, not technology) and Factor 3 (compatible partner) loaded negatively at the 0.05 level.

These results suggest that, as the perceived importance of a low-cost or low-price position increased, an increased emphasis was placed on the selection of a partner that could enhance the joint venture's ability (e.g., through providing critical inputs, facilities, locations, or skilled personnel) to produce efficiently and at low cost. Under these same circumstances, the respondents seemed to de-emphasize the importance of selecting a compatible partner, or a partner that could provide market-based, rather than technological, capabilities.

Factor 5: Local Identity and Governmental Policies

For both the original and the recoded samples, this fifth factor was positively correlated with both Factor 1 (knowledge of the local market, not technology) and Factor 2 (similar firm with local government influence) at a 0.05 level. In addition, Factor 7 (selection of a partner with access to strategically critical manufacturing capabilities, including a favorable site) evidenced a positive correlation significant at the 0.10 level.

These results suggest that, as the perceived importance of Factor 5 increased as a critical success factor, firms placed greater emphasis on the selection of partners that had knowledge of the local market and the ability to influence the joint venture's position positively vis-a-vis government policies. Under these circumstances, selection of a partner with access to critical manufacturing capabilities, particularly site, also appeared to have been emphasized.

Factor 6: Favorable Site

For both the original and the recoded data, the sixth factor was positively correlated at the 0.05 level with selection criteria Factor 7, selection of a partner with access to strategically critical manufacturing capabilities, including a favorable site.

These results imply that, as the importance of the joint venture's having access to a particularly favorable site increased, firms tended to place greater emphasis on the selection of a partner with access to such a site.

Factor 7: Governmental Promotion, Not Technology

For the original data, this seventh factor was positively correlated at the 0.05 level with four selection criteria factors: Factor 2 (similar firm with local government influence), Factor 5 (firm able to share in development efforts, including access to financing), Factor 6 (sales and service experience), and Factor 8 (opportunistic neighbor). For the recoded data, only Factor 1 (knowledge of local market, not technology) and Factor 2 were positively correlated at a 0.05 level; Factor 6 was significant at the 0.07 level.

These results suggest that, as the perceived importance of government promotion, not technology, increased, firms tended to place increased emphasis on the selection of partners that could enhance their market-related capabilities (e.g., marketing or service expertise, similar products and services to fill the joint venture's line, more rapid entry, or increased local government influence).

CHAPTER SUMMARY

This chapter discussed the results for the critical success factor variable. Sixteen categories were examined, fourteen of which were directly associated with the task-related partner selection criteria categories. Descriptive statistics were presented for each of the sixteen categories, including means, standard deviations, and frequencies. Based on these data, it appeared that government subsidies and government sales were perceived to be generally less important to the successful performance of a prospective joint venture than were other task-related critical success factor categories. It also appeared that there was a significant difference in the importance of alternative sources of financing, with nongovernmental sources being perceived as more critical to success than governmental sources.

Hypothesis 1, which predicted a positive correlation between the perceived importance of potential critical success factor categories and the valences of their associated partner selection criteria categories, appeared to be overwhelmingly supported by the data. Each of the fourteen correlations evidenced a positive relationship significant at the 0.01 level or less. In addition, all fourteen of the second-order partial correlation coefficients were significant at the 0.10 level or less.

Factor analysis of the sixteen critical success factor categories produced seven factors for both the original and recoded data samples. The principal loadings on these factors were interpreted and discussed. These factors were interpreted as:

1. Experienced technical personnel
2. Strong market presence
3. Rapid, self-financed market entry with service orientation
4. Low-cost, low-price position
5. Local identity and governmental policies
6. Favorable site
7. Governmental promotion, not technology

The statistical reliability of the factors seemed to be supported.

Each of the factors from the original and recoded data samples of the critical success factor variable was correlated with the nine selection criteria factors. The results of these correlations were presented and discussed.

NOTES

1. Detailed information on the factor analysis methods that were employed are presented in Appendix B.

2. Oblique rotation of the factors obtained for the original data was attempted, but the analysis failed to converge.

3. Several moderate intercorrelations were present between the factors of the task-related variables. Therefore, the tenth-order partial correlation coefficients were obtained for the relationship between each of the critical success factor factors and the partner selection criteria factors, correcting for the effects of all of the competitive position and difficulty of internal development factors simultaneously. Examination of these partial correlations suggested that the correlations that evidenced statistical significance without controlling for the effects of the other task-related variables also tended to evidence significant partial correlations. This was particularly true for those factor correlations previously significant at a 0.05 level or less, twelve of sixteen of which had partial correlations significant at a 0.10 level or less. (The 0.10 significance level was used for comparison for the partial correlation analysis because of the loss of an additional nine degrees of freedom in their calculation.)

The lack of complete substantiation between the data in Table 16 and the partial correlation analyses may be partially attributable to the substantial loss of degrees of freedom associated with the partial correlation procedure and to method differences (e.g., the use of Pearson r versus Kendall tau-b-based statistics), rather than solely to the effects of intercorrelations between the task-related variable factors. Nevertheless, the results of the partial correlation analysis tended to support further the results of the bivariate correlational analysis.

7

Competitive Position Variable

This chapter presents the results for the competitive position variable. The average (mean) values, standard deviations, and frequencies obtained for each of the competitive position categories are presented in Table 17. This table presents the results for both the original and recoded data samples, with the variables listed in descending order based on their average value for the original data.

There were no statistically significant differences between categories' average values when evaluated at the 0.05 level. This outcome was not unexpected, however. Hypothesis 2 asserted that a weaker perceived competitive position would be correlated with a higher valence on the associated partner selection criterion. No significant differences were hypothesized or expected regarding dimensions on which the respondents would consistently perceive themselves as having strong or weak competitive positions. Under these circumstances, case-by-case differences would tend to balance out, and similar means across competitive position categories would not seem an unlikely outcome.

HYPOTHESIS-TESTING EFFORTS

In Chapter 3, a negative correlation was hypothesized between managers' perceptions of their firm's relative competitive position and the valences of the associated partner selection criteria. To test this hypothesis, the competitive position categories were correlated with their associated partner selection criteria categories for both the original and the recoded data. The results of these correlations are listed in Table 18. Of the fourteen correlations calculated for each sample, nine correlations from each sample evidenced the hypothesized relationship at a 0.05 level of significance. None

Table 17

Descriptive Statistics for Competitive Position Categories

Variable Label	Unrecoded Data			Recoded Data		
	Mean	Std. Dev.	(n)	Mean	Std. Dev.	(n)
CPTRDMK	2.68	0.558	88	2.67	0.561	90
CPMGMT	2.59	0.620	87	2.57	0.619	90
CPEES	2.59	0.771	87	2.57	0.765	90
CP$	2.48	0.822	86	2.46	0.810	90
CPPATNT	2.44	0.876	82	2.40	0.845	90
CPFULL	2.13	0.826	64	2.09	0.697	90
CPSERV	2.05	0.839	59	2.03	0.678	90
CPMKTG	2.01	0.836	74	2.01	0.757	90
CPREGUL	1.93	0.834	68	1.94	0.725	90
CPLOWC	1.92	0.640	73	1.93	0.577	90
CPLOCAL	1.87	1.027	71	1.90	0.912	90
CPLOWP	1.82	0.552	78	1.84	0.517	90
CPGSALE	1.81	0.821	32	1.93	0.493	90
CPRAPID	1.80	0.658	75	1.83	0.604	90
CPSITE	1.80	0.971	65	1.86	0.829	90
CPGOVT$	1.76	0.913	38	1.90	0.601	90

The range of possible integer values for competitive position categories is 0 to 4. The maximum number of cases is 90.

Table 18
Tau-B Correlations between Task-Related Partner Selection Criteria Categories and Competitive Position Categories

Competitive Position Category	Partner Selection Criteria Category	Tau-B for Unrecoded Data	Tau-B for Recoded Data
CPREGUL	PSCREGUL	-.28**	-.29**
CP$	PSC$	-.35**	-.31**
CPGOVT$	PSCGOVT$	-.44**	-.36**
CPMGMT	PSCMGMT	-.15	-.10
CPEES	PSCEES	-.31**	-.27*
CPSITE	PSCSITE	-.34**	-.31*
CPLOWC	PSCLOWC	-.09	-.10
CPPATNT	PSCPATNT	-.40**	-.40**
CPTRDMK	PSCTRDMK	.03	.03
CPRAPID	PSCRAPID	.13	.11
CPGSALE	PSCGSALE	-.15	-.30
CPLOCAL	PSCLOCAL	-.57**	-.66**
CPMKTG	PSCMKTG	-.46**	-.31**
CPSERV	PSCSERV	-.34**	-.37**

** reflects P $\leq$ 0.01
* reflects P $\leq$ 0.05

of the bivariate relationships evidenced non-negative relationships significant at a 0.05 level. Based on these results, the second hypothesis did not appear to be clearly rejected.

The associated task-related variable categories frequently evidenced moderate intercorrelation. Therefore, to test Hypothesis 2 effectively, it was necessary also to calculate the partial correlation coefficients for the competitive position categories. The first- and second-order partial correlation coefficients for the competitive position categories are presented in Table 19, along with significance levels. The partial correlation data suggest that the hypothesized relationship between the competitive position variable and the selection criteria valences received less support than was suggested by the bivariate correlations. Only four of the fourteen categories evidenced partial correlation coefficients significant at the 0.05 level for the original data, plus an additional category significant at the 0.07 level, when the effects of the associated critical success factor and the difficulty of internal development variables' categories were controlled for. The competitive position variable evidenced five categories significant at the 0.05 level, plus an additional three categories significant at the 0.10 level, for the recoded data.

The results of the partial correlation analysis suggests several interesting insights. First, the lack of complete substantiation of the bivariate correlation data presented in Table 18 may be partially attributable to variance in the methods employed (e.g., the use of Pearson r versus Kendall tau-b-based statistics), rather than solely to the effects of intercorrelation between the task-related variable categories. Only two of the partial correlations for the original data and only one partial correlation for the recoded data evidenced a positive coefficient, and none of these was statistically significant at the 0.10 level.

In addition to the above, when the effects of the critical success factor variable were controlled for, the competitive position variable evidenced a strong relationship in the hypothesized direction with the task-related partner selection criteria valences. When the critical success factor variable was controlled for, ten of the fourteen categories for both samples evidenced partial correlation coefficients significant at the 0.05 level, as well as an additional category significant at the 0.10 level. Thus, the presence of the difficulty of internal development variable often appeared to confound the observed relationship between the competitive position and the task-related partner selection criteria variables. This is evidenced by only six partial correlations evidencing statistical significance at the 0.10 level for each sample when the effects of the difficulty of internal development variable were controlled for. The implication of these results is that, as operationalized, the competitive position variable tended to evidence extensive statistical overlap with the difficulty of internal development variable. Nevertheless, the results also strongly support the statistical significance of this con-

Table 19

First- and Second-Order Partial Correlations between Associated Categories of Competitive Position and Partner Selection Criteria Variables

PARTNER SELECTION CRITERIA CATEGORY	UNRECODED DATA			RECODED SAMPLE		
	CP CATEGORY CONTROLLING FOR CSF	CP CATEGORY CONTROLLING FOR DD	CP CATEGORY CONTROLLING FOR CSF & DD	CP CATEGORY CONTROLLING FOR CSF	CP CATEGORY CONTROLLING FOR DD	CP CATEGORY CONTROLLING FOR CSF & DD
PSCREGUL	-.39**	.12	-.07	-.33**	.00	-.14
PSCS	-.42**	-.05	-.10	-.38**	.01	-.11
PSCGOVT$	-.47**	-.27	-.33*	-.43**	-.23*	-.32**
PSCMGMT	-.22*	.01	.04	-.21*	.06	-.03
PSCEES	-.48**	-.07	-.22*	-.48**	-.14	-.29**
PSCSITE	-.38**	-.29*	-.34**	-.36**	-.18	-.30**
PSCLOWC	-.04	.17	.00	-.03	.15	.00
PSCPATNT	-.55**	.02	-.11	-.54**	.06	-.13
PSCTRDMK	-.06	.07	-.04	-.07	.11	-.06
PSCRAPID	.14	.22*	.08	.11	.30**	.10
PSCGSALE	-.25	.31*	-.13	-.18	.27**	-.05
PSCLOCAL	-.42**	-.23*	-.18	-.39**	-.09	-.20*
PSCMKTG	-.53**	-.11	-.12	-.50**	-.13	-.16
PSCSERV	-.49**	-.05	-.22*	-.49**	.10	-.23*

$*$ reflects $P \leq 0.05$

$**$ reflects $P \leq 0.01$

founded variable when the critical success factor variable was controlled for. This means that the combined competitive position/difficulty of internal development variable appeared to explain a significant amount of the variance in the task-related partner selection criteria valences, when controlling for the effects of the critical success factor variable. Thus, further efforts to examine and refine this combined variable construct seem to be warranted.

FACTOR ANALYSIS OF COMPETITIVE POSITION CATEGORIES

Because of the potential for conceptual overlap between the competitive position categories, we wanted to obtain statistically distinct categories for this variable's sample data. The most appropriate means of accomplishing this task involved the employment of factor analytic techniques.

The identical factor analysis methods discussed in Appendix B were employed in analyzing the competitive position categories. The only exception is that the factor analysis was performed on the recoded rather than on the original data. This was done because two categories, CPGSALE and CPGOVT$, exhibited very low frequencies in the unrecoded sample. Numerical values for these two categories occurred in only 32 and 38 cases, respectively. The resulting set of relevant cases was very small (n = 19), and factor analysis resulted in ill-conditioned correlation matrices and negative eigenvalues. To overcome this problem, the recoded data were used as input. The resulting factor analyses produced interpretable outputs without ill-conditioned matrices. Therefore, the following discussion is based primarily on these results for the recoded data.

The results of factor analysis of the competitive position categories are shown in Table 20. To guard against potential inaccuracies resulting from recoding of the data, a factor analysis was also conducted on the original sample with only the CPGSALE and CPGOVT$ categories recoded. The resulting correlation matrix was not ill conditioned, and the results are listed in Table 21. As a further reliability check, oblique rotation of the factors was attempted. Results of the oblique rotations are also listed in Table 21.

As can be discerned from Tables 20 and 21, the results for the three analyses were quite similar, supporting the reliability of the factors that were obtained. Factor analysis produced four interpretable factors from each sample, explaining a total of 62.5, 72.7, and 62.5 percent of the observed variance in the recoded, partially recoded (only two recoded categories), and oblique rotation samples, respectively.

The remainder of this section presents an interpretation of the recoded data's rotated factors and compares these results with those from the partially recoded and oblique rotation samples.

Table 20
Rotated Factors for Competitive Position Categories

RECODED DATA

	FACTOR 1	FACTOR 2	FACTOR 3	FACTOR 4
PARTNER SELECTION CRITERIA CATEGORY	Position Vis-a-vis Local Government Influence	Rapid Entry W/Low Priced Product Line	Strong Local Market Presence	Strong Reputation And Financial Capability
CPREGUL	.76*	.16	.11	.04
CP$	.04	-.09	.03	.85*
CPGOVT$	.58*	.05	.19	.36*
CPMGMT	-.21	.31*	.14	.60*
CPEES	-.67*	.28	.19	.31*
CPSITE	.58*	.21	.48*	-.11
CPLOWC	-.10	.79*	.00	.12
CPPATNT	-.75*	.24	.10	.03
CPTRDMK	.00	.21	.13	.72*
CPRAPID	.12	.71*	.08	.10
CPLOWP	-.08	.83*	.05	.06
CPFULL	-.30	.41*	.58*	.31*
CPGSALE	.56*	-.14	.28	-.07
CPLOCAL	.71*	.06	.42*	.07
CPMKTG	.28	.08	.79*	.06
CPSERV	.18	-.06	.81*	.27
EIGENVALUE	3.85	3.49	1.54	1.12
PCT. OF VAR.	24.1	21.8	9.6	7.0
CUM. PCT.	24.1	45.9	55.5	62.5

* FACTOR LOADINGS $\geq$ 0.30

Factor 1: Position vis-a-vis Local Government Influence, Not Technology

The first factor from the recoded sample was characterized by high positive loadings on the following competitive position categories: government regulation or pressure (CPREGUL), local or national identity of the joint venture (CPLOCAL), access to government subsidies (CPGOVT$), location of joint venture facilities (CPSITE), and ability to make sales to the government (CPGSALE). This first factor also had high negative loadings on two categories: possession of patents, licenses, or other know-how (CPPATNT), and possession of technically skilled employees (CPEES). Therefore, this first factor was interpreted as a firm's perceived competitive

Table 21
Rotated Factors for Competitive Position Variable

PARTNER SELECTION CRITERIA CATEGORY	PARTIALLY RECODED DATA				OBLIQUE ROTATION			
	FACTOR 1 — Position Vis-a-vis Local Government Influence, Not Technology	FACTOR 2 — Rapid Entry W/Low Priced Product Line	FACTOR 3 — Strong Reputation and Financial Capability	FACTOR 4 — Strong Market Presence, W/O Rapid Entry	FACTOR 1 — Position Vis-a-vis Local Government Influence, Not Technology	FACTOR 2 — Strong Reputation and Financial Capability	FACTOR 3 — Rapid Entry W/Low Priced Product Line	FACTOR 4 — Strong Local Market Presence
CSFREGUL	.81*	-.30*	.36*	.00	.76*	.06	.23	-.05
CSF$	-.20	.27	.82*	.24	.09	.89*	-.17	.04
CSFGOVT$	.53*	.01	.64*	-.08	.57*	.38*	.05	-.13
CSFMGMT	-.03	.74*	.09	.09	-.20	.56*	.22	-.07
CSFEES	-.65*	.49*	.07	.13	-.70*	.23	.16	-.19
CSFSITE	.86*	-.02	.00	.20	.47*	-.17	.22	-.47*
CSFLOWC	-.11	.72*	.40*	-.12	-.06	.04	.80*	.08
CSFPATNT	-.62*	.52*	-.13	.17	-.78*	-.05	.16	-.13
CSFTRDMK	.12	.26	.83*	-.05	.03	.71*	.13	-.05
CSFRAPID	.17	.41*	.12	-.76*	.14	.03	.73*	.00
CSFLOWP	-.12	.77*	.12	-.18	-.05	-.04	.85*	.03
CSFFULL	-.35*	.73*	.32*	.23	-.42*	.18	.28	-.57*
CSFGSALE	.63*	-.18	-.12	.03	.49*	-.07	-.12	-.29
CSFLOCAL	.83*	.00	.10	-.01	.62*	-.10	.08	-.42*
CSFMKTG	.62*	.37*	-.05	.54*	.09	-.05	-.01	-.83*
CSFSERV	.29	.28	.37*	.72*	-.01	.18	-.19	-.85*
EIGENVALUE	5.02	3.82	1.56	1.23	3.85	3.49	1.54	1.12
PCT. OF VAR.	31.4	23.9	9.8	7.7	24.1	21.8	9.6	7.0
CUM. PCT.	31.4	55.3	65.0	72.7	24.1	45.9	55.5	62.5

* FACTOR LOADINGS ≥ 0.30

position relative to local government influence rather than technological capability.

The reliability of this first factor was strongly supported by results from the other samples. The first factor from the oblique rotation had high positive and negative loadings on exactly the same categories as the recoded sample, plus a negative loading on the joint venture's competitive position vis-a-vis the ability to offer a full line of products or services (CPFULL). Similarly, Factor 1 from the partially recoded sample loaded on these same categories, plus a positive loading on access to marketing or distribution systems (CPMKTG). On the basis of these results, there was strong support for a factor comprising a firm's perceived competitive position relative to local government influence rather than technological capability.

Factor 2: Rapid Entry with Low-Priced Product Line

This factor had very high positive loadings on three categories: low price to customers (CPLOWP), low per-unit costs (CPLOWC), and rapid market entry (CPRAPID). Therefore, this factor was interpreted as a firm's perceived relative competitive position for rapid entrance into the target market with a line of low-priced products.

The pattern of loadings for Factor 2 was similar to the loadings for factors from the other samples. Both the third factor from the oblique rotation and Factor 2 from the partially recoded data evidenced high positive loadings on the same three categories. In addition, the partially recoded data evidenced high positive loadings on the CPMGMT, CPEES, CPPATNT, and CPFULL categories. The high loading of the additional high categories on the partially recoded sample is related to the possession of technically experienced personnel and related technical know-how, which would be likely to affect the joint venture's ability to enter a market rapidly through efficient, low-cost production. On the basis of these results, the reliability of Factor 2 from the recoded data seems to be supported.

Factor 3: Strong Local Market Presence

This factor had high positive loadings on five competitive position categories: access to post-sales service systems (CPSERV), access to marketing or distribution systems (CPMKTG), a full line of products or services (CPFULL), an important location for joint venture facilities (CPSITE), and local or national identity of the joint venture (CPLOCAL). Therefore, Factor 3 was interpreted as the relative strength of a firm's local market presence.

The statistical reliability of Factor 3 was supported by the results for the other samples. The fourth factor from the oblique rotation had high loadings on the same five categories, although the signs for each loading were reversed. Factor 3 was also supported by the partially recoded data's fourth factor, which had high positive loadings on the CPSERV and CPMKTG categories, and a negative loading on the CPRAPID category. Based on these results, the reliability of Factor 3 seemed to be supported.

Factor 4: Strong Reputation and Financial Capability

The fourth factor had high positive loadings on access to financing (CP$ and CPGOVT$), strong reputation or trademarks (CPTRDMK), and experienced management (CPMGMT). Therefore, this factor was interpreted as a firm's relative competitive position vis-a-vis the strength of its reputation and financial capability.

The partially recoded sample's Factor 3 and the oblique rotation Factor 2 had high positive loadings on CP$, CPGOVT$, and CPTRDMK, and the second factor from the oblique rotation had high positive loadings on CPMGMT. Thus, the reliability of this factor from the recoded data was strongly supported.

CORRELATION BETWEEN FACTORS OF COMPETITIVE POSITION AND PARTNER SELECTION CRITERIA VARIABLES

No specific hypotheses were developed regarding the relationship between the competitive position factors and the factors for the partner selection criteria categories. Nevertheless, the bivariate correlations between these two sets of factors were calculated, and the results were examined in an attempt to uncover additional insights into the partner selection process. This section discusses the results of these bivariate correlations.

Using the results of factor analysis as input, each of the four factors for the competitive position categories from the recoded and the partially recoded data samples was correlated with each of the nine factors obtained in Chapter 5 for the partner selection criteria categories. The results are listed in Table 22 for the recoded and partially recoded samples.[1] The following discussion examines the factors from the recoded data's competitive position categories and the partner selection criteria factors significantly correlated with each of them. The results from correlations involving the associated partially recoded sample's factors are also discussed.

Factor 1: Position vis-a-vis Local Government Influence, Not Technology

The first factor for the competitive position categories evidenced two negative and one positive correlations (significant at the 0.06 level or less) with the partner selection criteria factors. According to these results, a

Table 22
Tau-B Correlations between Factors of Competitive Position Categories and Factors of Partner Selection Criteria Categories

PARTNER SELECTION CRITERIA FACTORS	RECODED DATA				PARTIALLY RECODED DATA			
	CP FACTOR 1 Position Vis-a-vis Local Government Influence	CP FACTOR 2 Rapid Entry W/Low Priced Product Line	CP FACTOR 3 Strong Local Market Presence	CP FACTOR 4 Strong Reputation and Financial Capability	CP FACTOR 1 Position Vis-a-vis Local Government Influence	CP FACTOR 2 Rapid Entry W/Low Priced Product Line	CP FACTOR 3 Strong Reputation and Financial Capability	CP FACTOR 4 Strong Market Presence, W/O Rapid Entry
FACTOR 1 Knowledge of Local Market, Not Technology	-0.49**	0.11	-0.05	0.01	-0.54**	0.22#	0.00	0.01
FACTOR 2 Similar Firm with Local Government Influence	-0.14#	0.01	-0.12#	0.01	-0.29#	0.20#	-0.23#	0.03
FACTOR 3 Compatible Partner	0.04	-0.05	-0.10	-0.05	0.20#	-0.43**	-0.09	-0.05
FACTOR 4 Low Cost Production	-0.09	-0.15*	0.12#	0.05	-0.01	-0.11	-0.08	0.15
FACTOR 5 Shared Development	-0.01	0.02	-0.03	-0.05	-0.10	-0.13	-0.12	-0.16
FACTOR 6 Sales & Service Experience	0.06	0.04	-0.17*	0.02	-0.13	-0.01	-0.17	-0.29*
FACTOR 7 Strategically Critical Manufacturing Capabilities	-0.08	-0.07	-0.05	0.10	-0.23#	-0.09	0.14	0.04
FACTOR 8 Opportunistic Neighbor	0.22**	0.08	-0.08	0.02	0.11	0.04	0.38**	-0.04
FACTOR 9 Similar Respected Firm Controlling Inputs	0.01	-0.25**	0.04	0.19*	0.09	0.08	0.19#	0.26*

\# reflects $P \leq 0.10$
* reflects $P \leq 0.05$
** reflects $P \leq 0.01$

decline in a firm's competitive position relative to local government influence, rather than technological capability, was correlated with an increased importance placed on the selection of a partner with knowledge of the local market, not technology (Factor 1), and on selection of a similar partner with local government influence (Factor 2). These two correlations were both supported, at a 0.05 level or less, by results for the partially recoded sample. For the recoded data, declining competitive position on Factor 1 was also correlated with decreasing valences on the selection of an opportunistic neighbor firm (Factor 8).

These results suggest that, as the perceived competitive position of a firm declined relative to its ability to deal with nontechnology-based local government influence, the firm generally tried to rectify this situation by placing greater emphasis on selecting a partner that could provide strengths in knowledge of the local market, possibly including influence with the local government. When competitive position on Factor 1 declined, decreased emphasis frequently tended to be placed on the selection of a partner with technology-related expertise.

Factor 2: Rapid Entry with Low-Priced Product Line

The second factor was negatively correlated with two selection criteria factors: selection of a partner enabling low-cost production (Factor 4), and selection of a similar firm controlling important inputs (Factor 9). The partially recoded sample evidenced a negative correlation on Factor 3, the selection of a compatible partner.

These results suggest that, as the perceived competitive position for rapid entry with a low-priced product line diminished, firms tended to place increased emphasis on selection of a partner with the capability of enhancing the firm's low-price position. This could occur through the partner's ability to provide important inputs: low-priced labor, raw materials, or efficient production technology or know-how. As competitive position on Factor 2 declined, there tended to be an increased emphasis on the selection of a compatible partner, which might reflect the partner's ability to reduce barriers to rapid entry or operational efficiency.

Factor 3: Strong Local Market Presence

This third factor had a significant negative correlation with partner selection criteria Factor 6, a partner with sales and service experience. The partially recoded sample evidenced a positive correlation between competitive position Factor 3 and partner selection criteria Factor 8, selection of an opportunistic neighbor. Both samples had a negative correlation, significant at 0.10 or less, with selection criteria Factor 2, a similar firm with local government influence.

These results suggested that increased relative strength of a firm's local market presence was correlated with a greater tendency to seek an opportunistic neighbor (Factor 8) as a partner but a smaller tendency to seek a compatible partner that could provide sales and service experience, or increased influence with the local government (Factor 2).

Factor 4: Strong Reputation and Financial Capability

At a 0.05 level for both samples, Factor 4 loaded positively on the selection of a similar partner which controls important inputs (Factor 9). The partially recoded sample also evidenced a significant negative correlation with Factor 6, selection of a partner with sales and service experience.

These results suggested that, as the relative strength of a firm's reputation and financial capability was perceived to decline, there tended to be a decreased emphasis placed on the selection of a similarly respected (in this case, declining level of respect) firm which controlled important inputs and which could share development efforts, but there was an increased emphasis on selecting an opportunistic neighbor, preferably one with strengths in sales and service ability.

CHAPTER SUMMARY

This chapter presented and discussed the results for the competitive position variable. Sixteen categories were examined for this variable, fourteen of which were directly associated with the task-related partner selection criteria categories identified in Chapter 5. Descriptive statistics were presented for each of the sixteen categories, including means, standard deviations, and frequencies. Based on these data, it appeared that the results were relatively stable across both the original and the recoded data samples. In addition, no statistically significant differences between category means were obtained when they were evaluated at the 0.05 level.

Hypothesis 2, which predicted a negative correlation between perceived relative competitive position on a particular variable category and the valence of the associated task-related partner selection criterion, appeared to be only partially supported by the data. Nine of the fourteen correlations evidenced a negative relationship significant at the 0.05 level or less. None of the correlations was positive at the 0.05 level. However, partial correlation analysis suggested that the competitive position variable tended to be highly intercorrelated with the difficulty of internal development variable. Nevertheless, the intercorrelated competitive position/difficulty of internal development variable tended to exhibit a statistically significant relationship with the partner selection criteria variable when the effects of the critical success factor variable were controlled for.

Factor analysis of the competitive position categories produced four nonoverlapping factors for each of the recoded, partially recoded, and oblique rotation samples. The principal loadings on these factors were interpreted and discussed. The statistical reliability of the factors seemed to be supported.

Each of the four factors from the recoded and the partially recoded samples of the competitive position variable was correlated with each of the nine partner selection criteria factors obtained in Chapter 5. The results of these correlations were presented and discussed.

NOTES

1. Several moderate intercorrelations were present between the factors of the task-related variables. Therefore, the partial correlation coefficients were obtained for the relationship between each of the competitive position factors and the partner selection criteria factors, controlling for all of the critical success factor and difficulty of internal development factors simultaneously. Examination of these data showed that the factor correlations that evidenced statistical significance frequently did not evidence significant partial correlations when the effects of both the critical success factor and difficulty of internal development variables were controlled for. Only three of the six former significant correlations from the recoded sample evidenced partial correlation coefficients significant at the 0.10 level or less. None of the three correlations significant at the 0.05 to 0.10 level evidenced a partial correlation coefficient significant at 0.10.

These partial correlation results appear to suggest that the correlations received only partial support. The lack of complete substantiation may be partially attributable to the substantial loss of degrees of freedom associated with the partial correlation procedure and to method differences (e.g., the use of Pearson r versus Kendall tau-b–based statistics), rather than solely to the effects of intercorrelations between the task-related variable factors. However, it was expected that a substantial component of the differences would be attributable to extensive confounding produced by the difficulty of internal development factors. Therefore, seventh-order and sixth-order partial correlation coefficients were obtained for the relationship between the competitive position and partner selection criteria factors, controlling for the critical success factor and difficulty of internal development factors, respectively. These partial correlation coefficients demonstrated that when the effects of the critical success factor variable were controlled for, five of six correlations previously significant at the 0.05 level and one of three correlations previously significant at the 0.05 to 0.10 level evidenced significant partial correlations. On the other hand, when the effects of the difficulty of internal development variable were controlled for, four of six correlations previously significant at the 0.05 level and none of the three correlations previously significant at the 0.05 to 0.10 level evidenced significant partial correlations. Thus, the results of the bivariate correlational analyses tended to be supported further by the partial correlation analysis. However, the results also suggest that the differences that were obtained in the partial correlation analysis appeared to be attributable more to the possible confounding effects of the difficulty of internal development variable than to the critical success variable.

8

Difficulty of Internal Development Variable

This chapter presents and discusses the results derived for the difficulty of internal development variable. The average (mean) values, standard deviations, and frequencies obtained for each of the difficulty of internal development categories are presented in Table 23. This table presents the results for both the original and the recoded data; the variables are listed in descending order based on their average value for the unrecoded data. The results are relatively stable across the two samples. The principal exceptions occur for variables with relatively low frequencies in the original sample, particularly DDGOVT$ and DDGSALE.

There were no significant differences between average values for either sample. This was not unexpected. No significant differences were hypothesized regarding dimensions on which the respondents would consistently perceive themselves as facing higher or lower levels of difficulty in internal development efforts. Thus, case-by-case differences would tend to balance out, resulting in similar average values for all categories.

HYPOTHESIS TESTING

In Chapter 3, a positive correlation was hypothesized between management perceptions of the difficulty of internal efforts to achieve and maintain a competitive position vis-a-vis critical success factor categories and the valence of the associated partner selection criteria categories. To test this hypothesis, the difficulty of internal development variable's categories were correlated with their associated partner selection criteria categories for both the original and the recoded data samples. The results of these correlations are listed in Table 24. Twelve of the fourteen correlations from each sample

Table 23
Descriptive Statistics for Difficulty of Internal Development Categories

Variable Label	Unrecoded Data			Recoded Data		
	Mean	Std. Dev.	(n)	Mean	Std. Dev.	(n)
DDRAPID	2.32	0.619	75	1.93	1.036	90
DDLOWC	1.86	0.810	72	1.49	1.041	90
DDGSALE	1.78	0.832	32	0.63	0.988	90
DDREGUL	1.76	0.986	67	1.31	1.148	90
DDLOWP	1.76	0.668	78	1.52	0.864	90
DDMKTG	1.74	0.922	74	1.43	1.071	90
DDLOCAL	1.69	1.178	71	1.33	1.254	90
DDFULL	1.67	0.837	64	1.19	1.037	90
DDPATNT	1.62	0.989	82	1.48	1.052	90
DDEES	1.59	0.815	87	1.53	0.851	90
DD$	1.57	1.029	85	1.48	1.062	90
DDSITE	1.56	0.871	64	1.11	1.022	90
DDGOVT$	1.53	0.922	38	0.64	0.964	90
DDMGMT	1.51	0.745	87	1.46	0.781	90
DDSERV	1.42	0.855	59	0.93	0.969	90
DDTRDMK	1.41	0.705	88	1.38	0.728	90

The range of possible integer values for difficulty of internal development categories is 0 to 4. The maximum number of cases is 90.

Table 24

Tau-B Correlations between Task-Related Partner Selection Criteria Categories and Difficulty of Internal Development Categories

Difficulty of Internal Development Category	Partner Selection Criteria Category	Tau-B for Unrecoded Data	Tau-B for Recoded Data
DDREGUL	PSCREGUL	.50**	.55**
DD$	PSC$	.51**	.47**
DDGOVT$	PSCGOVT$	.51**	.54**
DDMGMT	PSCMGMT	.31**	.30**
DDEES	PSCEES	.53**	.53**
DDSITE	PSCSITE	.22*	.31*
DDLOWC	PSCLOWC	.32**	.28*
DDPATNT	PSCPATNT	.55**	.54**
DDTRDMK	PSCTRDMK	.12	.07
DDRAPID	PSCRAPID	.01	.02
DDGSALE	PSCGSALE	.46**	.56**
DDLOCAL	PSCLOCAL	.61**	.68**
DDMKTG	PSCMKTG	.55**	.50**
DDSERV	PSCSERV	.44**	.41**

* reflects P $\leq$ 0.05
** reflects P $\leq$ 0.01

evidenced the hypothesized relationship at a 0.05 level. Based on these results, the second hypothesis appeared to be strongly supported.

PARTIAL CORRELATIONS OF THE DIFFICULTY OF INTERNAL DEVELOPMENT CATEGORIES

The associated task-related variable categories frequently evidenced moderate levels of intercorrelation. Therefore, to effectively test Hypothesis 3, it was also necessary to calculate the partial correlation coefficients for the difficulty of internal development categories. The first- and second-order partial correlation coefficients are presented in Table 25, along with their significance levels. For both samples, eight of the fourteen categories evidenced positive correlations significant at the 0.05 level, when controlling for the effects of both the critical success factor and the competitive position variables. An additional two categories from the recoded data sample evidenced positive relationships significant at the 0.05 to 0.10 level. Therefore, the results of the partial correlation analysis supported Hypothesis 3.

FACTOR ANALYSIS OF THE DIFFICULTY OF INTERNAL DEVELOPMENT CATEGORIES

Because of potential conceptual overlap between the difficulty of internal development categories, we wanted to obtain statistically distinct categories for this variable. The most appropriate means of accomplishing this task involved the employment of factor analytic techniques.[1] The results of the factor analyses are shown in Table 26 for the fully recoded data and in Table 27 for the partially recoded data.[2]

Examination of Tables 26 and 27 reveals that the results for the two samples were quite similar, supporting the statistical reliability of the factors that were obtained. Factor analysis produced six interpretable factors from each sample, explaining a total of 71.8 and 69.2 percent of the observed variance in the fully recoded and partially recoded samples, respectively.

The remainder of this section discusses the interpretation of the factors from the fully recoded data, and compares these results with similar output from the partially recoded sample.

Factor 1: Rapid Entry with Full Line of Low-Priced Products

The first factor was characterized by high positive loadings on the following categories: low price to customers (DDLOWP); low per-unit costs (DDLOWC); full line of products or services (DDFULL); possession of patents, licenses, or other know-how (DDPATNT); technically skilled employees (DDEES); and rapid market entry (DDRAPID). It also had a small

Table 25
First- and Second-Order Partial Correlations between Associated Categories
of Difficulty of Internal Development and Partner Selection Criteria
Variables

PARTNER SELECTION CRITERIA CATEGORY	UNRECODED DATA			RECODED DATA		
	DD CATEGORY CONTROLLING FOR CSF	DD CATEGORY CONTROLLING FOR CP	DD CATEGORY CONTROLLING FOR CSF & CP	DD CATEGORY CONTROLLING FOR CSF	DD CATEGORY CONTROLLING FOR CP	DD CATEGORY CONTROLLING FOR CSF & CP
PSCREGUL	.46**	.50**	.26**	.33**	.50**	.14
PSC$	.49**	.41**	.31**	.45**	.47**	.28**
PSCGOVT$	.40**	.29*	.19	.33**	.47**	.14
PSCMGMT	.33**	.30**	.26**	.34**	.38**	.28**
PSCEES	.54**	.48**	.36**	.45**	.44**	.24**
PSCSITE	.21	.00	-.09	.21*	.31**	.01
PSCLOWC	.07	.37**	.06	.05	.46**	.05
PSCPATNT	.63**	.48**	.38**	.63**	.59**	.39**
PSCTRDMK	.05	.16	.02	.03	.21*	.00
PSCRAPID	-.13	.13	-.06	-.05	.51**	.01
PSCGSALE	.22	.61**	.07	.26*	.81**	.19*
PSCLOCAL	.46**	.42**	.26*	.41**	.63**	.23*
PSCMKTG	.62**	.42**	.39**	.57**	.49**	.35**
PSCSERV	.51**	.34**	.26*	.51**	.63**	.27**

*   reflects P $\leq$ 0.05
** reflects P $\leq$ 0.01

Table 26
Rotated Factors for Difficulty of Internal Development Categories for Recoded Data

PARTNER SELECTION CRITERIA CATEGORY	FACTOR 1 Rapid Entry W/Full Line of Low Priced Products	FACTOR 2 Strong Local Market Presence	FACTOR 3 Local Government Influence	FACTOR 4 Critical Site For Rapid Entry Into Local Market	FACTOR 5 Techno-Logical Capabili-ties	FACTOR 6 Financial Capability
DDREGUL	-.15	.27	.69 *	.10	.12	-.11
DD$	.13	.02	.00	-.04	.13	.85 *
DDGOVT$	.20	.08	.56 *	.41 *	-.19	.47 *
DDMGMT	.04	.58 *	-.24	.13	.41 *	.29
DDEES	.43 *	.05	-.26	-.26	.51 *	.30 *
DDSITE	-.07	.12	.04	.90 *	.10	.00
DDLOWC	.84 *	.03	-.02	.17	-.21	.07
DDPATNT	.55 *	-.18	-.17	-.29	.33 *	.09
DDTRDMK	.03	.10	.26	.22	.83 *	.02
DDRAPID	.40 *	.35 *	-.04	.40 *	.27	-.32 *
DDLOWP	.85 *	.01	.04	-.01	.07	.02
DDFULL	.61 *	.24	-.04	-.17	.27	.18
DDGSALE	.02	-.01	.87 *	-.07	.02	.06
DDLOCAL	-.34 *	.51 *	.47 *	.40 *	.16	-.12
DDMKTG	-.02	.84 *	.14	.20	-.08	.12
DDSERV	.18	.80 *	.20	-.06	.08	-.14
EIGENVALUE	3.41	3.18	1.54	1.27	1.07	1.02
PCT. OF VAR.	21.3	19.9	9.6	7.9	6.7	6.3
CUM. PCT.	21.3	41.2	50.8	58.8	65.4	71.8

* Factor loadings ≥ 0.30

Table 27

Rotated Factors for Difficulty of Internal Development Categories for Partially Recoded Data

PARTNER SELECTION CRITERIA CATEGORY	FACTOR 1 Full Line of Low Priced Products	FACTOR 2 Strong Local Market Presence	FACTOR 3 Access to Local Skilled Personnel	FACTOR 4 Access to Government Resources	FACTOR 5 Rapid Entry With Technology Based Reputation	FACTOR 6 Critical Site Not Government Regulation/Pressure
DDREGUL	.12	-.06	-.10	-.17	.13	-.73*
DD$	.66*	.18	.04	.29	-.04	-.19
DDGOVT$	-.12	-.04	-.06	.75*	-.06	-.07
DDMGMT	.08	.18	.90*	-.08	-.13	.12
DDEES	.00	.14	.88*	.13	.04	.14
DDSITE	.20	.13	.29	-.07	.29	.62*
DDLOWC	.70*	-.07	-.01	-.34*	.26	.22
DDPATNT	.10	.11	.00	-.05	.90*	-.04
DDTRDMK	.54*	-.26	.14	.14	.42*	-.35*
DDRAPID	.00	.45*	-.34*	-.14	.56*	.25
DDLOWP	.79*	.04	.03	-.26	.06	.00
DDFULL	.59*	.51*	-.04	.07	-.22	.17
DDGSALE	.01	-.11	-.16	.80*	-.01	.28
DDLOCAL	-.11	.58*	.34*	-.16	.19	.08
DDMKTG	.11	.77*	.07	.13	.14	.04
DDSERV	.08	.78*	.16	-.18	.01	.03
EIGENVALUE	3.37	2.23	1.70	1.58	1.17	1.01
PCT. OF VAR.	21.1	14.0	10.6	9.8	7.3	6.3
CUM. PCT.	21.1	35.0	45.7	55.5	62.9	69.2

* Factor Loadings $\geq$ 0.30

negative loading on local or national identity of the joint venture (DDLO-CAL). Therefore, this first factor was interpreted as the perceived difficulty of developing a strong competitive position via the joint venture's rapid entry with a full line of low-priced products or services.

The reliability of this first factor was strongly supported by the results from the partially recoded sample. Partially recoded Factor 1 had high positive loadings on the DDLOWP, DDLOWC, and DDFULL categories, as well as positive loadings on access to financing (DD$) and valuable reputation or trademark (DDTRDMK), both of which would be likely to influence the ease with which a firm could rapidly enter a market with a low-priced line. On the basis of these results, this first factor's reliability was strongly supported.

Factor 2: Strong Local Market Presence

This factor had high positive loadings on five categories: marketing or distribution systems (DDMKTG), post-sale service (DDSERV), experienced management (DDMGMT), local or national identity (DDLOCAL), and, to a lesser extent, rapid market entry (DDRAPID). Similar loadings were obtained for the other sample. Factor 2 from the partially recoded data had positive loadings on DDSERV, DDMKTG, DDLOCAL, and DDRAPID, as well as DDFULL, the possession of a full line of products or services. On the basis of these results, the reliability of this second factor was strongly supported, and it was interpreted as a firm's perceived difficulty in developing a strong local market presence.

Factor 3: Local Government Influence

This factor had high positive loadings on the following categories: sales to the government (DDGSALE), government regulations or pressure (DDREGUL), government financing or subsidies (DDGOVT$), and local or national identity (DDLOCAL). Factor 4 from the partially recoded sample had high positive loadings on DDGSALE and DDGOVT$, and a small negative loading on low per-unit costs (DDLOWC). Therefore, this factor was interpreted as a firm's perceived difficulties in the internal development and maintenance of a strong position vis-a-vis local government influence in the target market.

Factor 4: Critical Site for Rapid Entry into Local Market

This factor had a very high positive loading on access to critical site or facilities (DDSITE). It also had smaller positive loadings on access to government subsidies (DDGOVT$), local identity (DDLOCAL), and rapid market entry (DDRAPID). Factor 6 from the partially recoded sample also had a very high positive loading on DDSITE, and negative loadings on DDREGUL and DDTRDMK. Therefore, Factor 4 was interpreted as the perceived difficulty of internal efforts to develop a strong competitive position through access to a critical site or facilities that would enhance rapid entry into the local target market.

Factor 5: Technological Capability

The fifth factor had high positive loadings on four categories: trademark or reputation (DDTRDMK), technically skilled employees (DDEES), experienced management (DDMGMT), and patents, licenses, or other know-how (DDPATNT). For the partially recoded sample, the categories loading highly on the fifth factor seemed to have loaded on two different factors: Factor 3 (high positive loadings on DDMGMT and DDEES) and Factor 5 (high positive loadings on DDPATNT and DDTRDMK). The difference between the two factors on the partially recoded sample seems to be caused partly by the orientation toward rapidity of market entry: a positive loading for Factor 5 and a negative loading for Factor 3. Therefore, this fifth factor's loadings were interpreted as the perceived difficulty of developing a strong competitive position in terms of technological capability.

Factor 6: Financial Capability

The sixth factor loaded highly on access to financing (DD$) and, to a lesser extent, on government subsidies (DDGOVT$). The partially recoded sample did not have a similar factor; instead, the DD$ category loaded highly on Factor 1, the ability to enter the target market with a full line of low-priced products. Therefore, this sixth factor was interpreted as the perceived difficulty of developing a strong position via financial capability.

CORRELATION BETWEEN FACTORS OF DIFFICULTY OF INTERNAL DEVELOPMENT AND PARTNER SELECTION CRITERIA VARIABLES

No specific hypotheses were developed in regard to the relationship between the difficulty of internal development factors and the factors for the partner selection criteria categories. Nevertheless, the bivariate correlations between these two sets of factors were calculated, and the results were examined in an attempt to uncover additional insights into the partner selection process.

Using the results of factor analysis as input, each of the six factors for the difficulty of internal development categories from both the fully recoded and the partially recoded samples was correlated with each of the nine factors for the partner selection criteria categories from the original sample. The

Table 28
Tau-B Correlations between Factors of Difficulty of Internal Development and Partner Selection Criteria Categories

	RECODED SAMPLE				
FACTORS FOR PARTNER SELECTION CRITERIA CATEGORIES	DD FACTOR 1 Rapid Entry W/Full Line of Low Priced Prods.	DD FACTOR 2 Strong Local Market Pres.	DD FACTOR 3 Local Gov't Infl.	DD FACTOR 4 Crit. Site, Rapid Entry Into Local Market	DD FACTOR 5 Techno-logical Capab.
FACTOR 1 Knowledge of Local Market, Not Techn.	-0.33**	0.23**	0.16*	0.28**	0.03
FACTOR 2 Similar Firm W/Local Government Influence	0.11	0.07	0.46**	0.08	-0.10
FACTOR 3 Compatible Partner	-0.03	0.11	0.07	0.03	0.00
FACTOR 4 Low Cost Production	0.28**	0.01	0.05	0.11	-0.10
FACTOR 5 Shared Development	0.10	-0.02	0.15*	-0.06	0.02
FACTOR 6 Sales & Service Experience	0.23**	0.34**	0.12#	-0.02	0.02
FACTOR 7 Strategically Critical Mfg. Capabilities	-0.02	-0.03	-0.06	0.22**	0.02
FACTOR 8 Opportun. Neighbor	0.06	0.12#	-0.06	-0.10	-0.05
FACTOR 9 Similar firm Controlling Inputs	0.09	-0.03	0.00	0.07	0.04

reflects P ≤ 0.10, * reflects P ≤ 0.05,

Table 28 (continued)

PARTIALLY RECODED SAMPLE

DD FACTOR 6	DD FACTOR 1	DD FACTOR 2	DD FACTOR 3	DD FACTOR 4	DD FACTOR 5	DD FACTOR 6
	Rapid Entry W/Full Line of Low Priced Prods.	Strong Local Market Pres.	Local Gov't Infl.	Crit. Site, Rapid Entry Into Local Market	Techno-logical Capab.	
Fin'l Capab.						Fin'l Capab.
0.00	-0.09	0.11	-0.09	0.14#	-0.15*	0.13#
0.03	-0.02	-0.17*	-0.02	0.41**	-0.01	0.11
-0.16*	0.13#	-0.08	-0.03	0.05	-0.05	0.01
-0.06	-0.12#	-0.13#	0.06	0.14#	0.03	0.17*
0.33**	0.04	0.03	0.14#	0.22**	0.26**	-0.02
-0.10	-0.08	0.15*	0.15#	0.28**	-0.06	0.14#
-0.03	0.03	0.13#	-0.08	0.03	-0.13#	0.18*
-0.07	-0.07	-0.14#	0.05	-0.05	-0.06	0.09
-0.12*	0.26**	-0.03	-0.02	-0.07	0.08	0.02

** reflects $P \leq 0.01$

results are listed in Table 28 for the fully recoded and partially recoded samples. The following discussion examines the factors from the fully recoded sample's difficulty of internal development categories and the partner selection criteria factors significantly correlated with each of them.[3]

Factor 1: Rapid Entry with Full Line of Low-Priced Products

The first factor evidenced two positive and one negative correlations with the partner selection criteria factors. According to these results, an increase in the perceived difficulty of making a rapid entry into the target market with a full line of low-priced products was correlated with an increase in the importance of selecting a partner with the following skills: ability to enhance low-cost production (Factor 4) and sales and service experience (Factor 6). Increased difficulty on Factor 1 was also correlated with a decrease in the importance of selecting a partner with knowledge of the local market, but not technological capability (Factor 1).

For the partially recoded sample, an increase in perceived difficulty on Factor 1 was correlated with increased importance of selecting a similarly respected partner which controlled inputs (Factor 9). Increased difficulty on Factor 1 was also correlated with increased importance of selecting a compatible partner (Factor 3).

These results suggest that, as the perceived difficulty of achieving a strong competitive position on Factor 1 increased, firms tended to place greater emphasis on selecting partners that could help reduce the price level of the product or service line (e.g., low-cost production and control over inputs), or which could enhance the firm's ability to enter the market rapidly (e.g., by reducing delays due to incompatibility or by providing sales and service capabilities). However, it seemed that mere local market knowledge may not have been sufficient; the partner seemed to require also evidence of some basic minimum level of technological capability in order to be considered.

Factor 2: Strong Local Market Presence

The second factor was positively correlated with two selection criteria factors: selection of a partner with knowledge of the local market (Factor 1) and selection of a partner with sales and service experience (Factor 6). For the partially recoded sample, there was also a positive correlation with selection criteria Factor 6. The latter sample also evidenced a negative correlation with the selection of a similar firm with local government influence (Factor 2).

These results suggested that, as the perceived difficulty of developing a strong local market presence increased, firms exhibited a greater tendency to select partners that evidenced nongovernmentally based strengths in the local target market.

Factor 3: Local Government Influence

The third factor was positively correlated with three selection criteria factors: knowledge of the local target market (Factor 1), a similar firm with local government influence (Factor 2), and a firm able to share development efforts (Factor 5). For the partially recoded sample, these same three factors evidenced significantly positive correlations. Factor 6, selection of a firm with sales and service experience, also evidenced a significant positive correlation for the partially recoded data.

These results suggest that, as the perceived difficulty of developing a strong position vis-a-vis the influence of local government policies increased, firms tended to place greater emphasis on selecting partners with local market knowledge, including influence vis-a-vis local government policies. There also seemed to be a tendency, under these circumstances, to select a partner that could help share the development efforts, possibly through the ability to access governmental subsidies, as well as a tendency not to seek an opportunistic neighbor as a partner.

Factor 4: Critical Site for Rapid Entry into Local Market

For both samples, the fourth factor was positively correlated with Factor 1 (selection of a partner with knowledge of the local market) and Factor 7 (selection of a firm with strategically critical manufacturing capabilities). The partially recoded sample also evidenced a positive correlation with Factor 4, selection of a partner enhancing low-cost production.

These results suggested that, as the perceived difficulty of developing a strong position vis-a-vis the possession of a critical site for rapid entry into the local market increased, firms tended to place greater emphasis on selecting partners with strategically critical manufacturing capabilities, knowledge of the local market, and the ability to enhance low-cost production.

Factor 5: Technological Capability

For the fully recoded sample, none of the selection criteria factors was significantly correlated with Factor 5. Since the partially recoded sample's Factors 3 and 5 were interpreted as similar to the fully recoded sample's Factor 5, results for both of them will be reported here. Both Factor 3 and Factor 5 from the partially recoded sample were correlated with the fifth selection criteria factor (shared development). Factor 5 was also negatively correlated with partner selection criteria Factor 1 (knowledge of local market, not technology).

These results suggest that, as the perceived difficulty of developing a strong competitive position on technological capabilities increased, firms tended to place increased emphasis on the selection of partners that evidenced some degree of technological capability of their own.

Factor 6: Financial Capability

For the fully recoded sample, Factor 6 was positively correlated with selection criteria Factor 5 (shared development) and negatively correlated with Factor 3 (compatible partner). The partially recoded sample did not have a corresponding factor to use for comparison.

These results suggest that, when firms' perceptions of the difficulty of accessing financial resources increased, they placed greater emphasis on the selection of partners with the ability to access those resources. The perceived compatibility of the prospective partner was de-emphasized under those circumstances.

CHAPTER SUMMARY

This chapter presented and discussed the results for the difficulty of internal development variable. Sixteen categories were examined for this variable, fourteen of which were directly associated with the task-related partner selection criteria categories identified in Chapter 5. Descriptive statistics were presented for each of the sixteen categories, including means, standard deviations, and frequencies. Based on these data, it appeared that the results were relatively stable across the original and recoded data samples, with the exception of those variables (principally DDGOVT\$ and DDGSALE) that had a large number of "Not Applicable" (NA) responses. In addition, no statistically significant differences between category means were obtained when they were evaluated at the 0.05 level.

Hypothesis 3, which predicted a positive correlation between the perceived difficulty of internal development efforts on a particular variable category and the valence of the associated task-related partner selection criteria categories, appeared to be supported by the data. Twelve of the fourteen correlations evidenced a positive relationship significant at the 0.05 level or less. None of the correlations evidenced negative tau-b values for the sample data. These findings also received support from the results of the partial correlation analysis.

Factor analysis of the difficulty of internal development categories produced six orthogonal factors for both data samples. The principal loadings on these factors were presented and interpreted. The statistical reliability of the factors from the fully recoded sample seemed to have been supported. Each of the six factors from the fully recoded and the partially recoded samples was correlated with each of the nine selection criteria factors obtained in Chapter 5. The results of these correlations were presented and discussed.

NOTES

1. The identical factor analysis methods discussed in Appendix B were employed in analyzing the difficulty of internal development categories. The only exception is that the factor analysis was performed on the recoded rather than the unrecoded data. This was done because two categories, DDGSALE and DDGOVT$, exhibited very low frequencies in the unrecoded sample. Numerical values (non-NA, or not applicable, responses) for these two categories occurred in only 32 and 38 cases, respectively. The resulting set of relevant cases was very small (n = 19); therefore, factor analysis of the original data sample resulted in ill-conditioned correlation matrices. To overcome this problem, the fully recoded sample was used as input. The resulting factor analyses produced interpretable outputs without ill-conditioned matrices or factors with negative eigenvalues. Therefore, the discussion is based on the results for the recoded data sample.

2. Results from the oblique rotation were very consistent with the results from the recoded data sample.

3. Several moderate intercorrelations were present between the factors of the task-related variables. Therefore, the partial correlation coefficients were obtained for the relationship between each of the difficulty of internal development factors and the partner selection criteria factors, controlling for all of the factors of the critical success factor and competitive position variables simultaneously. The results suggested that the bivariate correlations among factors that evidenced statistical significance frequently did not evidence significant partial correlations when the effects of both the critical success factor and competitive position variables were controlled for. Only six of the twelve former correlations that were significant at the 0.05 level evidenced partial correlation coefficients significant at the 0.10 level or less. None of the three correlations previously significant at the 0.05 to 0.10 level evidenced a partial correlation coefficient significant at 0.10. These partial correlation results appear to suggest that the reported bivariate correlations received only partial support. The lack of complete substantiation may be partially attributable to the substantial loss of degrees of freedom associated with the partial correlation procedure and to method differences (e.g., the use of Pearson r versus Kendall tau-b-based statistics), rather than solely to the effects of intercorrelations between the task-related variable factors. However, it was expected that a not insubstantial component of the differences might be attributable to confounding produced by the competitive position and critical success factor variables' factors. Therefore, seventh- and fourth- order partial correlation coefficients were obtained for the relationship between the difficulty of internal development and partner selection criteria factors, controlling for the factors of the critical success factor and competitive position variables, respectively. When the effects of critical success factor were controlled for, seven of twelve correlations previously significant at the 0.05 level had partial correlation coefficients significant at the 0.10 level or less. Similarly, when the effects of competitive position were controlled for, ten of twelve correlations previously significant at the 0.05 level had partial correlation coefficients

significant at the 0.10 level or less. Thus, these results suggest that the partial correlation analyses tended to support and enhance most of the results of the bivariate correlational analyses discussed below. In addition, the partial correlation analysis suggested that, consistent with the findings for the competitive position variable's factors, confounding attributable to the competitive position factors seemed to account for more of the variation between the correlational and partial correlation analyses than was the case for the critical success factor variable's factors.

IV

RESULTS FOR PARTNER–RELATED VARIABLES

Based on a review of prior literature as well as on the responses from the pretest interviews, a set of eight, eight, and nine categories was obtained for the perceived task environment uncertainty, diversity of line functions, and extent of shared control variables, respectively. These categories are listed and briefly described in Table 29. The set of six prospective partner-related selection criteria categories, which was discussed in Chapter 5, are as follows:

PSCNEARU	Is close to respondent firm, geographically
PSCCOMIT	Has a strong commitment to the joint venture
PSCFREND	Top management of both firms are compatible
PSCLIKEU	Has similar national or corporate culture
PSCSIZE	Is similar in size or corporate structure
PSCPRIOR	Had satisfactory prior association with respondent firm

The presence of intercorrelation between categories of partner-related variables had the potential for confounding efforts to test the research hypotheses. Several of the partner-related categories evidenced moderate intercorrelations with other partner-related categories.[1] Twenty-four of 300 correlations (8 percent) evidenced coefficients of 0.40 or greater; 5 of these were 0.60 or greater. No correlations exceeded 0.70. Therefore, to control for these effects of intercorrelation, the analysis of each of the partner-related variables also includes analysis of the relevant partial correlation coefficients.

The discussion of partner-related variables begins with an analysis of the perceived task-environment uncertainty variable in Chapter 9. After addressing the issues related to that variable, a similar discussion will be

Table 29

Variable Labels and Descriptions for Partner-Related Variables

PERCEIVED TASK ENVIRONMENT UNCERTAINTY CATEGORIES

Variable Label	Description of Category
UNDESIGN	Product design
UNEQUIP	Production skills and equipment
UNRM	Sourcing and costs of raw materials and components
UNMKTG	Marketing and distribution policies
UNPRICE	Pricing of products
UNENVIR	Overall changes in the JV´s operating environment
UNDEMAND	Level of demand for the JV´s products or services
UNGOVT	Government regulations or nationalistic pressures

DIVERSITY OF LINE FUNCTIONS CATEGORIES

Variable Label	Description of Category
FMINE	Mining or other extractive activities
FBASIC	Basic, non-applied research
FAPPLY	Applied research and development
FMFG	Manufacturing of components, or raw materials refining or processing
FASSEM	Assembly of finished goods
FMKTG	Marketing
FDISTRIB	Distribution
FSERV	Post-sales service

EXTENT OF SHARED CONTROL CATEGORIES

Variable Label	Description of Category
SCDESIGN	Design of product or service
SCRM	Sourcing of raw materials or components
SCMFG	Determining manufacturing technology and set-up
SCHIRING	Hiring and firing joint venture managers
SCPRICE	Setting prices and sales targets
SCCOSTS	Overseeing costs and quality control
SCINVEST	Authorizing major capital expenditures for JV
SCMKTG	Determining marketing and distribution policies
SCMGMT	Day-to-day management of the joint venture

presented for the diversity of line functions variable in Chapter 10 and for the extent of shared control variable in Chapter 11.

NOTE

1. Several moderate intercorrelations were also present among the factors obtained from the data for the perceived task environment uncertainty and diversity

of line functions variable categories and the extent of shared control variable's categories. The presence of these intercorrelations was potentially troublesome for testing the research hypotheses as well as for efforts to examine the research data in greater depth for other potential insights. Because of the extent of intercorrelation, we undertook an extensive array of partial correlation analyses, which increased the conceptual and statistical complexity associated with the study. In addition, we examined the data for intercorrelations between task-related and partner-related categories. The incidence of moderate intercorrelations between task- and partner-related categories was quite minimal. Less than one percent of the correlations (9 of 1200) evidenced correlation coefficients of 0.40 to 0.60, and none evidenced coefficients over 0.60. Similar results were obtained for correlations between the variables' factors. These results enhance the apparent construct validity regarding the conceptual and statistical distinction between the task-related and the partner-related variables.

9

Perceived Task Environment Uncertainty Variable

This chapter presents the results for the perceived task environment uncertainty variable. The average (mean) values, standard deviations, and frequencies obtained for each of the eight perceived task environment uncertainty categories are presented in Table 30 for both the original and the recoded samples. The variables are listed in descending order, based on their average value for the unrecoded data. The results are relatively stable across both samples.

There were no significant differences between categories' average values when evaluated at the 0.05 level. No significant differences were expected regarding the dimensions of the task environment on which the respondents would consistently perceive higher or lower levels of uncertainty. Under these circumstances, case-by-case differences would tend to balance out. However, examination of Table 30 does suggest that, although not significant in a statistical sense, there tended to be greater perceived task environment uncertainty in the more macro, externally related environmental or market dimensions than in the more internally oriented dimensions of product design or production-related activities.

In Chapter 3, a positive correlation was hypothesized between management perceptions of the level of task environment uncertainty and the relative importance of partner-related selection criteria. To test this hypothesis, the categories of the perceived task environment uncertainty variable were correlated with each of the six prospective partner-related selection criteria categories. The results of these correlations are listed in Table 31 for the original and recoded data samples.

Examination of Table 31 provides several interesting insights. First, it appears that an increase in perceived task environment uncertainty is typically correlated with increased importance of selecting a partner within a

Table 30
Descriptive Statistics for Perceived Task Environment Uncertainty Categories

Variable Label	Unrecoded Data			Recoded Data		
	Mean	Std. Dev.	(n)	Mean	Std. Dev.	(n)
UNDEMAND	2.38	0.911	89	2.36	0.940	90
UNENVIR	2.31	1.002	90	2.31	1.002	90
UNMKTG	1.78	0.811	80	1.58	0.948	90
UNPRICE	1.72	0.839	89	1.70	0.854	90
UNGOVT	1.65	1.099	85	1.56	1.133	90
UNDESIGN	1.60	0.975	83	1.48	1.030	90
UNEQUIP	1.38	0.821	79	1.21	0.893	90
UNRM	1.16	0.737	80	1.03	0.785	90

The range of possible integer values for perceived task environment uncertainty categories is 0 to 4. The maximum number of cases is 90.

Table 31
Tau-B Correlations between Partner-Related Partner Selection Criteria
Categories and Perceived Task Environment Uncertainty Categories

| | Unrecoded Data | | | | | | Recoded Data | | | | | |
| | Partner-Related Partner Selection Criteria Categories | | | | | | Partner-Related Partner Selection Criteria Categories | | | | | |
Uncertainty Variable	PSC NEARU	PSC COMIT	PSC FREND	PSC LIKEU	PSC SIZE	PSC PRIOR	PSC NEARU	PSC COMIT	PSC FREND	PSC LIKEU	PSC SIZE	PSC PRIOR
UNDESIGN	.15#	-.02	.07	.24**	.12#	.00	.16*	.03	.04	.23**	.14#	-.07
UNEQUIP	.25**	-.07	-.04	.14#	-.11	-.10	.18*	-.06	-.01	.09	-.06	-.05
UNRM	.15#	-.10	-.18*	-.02	-.19*	.03	.13#	-.07	-.15#	-.02	-.09	.04
UNMKTG	.03	.04	-.03	.03	-.13#	-.02	.11	.01	-.03	.00	-.08	-.08
UNPRICE	.20*	-.03	-.01	.13#	-.09	-.10	.17*	-.02	-.01	.14#	-.07	-.12
UNENVIR	.14#	.11	.10	.21**	.04	-.03	.14#	.11	.10	.21**	.04	-.03
UNDEMAND	.14#	.10	.01	.05	-.10	-.24**	.14#	.11	-.01	.03	-.12	-.23**
UNGOVT	-.07	-.10	.06	.18*	.03	-.01	-.08	.10	.03	.21**	.06	-.01

** reflects P ≤ .01
* reflects P ≤ .05
# reflects P ≤ .10

relatively close geographical proximity (PSCNEARU). At a 0.10 level, the UNDESIGN, UNEQUIP, UNPRICE, UNENVIR, UNRM, and UNDEMAND categories were significantly positively correlated with PSCNEARU for both samples. UNMKTG and UNGOVT were the only perceived task environment uncertainty categories that evidenced no significant positive correlations with PSCNEARU for either sample.

There were no significant correlations between any of the perceived task environment uncertainty categories and the PSCCOMIT (strong commitment to the joint venture) and PSCFREND (compatibility of partners' top management teams) selection criteria categories. These results may be attributable to the very high average values obtained for both of these categories. The tendency to accord high importance to the PSCCOMIT and PSCFREND categories may have resulted in a relative degree of statistical insensitivity to variations in the perceived task environment uncertainty categories. The only exception was a negative correlation between the UNRM and PSCFREND categories for both samples. The latter exception suggests that, as the perceived uncertainty of raw materials or components increased, firms tended to place decreasing emphasis on the selection of partners with compatible top management.

According to the sample results, firms tended to place increased emphasis on selection of a partner similar in national or corporate culture (PSCLIKEU) when there was an increase in the perceived level of uncertainty in the following: product design (UNDESIGN), product price (UNPRICE), overall changes in the joint venture's operating environment (UNENVIR), governmental regulations or nationalistic pressures (UNGOVT), and production skills and equipment (UNEQUIP). No significant correlations were found between PSCLIKEU and the UNRM, UNMKTG, or UNDEMAND categories.

Data from the sample firms evidenced a positive correlation between the UNDESIGN and the PSCSIZE categories. This suggests that increased perceived uncertainty regarding the design of a product was correlated with increased importance being placed on the selection of a partner with similar organizational size or structure.

In contrast to the results for UNDESIGN, both UNRM and UNMKTG evidenced significant negative correlations with the PSCSIZE category for the unrecoded data. These results suggest that increased perceived uncertainly in raw materials or components and in marketing or distribution of a product tended to be associated with a decreased emphasis on selecting a partner of similar organizational size or structure.

Finally, for both samples, there was a significant negative correlation between the perceived level of uncertainty of demand for a joint venture's products and services (UNDEMAND) and the selection of a partner with which the firm had favorable prior association (PSCPRIOR). No other positive or negative correlations between the perceived task environment uncertainty categories and the partner-related selection criteria categories were significant at the 0.10 level or less.

Based on the above results, the fourth hypothesis seemed to have received mixed support. Although the hypothesized relationship was upheld in approximately a dozen of the correlated pairs of categories, the remaining correlations did not produce clear support for the hypothesis. The lack of support in certain cases, specifically for correlations involving the PSCCOMIT and PSCFREND categories, may be partially a result of the high average values associated with these categories. However, this explanation does not readily account for the remainder of the nonconforming results. The hypothesized relationship seemed to be clearly rejected in several instances, particularly in the relationship between the following pairs of variables: UNRM and PSCFREND, UNMKTG and PSCSIZE, and UNDEMAND and PSCPRIOR. Although several of the remaining deviations may be explainable on a case-by-case basis, the general conclusion is that the fourth hypothesis received only limited support.[1]

FACTOR ANALYSIS OF PERCEIVED TASK ENVIRONMENT UNCERTAINTY CATEGORIES

Because of the potential conceptual overlap between the perceived task environment uncertainty categories, we wanted to obtain statistically distinct categories for this variable's data. The most appropriate means of accomplishing this task involved use of factor analysis.

Results of the factor analysis are presented in Table 32 for the original and recoded samples, as well as for the oblique rotation of the original sample's factors. As evident from examination of Table 32, the results from the three analyses are quite similar, supporting the reliability of the factors that were obtained. Factor analysis produced two interpretable factors for each of the samples. These factors explained 57.4, 55.3, and 57.4 percent of the variance for the original, recoded, and oblique samples, respectively. The interpretations of the original sample's rotated factors are presented below, along with comparisons with the results from the other two samples.

Factor 1: Uncertainty of Overall Market Environment

The first factor had very high loadings on the following perceived task environment uncertainty categories: product pricing (UNPRICE), marketing and distribution policies (UNMKTG), overall changes in the venture's operating environment (UNENVIR), and the level of demand for the venture's products or services (UNDEMAND). There were also lower positive loadings on the categories of government regulations or nationalistic pressures (UNGOVT) and product design (UNDESIGN).

Oblique rotation Factor 1 had positive loadings on the same six categories,

Table 32
Rotated Factors for Perceived Task Environment Uncertainty Categories

	UNRECODED DATA		RECODED DATA		OBLIQUE ROTATION	
	FACTOR 1	FACTOR 2	FACTOR 1	FACTOR 2	FACTOR 1	FACTOR 2
	Uncertainty of Overall Market Environment	Uncertainty of Manufacturing Operations	Uncertainty of Overall Market Environment	Uncertainty of Manufacturing Operations	Uncertainty of Overall Market Environment	Uncertainty of Manufacturing Operations
UNDESIGN	.39*	.39*	.64*	.15	.47*	.27
UNEQUIP	.22	.75*	.36*	.80*	.34*	.67*
UNRM	.03	.90*	.07	.90*	-.09	.93*
UNMKTG	.75*	.01	.69*	.22	.80*	-.20
UNPRICE	.79*	.20	.73*	.25	.82*	-.01
UNENVIR	.72*	.21	.72*	-.04	.77*	.01
UNDEMAND	.72*	.22	.80*	.10	.74*	.04
UNGOVT	.45*	.23	.05	.13	.45*	.12
Eigenvalue	3.55	1.04	3.27	1.15	3.55	1.04
Pct. of Variance	44.4	13.0	40.9	14.4	44.4	13.0
Cumulative Pct. of Variance	44.4	57.4	40.9	55.3	44.4	57.4

*reflects factor loadings $\geq$ 0.30

as well as on UNEQUIP, the uncertainty of the production skills and equipment. Recoded Factor 1 had high positive loadings on UNDEMAND, UNPRICE, UNENVIR, UNMKTG, and UNDESIGN, as well as a small positive loading on UNEQUIP. Therefore, results from the oblique and recoded samples support the reliability of this first factor, which was interpreted as the perceived uncertainty of the overall market environment of the joint venture.

Factor 2: Uncertainty of Manufacturing Operations

This second factor had high positive loadings on the uncertainty of the sourcing and costs of raw materials and components (UNRM) and on production skills and equipment (UNEQUIP), as well as a smaller positive loading on the uncertainty of product design (UNDESIGN). The pattern of loadings for Factor 2 was similar to the loadings for the second factor from the recoded and the oblique rotation samples, both of which had high positive loadings on UNEQUIP and UNRM. This supports the statistical reliability of the original sample's Factor 2, which was interpreted as the perceived uncertainty associated with manufacturing operations.

CORRELATION BETWEEN PERCEIVED TASK ENVIRONMENT UNCERTAINTY FACTORS AND PARTNER-RELATED SELECTION CRITERIA CATEGORIES

Correlations between the perceived task environment uncertainty factors and the partner-related selection criteria categories were calculated in an attempt to further test the fourth research hypothesis. Since the factors represented statistical reformulations of the perceived task environment uncertainty categories, the fourth hypothesis would suggest that there would be a positive correlation between these factors and the valences of the partner-related selection criteria categories.

Using the results of the factor analysis of the perceived task environment uncertainty categories as input, both of the interpretable factors from the original and the recoded samples were correlated with each of the six partner-related selection criteria categories. The results are listed in Table 33. The following discussion examines the factors from the original sample's perceived task environment uncertainty categories and the partner-related selection criteria significantly correlated with each of them. The results from the correlations involving the associated factors from the recoded sample are also discussed.[2]

Factor 1: Uncertainty of Overall Market Environment

The first factor for the perceived task environment uncertainty categories evidenced three positive and one negative correlations with the partner-

Table 33

Tau-B Correlations between Partner-Related Partner Selection Criteria Categories and Perceived Task Environment Uncertainty Factors

	UNRECODED DATA		RECODED DATA	
PARTNER- RELATED SELECTION CRITERIA CATEGORY	PTEU FACTOR 1 Overall Market	PTEU FACTOR 2 Manufacturing Operation	PTEU FACTOR 1 Overall Market	PTEU FACTOR 2 Manufacturing Operation
PSCNEARU	.13#	.07	.17*	.11#
PSCCOMIT	.11#	-.10	.13#	-.07
PSCFREND	.08	-.17#	.05	-.12
PSCLIKEU	.13*	-.01	.09	-.04
PSCSIZE	-.04	-.12#	-.03	-.09
PSCPRIOR	-.11#	-.05	-.11#	.03

*   reflects P $\leq$ 0.05
\#   reflects P $\leq$ 0.10

related selection criteria categories. According to these results, an increase in the perceived level of uncertainty of the joint venture's overall market environment was correlated with an increased valence on the following: selection of a partner in close geographical proximity (PSCNEARU), selection of a partner committed to the joint venture (PSCCOMIT), and selection of a partner with similar national or corporate culture (PSCLIKEU). Under these same circumstances, there tended to be a decreased emphasis on selecting a partner with which the firm had a favorable prior association (PSCPRIOR). The results for the recoded sample's first factor were similar to those for the original data sample. Recoded Factor 1 was positively correlated, at the 0.10 level or less, with both PSCNEARU and PSCCOMIT and negatively correlated at that same level with PSCPRIOR.

The results suggest that, as the perceived uncertainty of the joint venture's overall market environment increased, firms tended to place greater emphasis on the selection of partners in close geographical proximity which evidenced a strong commitment to the joint venture and which might have been similar in culture. Under these same circumstances, firms tended to place less emphasis on the selection of a partner with which they had favorable prior association.

Factor 2: Uncertainty of Manufacturing Operations

The second factor was negatively correlated with two partner-related selection criteria categories: a partner with compatible top management (PSCFREND) and a partner of similar organizational size or structure (PSCSIZE). For recoded Factor 2, there was a positive correlation with the selection of a partner in close geographical proximity (PSCNEARU) and a negative correlation with PSCFREND.

These results suggest that, as the perceived uncertainty of manufacturing operations increased, firms tended to place greater emphasis on selecting firms that were in close geographical proximity, and they placed reduced emphasis on the selection of firms that evidenced compatible top management teams or similar organizational size or structure.

On the basis of the results presented in this section, Hypothesis 4 seemed to be supported by only about 20 to 25 percent of the correlations that were examined, and it seemed to be rejected by results from nearly as many other correlations.

CORRELATIONS BETWEEN FACTORS OF PERCEIVED TASK ENVIRONMENT UNCERTAINTY AND PARTNER SELECTION CRITERIA VARIABLES

No specific hypotheses were developed regarding the relationship between the factors for the perceived task environment uncertainty categories and the factors for the partner selection criteria categories. Nevertheless, the correlations between these two sets of factors were calculated in an attempt to gain additional insights into the partner selection process.

Using the results of the factor analysis as input, both of the factors for the perceived task environment uncertainty categories from both the original and the recoded samples were correlated with each of the nine factors for the original sample's partner selection criteria categories. The results are listed in Table 34.[3] The following discussion examines each of the two factors from the original sample's perceived task environment uncertainty categories and the partner selection criteria factors significantly correlated with each. The results from correlations involving the corresponding factors from the recoded sample are also discussed.

Factor 1: Uncertainty of the Overall Market Environment

The first factor for the perceived task environment uncertainty categories evidenced a positive correlation with four partner selection criteria factors. According to these results, as the perceived uncertainty of the joint venture's overall market increased, selection of partners with the following characteristics were also perceived to be of increasing importance: a similar firm with local government influence (Factor 2), a compatible partner (Factor 3), a firm with sales and service experience (Factor 6), and an opportunistic neighbor (Factor 8).

The results for the recoded sample were similar. For recoded Factor 1, there were positive correlations between the perceived uncertainty of the joint venture's overall market and the relative importance of the same four

Table 34

Correlations between Perceived Task Environment Uncertainty Factors and Partner Selection Criteria Factors

PARTNER SELECTION CRITERIA FACTOR	ORIGINAL DATA		RECODED DATA	
	PTEU FACTOR 1 Overall Market	PTEU FACTOR 2 Manufacturing Operations	PTEU FACTOR 1 Overall Market	PTEU FACTOR 2 Manufacturing Operations
FACTOR 1 Knowledge of Local Market, Not Technology	.05	-.12#	.16*	-.02
FACTOR 2 Similar Firm with Local Government Influence	.21*	.11	.19	.01
FACTOR 3 Compatible Partner	.16*	-.21**	.12#	-.19*
FACTOR 4 Low Cost Production	-.10	.04	-.08	.07
FACTOR 5 Shared Development	.04	.08	.13#	.10
FACTOR 6 Sales & Service Experience	.24**	.04	.28**	.12#
FACTOR 7 Strategically Critical Manufacturing Capabilities	-.12	.12#	-.10	.15*
FACTOR 8 Opportunistic Neighbor	.21*	-.07	.23**	-.04
FACTOR 9 Similar Respected Firm Controlling Inputs	-.10	.12#	-.09	.04

** reflects P < .01
* reflects P |<| .05
# reflects P |<| .10

factors, as well as with two other selection criteria factors: knowledge of the local market, not technology (Factor 1) and capability for shared development (Factor 5)., These correlations suggest that, as the perceived uncertainty of the joint venture's overall market environment increased, firms tended to place greater emphasis on selecting compatible partners that had market-related knowledge and government influence.

Factor 2: Uncertainty of Manufacturing Operations

The second factor was positively correlated with two partner selection criteria factors: a firm with strategically critical manufacturing capabilities (Factor 7) and a similar respected firm controlling inputs (Factor 9). The second factor was negatively correlated with two additional selection criteria factors: a firm with knowledge of the local market, not technology (Factor 1) and a compatible partner (Factor 3).

For recoded Factor 2, there was a positive correlation with two partner selection criteria factors: strategically critical manufacturing capabilities (Factor 7) and sales and service experience (Factor 6), and a negative correlation with the selection of a compatible partner (Factor 3).

These results suggest that an increase in the perceived level of uncertainty regarding the joint venture's manufacturing operations was correlated with increased efforts to select a partner that could provide important inputs (e.g., raw materials, components, a critical site, or technological knowledge) for the manufacturing operations of the joint venture. Under these same circumstances, firms placed less emphasis on the selection of a partner with market-related capabilities, and compatibility of the partner was also seen as declining in relative importance.

CHAPTER SUMMARY

This chapter discussed the results for the perceived task environment uncertainty variable. Descriptive statistics were presented for each of the eight categories of this variable, including average (mean) values, standard deviations, and frequencies. Based on these data, it appeared that the results were relatively stable across both the original and the recoded data samples. In addition, no statistically significant differences between category means were obtained, when they were evaluated at the 0.05 level.

Hypothesis 4, which predicted a positive correlation between perceived task environment uncertainty and the valences of partner-related selection criteria, was not strongly supported by the data. The data seemed clearly to reject the hypothesis for a few of the bivariate correlations, while the results for many of the pairs of variables neither supported nor rejected the hypothesis. The hypothesis seemed to be supported for approximately 20 to 25 percent of the bivariate correlations involving the categories measured in the questionnaire, and on approximately the same number of correlations involving the factors for the perceived task environment uncertainty categories with the partner-related selection criteria categories.

Factor analysis of the perceived task environment uncertainty categories produced two interpretable orthogonal factors for both the original and the recoded data samples. The principal loadings on these factors were presented and interpreted. The statistical reliability of these factors seemed to have been supported.

The correlations between each of the factors from the original and the recoded samples of the perceived task environment uncertainty categories and each of the six partner-related selection criteria categories, as well as with each of the nine partner selection criteria factors obtained in Chapter 5, were calculated. The results of these correlations were presented and discussed.

NOTES

1. The partner-related variable categories evidenced several moderate intercorrelations. Therefore, to test Hypothesis 4 effectively, it was also necessary to calculate the tenth-order partial correlation coefficients for the perceived task environment uncertainty categories. Examination of these partial correlations suggested that there were some differences between these data and the data presented for the bivariate correlations. The latter correlations evidencing statistical significance at the 0.05 level without controlling for the effects of the other partner-related variables frequently did not evidence significant partial correlations. For the original sample, only four of the eight correlations evidenced partial correlation coefficients significant at the 0.10 level, and only two of eight correlations formerly significant at the 0.10 level evidenced partial correlations significant at that same level.

The lack of complete substantiation of the earlier results may be at least partially due to the substantial loss of degrees of freedom attributable to the partial correlation procedure, as well as to method differences (e.g., the use of Pearson r versus Kendall tau-b-based statistics). Nevertheless, the results suggest that Hypothesis 4 did not receive clear-cut support, although it also did not appear to be clearly rejected.

2. Several moderate correlations were present among the factors of the perceived task environment uncertainty and diversity of line functions variables and the categories of the extent of shared control variable. Therefore, the twelfth-order partial correlation coefficients were obtained for the relationship between each of the perceived task environment uncertainty factors and the partner-related selection criteria categories, controlling for the effects of the diversity of line functions factors and the extent of shared control categories. Examination of the results suggested that the correlations in Table 34 tended to be supported by the results of the partial correlation analysis.

3. Several moderate correlations were present among the factors of the perceived task environment uncertainty and diversity of line functions variables and the categories of the extent of shared control variable. Therefore, the partial correlation coefficients were obtained for the relationship between each of the perceived task

environment factors and the partner selection criteria factors, controlling for the diversity of line functions factors and the extent of shared control categories simultaneously. These twelfth-order partial correlation coefficients suggest that the bivariate factor correlations evidencing statistical significance at the 0.05 level without controlling for the effects of the other partner-related variables also tended to evidence partial correlation coefficients significant at the 0.10 level or less. (The 0.10 significance level was used for comparison for the partial correlation analysis, due to loss of an additional eleven degrees of freedom in their calculation.) Three of five correlations previously significant at the 0.05 level, without controlling for the effects of the other partner-related variables, evidenced significant partial correlation coefficients. The lack of complete substantiation between the data in Table 34 and the partial correlations may be partially attributable to the substantial loss of degrees of freedom associated with the partial correlation procedure and to method differences, rather than solely to the effects of intercorrelations between the partner-related variables. Nevertheless, the results of the partial correlation analysis tended to support further the results of the bivariate correlation analysis.

10

Diversity of Line Functions Variable

This chapter presents the results for the diversity of line functions variable. The frequencies obtained for each of the eight diversity of line functions categories for the original data sample were as follows:

Category	Frequency
FMINE	2
FBASIC	1
FAPPLY	45
FMFG	42
FASSEM	43
FMKTG	65
FDISTRIB	31
FSERV	38

Because these categories were coded as "dummy" variables, with values of either 0 (if the function was not expected to be engaged in by the joint venture) or 1 (if the function was expected to be engaged in), the average (mean) values and standard deviations were less relevant statistics and were therefore not calculated.

As is evident from examination of the above data, the line function most commonly expected in the joint ventures, marketing (FMKTG), occurred in 65 of the 90 sample ventures. The line functions of applied research and development (FAPPLY), manufacturing of components (FMFG), manufacturing or assembly of finished goods (FASSEM), post-sale service

(FSERV), and distribution (FDISTRIB), were expected to be engaged in by 45, 42, 43, 38, and 31 of the ventures, respectively. The functions of mining or extraction (FMINE) and basic research (FBASIC), were expected to occur in only 2 and 1 joint ventures, respectively.

Because missing values occurred for only one of the joint ventures, re-coding of the diversity of line functions data was not attempted.

CORRELATIONS BETWEEN DIVERSITY OF LINE FUNCTIONS VARIABLE AND PARTNER-RELATED SELECTION CRITERIA CATEGORIES

In Chapter 3, a positive correlation was hypothesized between the number of line functions which the joint venture was expected to engage in and the valences of partner-related selection criteria. To test this fifth hypothesis, it was necessary to create a new variable, labelled NUMBERF, which represented the total number of functions that each individual joint venture was expected to engage in. The average values, standard deviations, and frequencies obtained for the NUMBERF variable are as follows:

Average value	3.00
Standard deviation	1.48
Frequency	89
Range of values	1 to 6

The average number of functions expected to be engaged in was approximately three, although the absolute number of functions expected to be engaged in ranged from one to six.

To test Hypothesis 5, the NUMBERF variable was correlated with each of the six prospective partner-related selection criteria categories. The results of these correlations are as follows:

PSC Category	Tau-B
PSCNEARU	.16 (p ≤ 0.05)
PSCLIKEU	.12 (p ≤ 0.10)
PSCSIZE	.04
PSCPRIOR	.05
PSCCOMIT	− .01
PSCFREND	.11 (p ≤ 0.10)

Analysis of these results shows that positive correlations, significant at the 0.10 level or less, were found for three of the six relationships, as noted in parentheses. The partner-related selection criteria categories which evidenced these positive correlations with the NUMBERF variable were: a partner in close geographical proximity (PSCNEARU), a partner with similar national or corporate culture (PSCLIKEU), and a partner with compatible top management (PSCFREND). There were no negative correlations significant at the 0.10 level.

The results suggest that Hypothesis 5 was not rejected. Furthermore, these results suggest that increases in the expected number of line functions tended to be associated with greater emphasis upon the selection of a nearby firm that had compatible top management and a similar culture.

PARTIAL CORRELATIONS OF THE NUMBERF VARIABLE WITH THE PARTNER-RELATED SELECTION CRITERIA CATEGORIES

The partner-related variable categories frequently evidenced moderate levels of intercorrelation. Therefore, to test Hypothesis 5 effectively, it was necessary not only to calculate the correlations between the NUMBERF variable and the partner-related selection criteria categories, but also to calculate the partial correlation coefficients for the NUMBERF variable.

The seventeenth-order partial correlation coefficients for the NUMBERF variable, controlling for the perceived task environment uncertainty and the extent of shared control categories, were as follows:

PSC Category	Partial Correlation Coefficient
PSCNEARU	.11
PSCCOMIT	.08
PSCFREND	.19 ($p \leq 0.10$)
PSCLIKEU	.28 ($p \leq 0.05$)
PSCSIZE	.15
PSCPRIOR	.07

Those coefficients that were significant at 0.10 or less are noted in parentheses. The results suggest that there were only minor differences between these data and the data previously presented for the bivariate correlations. Two of the three correlations significant at the 0.10 level evidenced partial correlation coefficients significant at that same level. Furthermore, all six of the partial correlations evidenced positive coefficients, which was the hypothesized outcome.

The lack of complete substantiation of the earlier results appears to have been at least partially due to the substantial loss of degrees of freedom attributable to the partial correlation procedure, and possibly also to method differences (e.g., the use of Pearson r versus Kendall tau-b-based statistics). Some or all of the differences may have also been the result of controlling for the effects of intercorrelations among the partner-related variable categories. Nevertheless, the results provide further support for the assertion that Hypothesis 5 was not rejected.

CORRELATIONS BETWEEN DIVERSITY OF LINE FUNCTIONS VARIABLE AND PARTNER SELECTION CRITERIA FACTORS

No hypotheses were explicitly developed regarding the relationship between the diversity of line functions variable and the partner selection criteria factors obtained in Chapter 5. However, the bivariate correlations between these two sets of variables were calculated in an attempt to gain additional insight into the partner selection process. Using the results of the factor analysis of the partner selection criteria variable as input, the NUMBERF variable was correlated with each of the nine selection criteria factors for the original sample. The results were as follows:[1]

PSC Factor	Tau-B
Factor 1	.01
Factor 2	.12 ($p \leq 0.10$)
Factor 3	−.03
Factor 4	.10
Factor 5	.31 ($p \leq 0.01$)
Factor 6	.19 ($p \leq 0.05$)
Factor 7	−.04
Factor 8	−.03
Factor 9	.01

As shown, three of the selection criteria factors evidenced significant positive correlations with the NUMBERF variable at a 0.10 level or less. According to these results, an increase in the number of line functions (NUMBERF) expected to be engaged in by the joint venture was associated with increased emphasis on selecting a partner with the following traits: the ability to share development tasks (Factor 5), sales and service experience (Factor 6), and a similar firm with local government influence (Factor 2). Therefore, increased diversity of line functions was correlated with the selection of a similar firm that could share the development efforts, particularly in sales and service, and had influence vis-a-vis local government policies.

Table 35
Rotated Factors for Diversity of Line Functions Categories

UNRECODED DATA

DIVERSITY OF LINE FUNCTIONS CATEGORY	FACTOR 1 Marketing Functions	FACTOR 2 Production Functions
FMINE	-.44*	-.41*
FBASIC	-.03	-.09
FAPPLY	-.16	.78*
FMFG	.00	.79*
FASSEM	.20	.44*
FMKTG	.79*	.09
FDISTRIB	.66*	-.24
FSERV	.67*	.02
EIGENVALUE	1.87	1.64
PCT. OF VAR.	23.4	20.6
CUM. PCT. OF VAR.	23.4	44.0

* reflects factor loadings $\geq$ 0.30

FACTOR ANALYSIS OF DIVERSITY OF LINE FUNCTIONS CATEGORIES

Because of the potential conceptual overlap between the diversity of line functions categories, we wanted to obtain statistically distinct categories for this variable's sample data. The most appropriate means of accomplishing this task involved the employment of factor analytic techniques.

The results of the factor analysis are presented in Table 35. Factor analysis produced two interpretable factors explaining a total of 44.0 percent of the sample's variance. The following discussion presents the interpretation of these two rotated factors.

Factor 1: Marketing Functions

The first factor had high positive loadings on three diversity of line functions categories: marketing (FMKTG), distribution (FDISTRIB), and post-sale service (FSERV). There was also a negative loading on the function of mining or extraction (FMINE). Factor 1 was therefore interpreted as the customer-oriented, or marketing, line functions.

Factor 2: Production Functions

The second factor had high positive loadings on three diversity of line functions categories: manufacturing of components (FMFG), applied research or development (FAPPLY), and manufacturing or assembly of finished goods (FASSEM). There was also a negative loading on the function of mining or extraction (FMINE). Factor 2 was therefore interpreted as the production-oriented line functions.

CORRELATIONS BETWEEN DIVERSITY OF LINE FUNCTIONS FACTORS AND PARTNER-RELATED SELECTION CRITERIA CATEGORIES

No hypotheses were explicitly developed regarding the relationship between the diversity of line functions factors and the partner-related selection criteria categories. However, the bivariate correlations between these two sets of variables were calculated in an attempt to gain further insights into the partner selection process. Using the results of the factor analysis of the diversity of line functions categories as input, both of the factors were correlated with each of the six partner-related selection criteria categories. However, only one of these correlations was significant at the 0.10 level: Factor 2 with the PSCLIKEU category. This result suggests that, as the number of nonmarketing-oriented line functions increased, a corresponding emphasis was placed on the selection of a culturally similar partner.

CORRELATIONS BETWEEN DIVERSITY OF LINE FUNCTIONS FACTORS AND PARTNER SELECTION CRITERIA FACTORS

No specific hypotheses were developed regarding the relationship between the factors for the diversity of line functions categories and for the PSC categories. Nevertheless, the bivariate correlations between these two sets of factors were calculated in an attempt to uncover additional insights into the partner selection process. Using the results of the factor analysis as input, both of the factors for the diversity of line functions categories were correlated with each of the nine factors for the partner selection criteria categories. The results are listed in Table 36.[2] The following discussion examines each of the factors for the diversity of line functions variable and the partner selection criteria factors significantly correlated with each of them.

Factor 1: Marketing Functions

The first factor evidenced a positive correlation with the sixth selection criteria factor: sales and service experience. The first factor was also negatively correlated with selection criteria Factor 4, a firm that enhances low-cost production. These results suggest that, as the number of customer-oriented, or marketing, functions increased, firms tended to place greater emphasis on selecting partners with marketing-related skills (e.g., sales and service) and less emphasis on partners with production-oriented capabilities.

Table 36
**Tau-B Correlations between Diversity of Line Functions Factors and Partner
Selection Criteria Factors**

	UNRECODED DATA	
PARTNER SELECTION CRITERIA FACTOR	DLF FACTOR 1 Marketing Functions	DLF FACTOR 2 Production Functions
FACTOR 1 Knowledge of Local Market, Not Technology	.03	-.01
FACTOR 2 Similar Firm with Local Government Influence	-.08	.16*
FACTOR 3 Compatible Partner	-.02	-.08
FACTOR 4 Low Cost Production	-.12#	.19*
FACTOR 5 Shared Development	.08	.28**
FACTOR 6 Sales & Service Experience	.17*	.07
FACTOR 7 Strategically Critical Manufacturing Capabilities	-.10	.10
FACTOR 8 Opportunistic Neighbor	-.05	-.09
FACTOR 9 Similar Respected Firm Controlling Inputs	-.01	.04

```
** reflects P ≤ .01
 * reflects P ≤ .05
 # reflects P ≤ .10
```

Factor 2: Production Functions

The second factor was positively correlated with three selection criteria
factors: low-cost production (Factor 4), shared development (Factor 5), and
a similar firm with local government influence (Factor 2). These results
suggest that, as the number of production-related functions increased, firms
tended to place greater emphasis on selecting similar firms with production-

related capabilities, including the ability to influence government policies and the ability to provide strategically critical manufacturing capabilities.

CHAPTER SUMMARY

This chapter discussed the results for the diversity of line functions variable. Frequencies were presented for each of the eight categories of this variable. From this data, it was apparent that marketing was the most common function expected to be engaged in by the sample firms' joint ventures, and the functions of mining or extraction and of basic research were almost never expected to be engaged in.

Hypothesis 5 predicted a positive correlation between diversity of line functions and the relative importance of partner-related selection criteria. In order to test this hypothesis, the NUMBERF variable was calculated, and the descriptive statistics for it were presented. These statistics showed that the average number of expected line functions was exactly three for the sample joint ventures.

The NUMBERF variable was correlated with the six partner-related selection criteria categories in an effort to test Hypothesis 5. The results of the correlational analyses suggested that this hypothesis was not rejected. Three of the six bivariate correlations were significantly positive at the 0.10 level or less, and none evidenced a significant negative relationship. The results suggested that an increase in the expected number of line functions was associated with an increased emphasis on the selection of partners in close geographical proximity with similar cultures and compatible top management.

The NUMBERF variable was also correlated with the nine partner selection criteria factors obtained in Chapter 5. Three of these factors evidenced significant positive correlations with the NUMBERF variable, at a 0.10 level or less, and none evidenced a significant negative relationship. The selection criteria factors with positive correlations included Factor 2 (similar firm with local government influence), Factor 5 (shared development), and Factor 6 (sales and service experience).

Factor analysis of the diversity of line functions categories produced two interpretable factors. The principal loadings on these factors were presented and interpreted. These factors were interpreted as follows: Factor 1 as marketing-oriented line functions and Factor 2 as production-oriented line functions.

Each of the factors was correlated with each of the six partner-related selection criteria categories, as well as with each of the nine partner selection criteria factors obtained in Chapter 5. The results of these correlations were presented and discussed.

NOTES

1. The partner-related variable categories frequently evidenced moderate levels of intercorrelation. Therefore, to increase confidence in the correlational results, it was necessary to calculate the partial correlation coefficients for these relationships. The seventeenth-order partial correlation coefficients for the NUMBERF variable, controlling for the perceived task environment uncertainty and extent of shared control categories, and the eleventh-order partial correlation coefficients for the NUMBERF variable, controlling for the extent of shared control categories and the factors for the perceived task environment uncertainty variable, were calculated. Examination of the results suggested that the results discussed above received only partial support. For the seventeenth-order partial correlations, only one of the three correlations that had correlation coefficients significant at the 0.10 level evidenced a partial correlation coefficient significant at that same level. For the eleventh-order partial correlations, both of the correlations that had correlation coefficients significant at the 0.05 level evidenced partial correlation coefficients significant at the 0.10 level.

The lack of complete substantiation of the earlier results may have been at least partially due to the substantial loss of degrees of freedom attributable to the partial correlation procedure. The differences between the eleventh- and the seventeenth-order partial correlation coefficients seems to lend some support to this prospective interpretation. In addition, some of the differences may have been attributable to method differences (e.g., the use of Pearson r versus Kendall tau-b-based statistics). Nevertheless, the results of the partial correlation analysis suggest that the bivariate correlation results received at least partial confirmation.

2. The presence of moderate correlations among the factors of the perceived task environment uncertainty and diversity of line functions variables and the categories of the extent of shared control variable was potentially troublesome. Therefore, the partial correlation coefficients were obtained for the relationship between each of the diversity of line functions factors and the partner selection criteria factors, controlling for the perceived task environment uncertainty factors and the extent of shared control categories. The results from these eleventh-order partial correlations suggested that the factor correlations evidencing statistical significance at the 0.05 level without controlling for the effects of the other partner-related variables also tended to evidence partial correlation coefficients significant at the 0.10 level or less. (The 0.10 significance level was used for comparison for the partial correlation analysis due to the loss of an additional 10 degrees of freedom in their calculation.) Five of seven correlations previously significant at the 0.05 level, without controlling for the effects of the other partner-related variables, evidenced significant partial correlation coefficients.

The lack of complete substantiation may be partially attributable to the substantial loss of degrees of freedom associated with the partial correlation procedure and to method differences (e.g., the use of Pearson r versus Kendall tau-b-based statistics), rather than solely to the effects of intercorrelations between the partner-related variables. Nevertheless, the results of the partial correlation analyses tended to support further the results of the bivariate correlational analyses.

11

Extent of Shared Control Variable

This chapter presents the results for the extent of shared control variable. Nine categories of this variable were examined. On the questionnaire, the respondents were asked to evaluate the extent to which their firms sought to share control over each of these categories. Responses were scored on a scale of 0 to 4, with 0 representing expected control of that function by the respondent's company, 2 representing shared control of the function by the two partner organizations, and 4 representing anticipated control over that function by the partner firm. Therefore, results from this five-point Likert-type scale represent the level of control that firms sought to allocate to their partner firm, with the relative level of the partner's control over a dimension increasing as the reported value ascended from 0 to 4.

In addition to the analysis conducted with responses on the 0 to 4 scale, the extent of shared control variable was also recoded to a 0 to 2 scale, where 0 represented full allocation of control to one of the partners (a response of either 0 or 4 on the questionnaire), 1 represented partial allocation of control (a response of either 1 or 3 on the questionnaire), and 2 represented equally shared control over a particular dimension. Use of the 0 to 2 scale permitted analyses based on absolute sharing or nonsharing of control over a particular dimension, regardless of which partner the control had been allocated to. Comparison of results of the 0 to 2 scale with similar results from the 0 to 4 scale enhanced opportunities for determining whether responses on one or more dimensions tended toward extreme (unshared) or toward middle (shared) values.

Table 37 presents the means, standard deviations, and frequencies for the extent of shared control categories, as calculated using the 0 to 4 scale for the original and recoded samples. The categories are listed in descending order based on their average value for the original sample. Table 37 also

Table 37
Descriptive Statistics for Extent of Shared Control Categories

| | 0 to 4 Scaled Data | | | | | | 0 to 2 Scaled Data | | | | | |
| | Unrecoded Data | | | Recoded Data | | | Unrecoded Data | | | Recoded Data | | |
Variable Label	Mean	Std. Dev.	(n)	Mean	Std. Dev.	(n)	Mean	Std. Dev.	(n)	Mean	Std. Dev.	(n)
SCMGMT	1.90	1.578	87	1.90	1.551	90	0.68	0.856	87	0.72	0.874	90
SCINVEST	1.85	0.578	88	1.86	0.572	90	1.81	0.564	88	1.81	0.559	90
SCCOSTS	1.77	1.142	88	1.78	1.130	90	1.18	0.824	88	1.20	0.824	90
SCMFG	1.68	1.336	74	1.73	1.216	90	0.92	0.840	74	1.11	0.867	90
SCMKTG	1.67	1.140	79	1.71	1.073	90	1.17	0.839	79	1.27	0.832	90
SCRM	1.63	1.209	76	1.69	1.118	90	1.11	0.888	76	1.24	0.878	90
SCPRICE	1.63	0.861	84	1.66	0.837	90	1.46	0.768	84	1.50	0.753	90
SCHIRING	1.61	0.808	88	1.62	0.801	90	1.55	0.772	88	1.56	0.766	90
SCDESIGN	1.32	1.253	84	1.37	1.222	90	0.89	0.892	84	0.97	0.905	90

presents the same data obtained by using the 0 to 2 scale. Examination of the data in this table shows that the results for the original and recoded samples were quite similar within the same (i.e., 0 to 4 or 0 to 2) scale.

For both the 0 to 2 and the 0 to 4 scale data, there were no statistically significant differences between the categories' means when tested at the 0.10 level. However, comparison of the data in Table 37 uncovers several interesting characteristics of the data when it is coded 0 to 4 versus 0 to 2. For instance, when coded on a 0 to 4 scale, the highest mean was the SCMGMT category; however, this same category evidenced the lowest mean when a 0 to 2 scale was employed. This suggests that day-to-day management of the joint ventures tended to be allocated to one partner or the other, rather than being shared between partners, and it also highlights the usefulness of employing both the 0 to 4 and 0 to 2 scales in analysis of the data. Similar, but less dramatic, change was observed for the SCMFG category; both the SCPRICE and the SCHIRING categories evidenced a substantial, but opposite, change in their means' relative position vis-a-vis the other categories of shared control.

In contrast to the movements noted above, especially for the SCMGMT category, it is interesting to note the stability of the statistical mean of the SCINVEST category between the 0 to 4 and the 0 to 2 scales. The stability and the absolute value of the SCINVEST means, as well as their relatively low standard deviations, suggest that control over major capital investments made by the joint venture were almost universally shared between the partners. On the other hand, data on the SCDESIGN category, which consistently evidenced one of the lowest means, suggests that control over the design dimension is typically not shared between the partners, and particularly not shared with non-U.S. partners. These assertions, as well as the findings on the SCMGMT category, were strongly supported by the interview responses of the participating executives.

CORRELATIONS BETWEEN EXTENT OF SHARED CONTROL CATEGORIES AND PARTNER-RELATED SELECTION CRITERIA CATEGORIES

In Chapter 3, a positive correlation was hypothesized between the sharing of control over joint venture activities and the relative importance of partner-related selection criteria. To test this hypothesis, the nine categories of the extent of shared control variable were correlated with each of the six prospective partner-related selection criteria categories for the original and recoded data samples for both the recoded 0 to 2 scaled data and the 0 to 4 scaled data. The results of these correlations for the 0 to 2 scaled data are listed in Table 38 for the original and recoded samples, respectively. The results of these correlations for the 0 to 4 scaled data are listed in Table 39 for the original and recoded samples, respectively.[1]

Table 38
Tau-B Correlations between Categories of Partner-Related Selection
Criteria and Extent of Shared Control Variables for 0 to 2 Scaled Data

Unrecoded Data (Recoded Data)

EXTENT OF SHARED CONTROL CATEGORY	PSCNEARU	PSCLIKEU	PSCSIZE	PSCPRIOR	PSCCOMIT	PSCFREND
SCDESIGN	.01 (.00)	-.01 (-.05)	.12 (.11)	.08 (.09)	-.02 (-.03)	-.06 (-.08)
SCRM	.05 (.04)	.00 (.00)	.16# (.11)	.00 (.00)	-.04 (-.03)	-.08 (-.09)
SCMFG	.03 (.05)	-.14# (-.13*)	.00 (-.08)	.07 (.07)	-.10 (-.12)	-.12 (-.20*)
SCHIRING	-.09 (-.10)	-.10 (-.11)	-.08 (-.08)	-.11 (-.12#)	.04 (.05)	-.08 (-.08)
SCPRICE	-.10 (-.11)	-.08 (-.06)	.04 (.03)	-.11 (-.07)	.15# (.12)	.10 (.11)
SCCOSTS	-.04 (-.05)	-.06 (-.06)	-.06 (-.05)	-.10 (-.12)	.00 (.01)	-.10 (-.10)
SCINVEST	-.19* (-.19*)	.06 (.05)	.08 (.07)	-.02 (-.03)	.00 (.00)	-.01 (-.01)
SCMKTG	-.22* (-.24**)	.01 (.03)	.13# (.11)	.03 (.01)	.23 (.20*)	.07 (.04)
SCMGMT	-.02 (-.05)	-.05 (-.10)	.01 (-.03)	.04 (-.01)	.08 (.11)	-.01 (-.03)

* reflects P $\leq$ .05
# reflects P $\leq$ .10

Table 39
Tau-B Correlations between Categories of Partner-Related Selection
Criteria and Extent of Shared Control Variables for 0 to 4 Scaled Data

Unrecoded Data (Recoded Data)

EXTENT OF SHARED CONTROL CATEGORY	PSCNEARU	PSCCOMIT	PSCFREND	PSCLIKEU	PSCSIZE	PSCPRIOR
SCDESIGN	.12 (.11)	-.02 (-.02)	-.09 (-.09)	-.01 (-.04)	.13# (.12#)	.02 (.03)
SCRM	-.07 (-.06)	-.03 (-.02)	.07 (.05)	.05 (.05)	.13# (.11)	-.01 (-.03)
SCMFG	.19* (.18*)	-.19* (-.15#)	-.08* (-.07)	-.01 (-.01#)	-.07 (-.09)	-.02 (-.01)
SCHIRING	-.14# (-.15#)	.08 (.08)	.02 (.02)	-.12 (-.13#)	-.08 (-.08)	-.12# (-.14#)
SCPRICE	-.15# (-.16#)	.11 (.10)	.10 (.10)	.00 (.01)	.07 (.07)	-.17# (-.14#)
SCCOSTS	-.11 (-.11)	-.13# (-.13#)	-.10# (-.10)	-.13# (-.13#)	-.11 (-.11)	-.14* (-.15*)
SCINVEST	-.14* (-.14#)	.05 (.05)	.05 (.05)	.03 (.03)	-.01 (-.02)	-.17* (-.18*)
SCMKTG	-.24** (-.24**)	.12 (.11)	.05 (.04)	.13# (.13#)	.13# (.11)	-.12 (-.11)
SCMGMT	-.01 (-.02)	.00 (.00)	.05 (.05)	-.12# (-.12#)	-.10 (-.10)	.02 (.01)

** reflects P ∨ .01
* reflects P ∨|∨|∨ .05
# reflects P ∨|∨| .10

Analysis of the results presented in Tables 38 and 39 suggests that Hypothesis 6 was generally not supported by the sample data. For the 0 to 2 scaled data, only 12 of the 108 correlations evidenced relationships that were statistically significant at the 0.10 level, and two-thirds of these were negative correlations. Furthermore, only 3 of the 54 correlated pairs of categories evidenced significant relationships for both of the samples, thereby questioning the reliability of the remaining significant correlations that were observed. The lack of support for Hypothesis 6 was similar for the 0 to 4 scaled data, where 36 of 108 correlations were significant, but only 8 of these were in the hypothesized positive direction.

Despite these limitations, several insights can be garnered from examination of Table 38. First, it appears that similar partner size and structure (PSCSIZE) may evidence a relationship with the extent of shared control variable. Both the SCRM and the SCMKTG categories evidenced significant positive correlations with PSCSIZE for the unrecoded data.

The data in Table 38 also suggest that a geographically close partner (PSCNEARU) tended to be accorded less importance as a selection criterion when firms sought more equally shared control over major capital investments (SCINVEST) and over marketing and distribution policies (SCMKTG). Similarly, selection of a partner with similar national or corporate culture (PSCLIKEU) tended to receive lower valences when firms sought more equal control over the manufacturing setup (SCMFG). Furthermore, selection of a partner with compatible top management (PSCFREND) tended to receive less emphasis as a selection criterion when firms sought more equal control of manufacturing setup (SCMFG).

Although more equally shared control over marketing and distribution (SCMKTG) tended to be associated with less emphasis on selecting a partner in close geographical proximity (PSCNEARU), it also tended to be positively correlated with selection of a partner of similar size or organization structure (PSCSIZE) and of a partner that evidenced a strong commitment to the joint venture (PSCCOMIT).

Comparison of the results for the 0 to 2 scaled data (Table 38) with those for the 0 to 4 scaled data (Table 39) provides some interesting insights into the samples. First, as the firms sought to give increasing control over joint venture activities to their partners (movement from 0 to 4 values), they tended to de-emphasize the selection of partners in close geographical proximity (PSCNEARU) (except in regard to control over manufacturing setup, or SCMFG), with similar national or corporate culture (PSCLIKEU) (except in regard to control over marketing and distribution policies, or SCMKTG), which evidenced a strong commitment to the joint venture (PSCCOMIT), and with which they had favorable prior association (PSCPRIOR). Under these same circumstances, there was not a distinguishable tendency to de-emphasize the selection of partners with a similar size or organizational structure (PSCSIZE), or the selection of partners with compatible top management (PSCFREND) (except in regard to manufacturing setup, or SCMFG). Finally, examination of Table 39 suggests that firms tended to seek partners with similar size or structure when they anticipated increased delegation of control to their partner over design (SCDESIGN), raw materials (SCRM), or marketing and distribution policies (SCMKTG).

FACTOR ANALYSIS OF EXTENT OF SHARED CONTROL CATEGORIES

As mentioned in Appendix B, in order to utilize factor analytic methods on the sample data, the data should embody certain characteristics. These characteristics include normality of distributions, linearity of relationships, and homoscedasticity. For the extent of shared control data, both when scaled 0 to 4 and when scaled 0 to 2, the linearity of relationships characteristic was only approximated, and the normality of distributions and homoscedasticity requirements were clearly not satisfied. Therefore, the exploratory use of factor analytic techniques on the data for this research variable was not justified, and no factor analysis was performed.

CORRELATIONS BETWEEN EXTENT OF SHARED CONTROL CATEGORIES AND PARTNER SELECTION CRITERIA FACTORS

No hypotheses were explicitly developed regarding the relationship between the extent of shared control variable and the partner selection criteria factors developed in Chapter 5. However, the bivariate correlations between these two sets of variables were calculated, and the results were examined in an attempt to gain additional insights into the partner selection process.

Using the results of factor analysis of the partner selection criteria variable as input, each of the nine extent of shared control categories from both the original and recoded data samples was correlated with each of the nine selection criteria factors for the original sample. This was done for both the 0 to 2 and the 0 to 4 scaled data sets.[2] The following discussion examines the extent of shared control categories and the partner selection criteria which were significantly correlated with each of them, for the original and recoded samples and for both the 0 to 2 and 0 to 4 scaled data sets.

SCDESIGN

For the 0 to 2 scaled data, the SCDESIGN category evidenced negative correlations with two selection criteria factors: Factor 1 and Factor 6. According to these results, as firms sought more equal control over product design, they placed less emphasis on the selection of a partner with knowledge of the local market, not technology (Factor 1), and on the selection of a partner with sales and service experience (Factor 6). In other words, nontechnological, customer-oriented skills received less emphasis as partner selection criteria when a firm was seeking to share more of the product design activities.

For the 0 to 4 scaled data, the SCDESIGN category evidenced a significant negative correlation with partner selection criteria Factor 1. This result suggests that, as firms sought to allocate more control over product design to their joint venture partners, they tended to de-emphasize the selection of a partner with nontechnological, local-market-knowledge-based capabilities.

SCRM

For the 0 to 2 scaled data, the SCRM category was negatively correlated with selection criteria Factor 1 for both the original and recoded samples. The SCRM category was also positively correlated with Factors 5 and 7 for the original sample. These results suggest that, as firms sought more equal control over raw materials sourcing, they tended to de-emphasize selection of partners with nontechnological, local market knowledge (Factor 1) and to emphasize selection of partners able to share development efforts, including provision of strategically critical manufacturing capabilities (Factors 5 and 7).

For the 0 to 4 scaled data, the SCRM category was negatively correlated with Factors 1 and 7 and positively correlated with Factors 4 and 9, for both samples. The implication is that, as firms sought to place more of the control over raw materials sourcing into the hands of their partners, they tended to emphasize selection of partners able to enhance low-cost production (Factor 4), including the ability to control important inputs (Factor 9). Under these same circumstances, firms tended to de-emphasize the selection of partners with nontechnological, local market knowledge (Factor 1) and, somewhat surprisingly, partners with strategically critical manufacturing capabilities (Factor 7).

SCMFG

For the 0 to 2 scaled data, the SCMFG category was negatively correlated with Factors 3 and 8 for both samples and positively correlated with Factor 5 for the original sample. These results suggest that, as firms sought to share control over manufacturing setup more equally, they tended to place less emphasis on the selection of compatible partners (Factor 3) and opportunistic neighbors (Factor 8), and they tended to place greater emphasis on selecting a partner able to share in the joint venture's development efforts (Factor 5).

For the 0 to 4 scaled data, the SCMFG category was negatively correlated with Factor 1 and positively correlated with Factors 4 and 9. This suggests that, as firms sought to allocate more control over manufacturing setup to their partners, they tended to place greater emphasis on selecting similar respected firms that controlled inputs (Factor 9) and could enhance low-cost production (Factor 4). Under these circumstances, they also tended to place less emphasis on selecting a partner with knowledge of the local market, not technology (Factor 1).

SCHIRING

For the 0 to 2 scaled data, the SCHIRING category was positively correlated with Factor 4 and negatively correlated with Factor 8 for the original sample. This suggests that, as firms sought to share more equally control over hiring of joint venture managers, they tended to place greater emphasis on selecting partners able to enhance low-cost production (Factor 4) and less emphasis on selecting opportunistic neighbors (Factor 8) as partners.

For the 0 to 4 scaled data, the same results were obtained; in addition, there was a positive correlation with Factor 6. Therefore, in addition to the interpretation of the results for the 0 to 2 data, firms under the same circumstances also tended to place greater emphasis on selecting partners with sales and service experience (Factor 6).

SCPRICE

For the 0 to 2 scaled data, the SCPRICE category was positively correlated with Factors 4 and 7 and negatively correlated with Factor 8 for both samples. This means that, as firms sought to share more equally control over pricing and sales targets, they tended to place greater emphasis on selection of partners that could enhance low-cost production (Factor 4), including the provision of strategically critical manufacturing capabilities (Factor 7), but the selection of an opportunistic neighbor (Factor 8) as a partner tended to be de-emphasized.

For the 0 to 4 scaled data, the SCPRICE category was positively correlated with Factor 6 and negatively correlated with Factor 8 for both samples, and was also positively correlated with Factor 7 for the recoded sample. These results suggest that, as firms sought to place increasing control over pricing and sales targets into the hands of their partners, they tended to place greater emphasis on selecting partners with sales and service experience (Factor 6) with strategically critical manufacturing capabilities (Factor 7), but de-emphasized selection of an opportunistic neighbor (Factor 8) as a partner.

SCCOSTS

For the 0 to 2 scaled data, there was a negative correlation with Factor 3 and a positive correlation with Factor 6 for both samples. This suggests that, as firms sought to share more equally cost and quality control with their partners, they tended to place more emphasis on selecting partners with sales and service experience (Factor 6) and less emphasis on selecting compatible partners (Factor 3).

For the 0 to 4 scaled data, there again was a negative correlation with Factor 3 but also a positive correlation with Factor 4 (low-cost production). Therefore, as firms sought to allocate increasing levels of control over costs and quality control to their partners, they tended to place less emphasis on selecting compatible partners (Factor 3) but greater emphasis on selecting partners that would enhance low-cost production (Factor 4).

SCINVEST

For both the original and the recoded samples of both the 0 to 2 and 0 to 4 data sets, there was a negative correlation between SCINVEST and selection criteria Factor 8. This means that, as firms sought to increase the amount of control over major capital investment allocated to the partner, they tended to de-emphasize the selection of an opportunistic neighbor as a partner.

SCMKTG

For both the original and the recoded samples of the 0 to 2 scaled data, there was a positive correlation between the SCMKTG category and Factors 1, 3, and 5 and a negative correlation between SCMKTG and Factor 8. These results suggest that when firms sought to share more equally control over marketing and distribution, they tended to place greater emphasis on selecting a compatible partner (Factor 3) with knowledge of the local market, not technology (Factor 1), who could help share in the joint venture's development efforts (Factor 5). Under these same circumstances, selection of an opportunistic neighbor (Factor 8) as a partner tended to be de-emphasized.

For the 0 to 4 scaled data, there was a positive correlation between SCMKTG and Factors 1, 6, and 9 for both the original and the recoded samples. This suggests that, as firms sought increasingly to allocate control over marketing and distribution to their partner, they tended to place greater emphasis on selecting a similar respected firm which controlled inputs (Factor 9) and had sales and service experience (Factor 6) and knowledge of the local market, not technology (Factor 1).

SCMGMT

For the 0 to 2 scaled data, there were no significant correlations between the SCMGMT category and the selection criteria factors. For the 0 to 4 scaled data, there were positive correlations between this category and Factors 1, 4, and 7. These results suggest that, as firms sought increasingly to allocate control over day-to-day management to their partner, they tended to place greater emphasis on selecting partners with knowledge of the local market, not technology (Factor 1), with the ability to enhance low-cost production (Factor 4), which evidenced strategically critical manufacturing capabilities (Factor 7). In other words, when firms sought to place greater control over day-to-day management in their partners' hands, they generally tried to select partners with strong marketing or production capabilities.

CHAPTER SUMMARY

This chapter discussed the results for the extent of shared control variable. Descriptive statistics were presented for each of the nine categories of this variable, including means, standard deviations, and frequencies, for the original and recoded data samples of the 0 to 2 and the 0 to 4 scaled data sets. Based on these data, it appeared that the results were relatively stable across each sample within a particular data scaling system. However, there were several significant differences in these statistics when comparisons were made across the two different scaling systems. These differences were identified and discussed.

Hypothesis 6, which predicted a positive correlation between the extent of shared control variable and the valences of partner-related selection criteria, did not appear to be supported by the data. Less than 20 percent of the correlations that were calculated evidenced statistical significance at the 0.10 level or less; more than half of the significant relationships were in the opposite direction from what had been hypothesized.

Each of the categories of the extent of shared control variable was correlated with each of the partner-related selection criteria categories, as well as with each of the selection criteria factors. These correlations were performed for both the 0 to 2 and the 0 to 4 scaled data sets. The results of these correlations and the relevant partial correlation analyses were presented and discussed.

NOTES

1. The partner-related variable categories frequently evidenced moderate intercorrelation. Therefore, to test Hypothesis 6 effectively, it was necessary not only to calculate the Kendall tau-b correlation coefficients between the extent of shared control and partner-related selection criteria categories, but also to calculate the partial correlation coefficients. Examination of these ninth-order partial correlation coefficients for the extent of shared control categories from the original sample, controlling for the effects of the perceived task environment uncertainty categories and the NUMBERF variable, suggests that there were substantial differences between these data and the results for the bivariate correlations. For the 0 to 2 scaled

data, only one of three correlations significant at the 0.05 level and none of the four correlations significant at the 0.05 to 0.10 level evidenced partial correlation coefficients significant at the 0.10 level. For the 0 to 4 scaled data, only one of six correlations significant at the 0.05 level evidenced a partial correlation coefficient significant at the 0.10 level.

However, the consistency between partial correlation results and the bivariate correlations increased significantly when the partial correlations controlled for the *factors* of the perceived task environment uncertainty and diversity of line functions variables, instead of controlling for the *categories* of the perceived task environment uncertainty variable and the NUMBERF variable. In this latter case, for the 0 to 2 scaled data, two of three correlations significant at the 0.05 level and two of four correlations significant at the 0.05 to 0.10 level evidenced partial correlation coefficients significant at the 0.10 level. For the 0 to 4 scaled data, three of six correlations significant at the 0.05 level and six of eleven correlations significant at the 0.05 to 0.10 level evidenced partial correlation coefficients significant at the 0.10 level.

The lack of complete substantiation of the earlier results appears to have been at least partially due to the substantial loss of degrees of freedom attributable to the partial correlation procedure, and possibly also to method differences (e.g., the use of Pearson r versus Kendall tau-b-based statistics). Nevertheless, the results provide further support for the assertion that Hypothesis 6 appeared generally not to have been supported by the sample results.

2. Several moderate correlations were present among the factors of the perceived task environment uncertainty and diversity of line functions variables and the categories of the extent of shared control variable. Therefore, the partial correlation coefficients were calculated for the relationship between each of the extent of shared control categories and the partner selection criteria factors, simultaneously controlling for the perceived task environment uncertainty and diversity of line functions factors.

The results from the partial correlation analysis suggested that the correlations evidencing statistical significance at the 0.10 level without controlling for the effects of the other partner-related variables exhibited an overwhelming tendency to also evidence partial correlation coefficients significant at the 0.10 level. For the 0 to 2 scaled data, six of seven correlations previously significant at the 0.05 level and six of thirteen correlations previously significant at the 0.05 to 0.10 level evidenced partial correlation coefficients significant at the 0.10 level or less. Similarly, for the 0 to 4 scaled data, all thirteen of the correlations previously significant at the 0.05 level and seven of nine correlations previously significant at the 0.05 to 0.10 level evidenced partial correlation coefficients significant at the 0.10 level. The lack of complete substantiation between the data analyses may be partially attributable to the loss of degrees of freedom associated with the partial correlation procedure and to method differences (e.g., the use of Pearson r versus Kendall tau-b-based statistics), rather than solely to the effects of intercorrelations between the partner-related variables. Nevertheless, the results of the partial correlation analysis very strongly supported the results of the bivariate correlational analyses.

V

CONCLUSIONS AND IMPLICATIONS

12

Conclusions

This chapter presents our conclusions regarding the selection of partners for joint ventures in developed countries. The discussion of results in Chapters 5 through 11 was limited primarily to analysis of quantitative, empirically based "facts" based upon "objective" data from the questionnaire. This chapter, in contrast, not only presents the principal conclusions drawn from the preceding chapters' quantitative analyses, but also supplements these findings with qualitative data gathered in the field interviews. Possible explanations for our results will also be discussed.

The chapter begins with a review of the purpose for which the study was conducted. An examination is made of the characteristics of the research sample, highlighting the traits of the sample joint ventures and some of the circumstances surrounding their formation. This discussion permits the reader to evaluate the probable extent to which the results will be generalizable beyond the sample joint ventures themselves. Next, the perspectives of the participating managers and ourselves regarding important aspects of the partner selection process are considered. The discussion also examines the characteristics of the selection criteria and their valences, both individually and vis-a-vis the other criteria categories. Conclusions are presented regarding the apparent relationships between selection criteria valences and the other research variables examined in the study.

PURPOSE OF THE STUDY

The purpose of this study was to examine one type of collaborative business activity: joint ventures. The focus was on the criteria, and their valences, which were employed by organizations when selecting partners for bilateral joint ventures. The focus was limited to those ventures in which the principal target market included one or more developed country and the joint venture partner selection process was terminated or final agreement was reached between January 1, 1979, and March 1, 1985.

In the past, the issue of partner selection received scant attention in the joint venture literature, particularly for joint ventures in the developed countries. Yet, the selection decision may critically affect the performance of joint ventures, as well as the structure, conduct, and performance of the partner firms and other organizations in the same or related industries. Therefore, improved understanding of the most salient characteristics of the joint venture partner selection process was perceived as an important objective for the relevant stakeholder groups affected by the joint ventures. To further that objective, we examined which partner selection criteria were used by U.S.-based organizations and what, if any, relationship might be observed between these criteria and selected variables culled from the strategic management literature. The results were expected to assist stakeholding groups in a variety of ways, including the following:

1. Assist managers considering entry or expansion of their market presence through use of joint ventures by highlighting others' joint venture experiences
2. Assist governmental or quasi-governmental entities in anticipating the probable influence of alternative policy options available to them for influencing the joint venture formation process
3. Assist firms in positioning themselves for selection as joint venture partners, or for greater success when approaching another firm for a prospective joint venture
4. Assist firms in establishing negotiating strategies for joint ventures, vis-a-vis the anticipated objectives of their prospective partners
5. Assist firms in determining what "types" of partners a competitor is likely to seek if it were to attempt to establish a joint venture

Review of the literature suggested that specific criteria did seem to be employed when selecting prospective joint venture partners and that, if an appropriate data collection methodology were utilized, these criteria could be obtained in an *ex post* manner from the key individuals involved in the partner selection process. Therefore, we utilized both questionnaires and semistructured interviews to collect data from 101 executives, principally from senior levels of their corporate hierarchies, who were intimately involved in selecting partners for 90 randomly selected joint ventures. The resulting quantitative and qualitative data were analyzed using a range of univariate and multivariate techniques, and the results and their implications were examined.

CHARACTERISTICS OF THE RESEARCH SAMPLE

Examination of the characteristics of the research sample is important for evaluating representativeness of the sample vis-a-vis the universe of prospective joint ventures and, thus, the prospects for generalizing results to nonsampled joint ventures. Random selection of the sample and a high participation rate (82.6 percent of the qualifying joint ventures) supports generalizability of the results to the remaining firms in the sampling frame. However, applicability of the research findings for specific joint ventures may be influenced by unique traits of the overall sample. Therefore, this section summarizes the results relating to five dimensions of the sample: the joint ventures' expected target market, industry, and line functions; the perceived critical success factors; the number of prospective partners; the perceived task environment uncertainty; and the ownership and control of the joint ventures.

Expected Target Market, Industry, and Line Functions

Due to the limitations imposed on the research focus, the sample joint ventures had expected target markets that included one or more developed country. The sample therefore sharply contrasts with those of several earlier joint venture studies,[1] since participants almost never anticipated that less developed countries would constitute a significant component of the ventures' expected target markets. In addition, the sample joint ventures included a wide range of industries, although the industrial focus predominately involved manufacturing-related activities (SIC codes 20 to 39).

The range of line functions expected to be engaged in by the joint ventures ranged from one to six, with a mean of approximately three functions. Factor analysis of the diversity of line functions variable suggested that there were two principal underlying dimensions for this variable: marketing-related functions and production-related functions. The data indicated a greater prevalence for the marketing-related, rather than the production-related, functions. Mining/extraction and basic, nonapplied research activities were virtually nonexistent as expected joint venture functions.

Perceived Critical Success Factors

Technological capabilities were most frequently perceived as the most important critical success factor dimensions confronting a proposed joint venture. Sales to, and financing from, government sources generally were perceived to have relatively little importance as critical success factors. In addition, financing from nongovernmental sources tended to be viewed as much more critical to joint venture performance than financing or subsidies from governmental sources.

Number of Prospective Partners

In most cases, participants perceived that there were several prospective partner organizations at the time they were pursuing joint venture formation. Under these circumstances, selection criteria were able to assist not only in the decision of whether or not to pursue a joint venture, but also for discriminating the most suitable partner prospect.

Perceived Task Environment Uncertainty

Results for the perceived task environment uncertainty variable revealed that managers tended to perceive greater uncertainty vis-a-vis environmental and market-based dimensions of the joint venture's task environment than in the design and production-related areas. Although not statistically significant, these distinctions were supported by factor analysis results which identified two underlying dimensions of task environment uncertainty: uncertainty of the overall market environment and uncertainty of manufacturing operations.

Ownership and Control

There was a strong tendency for the sample joint ventures to share ownership equally between the partners. Of the 86 joint ventures for which ownership data were available, 60 ventures split equity holdings on a 50/50 basis. However, executives noted that control over specific activities of the joint venture often was not expected to be shared as equally as ownership. In particular, control over major capital investments, hiring of joint venture managers, and the establishment of prices and sales targets tended to be more equally shared than were control over product design, manufacturing setup and day-to-day management of the joint venture.

THE PROCESS OF PARTNER SELECTION

The process of selecting a joint venture partner was an important concern of virtually all of the participating managers. Very few of the contacted companies or individuals refused to participate in the study, and those who did decline participation reported other compelling reasons for not participating (e.g., pending lawsuits preventing discussion of the joint venture, or nonavailability due to travel commitments). Furthermore, those executives who did participate frequently commented that the topic of partner selection was important to them. A further indication of the topic's importance was senior managers' willingness to devote a significant amount of time to the interviews, which averaged approximately 50 percent more time than was initially requested.

Consistent with prior research, the selection of a partner generally constituted a distinct and separable decision in the joint venture formation process.[2] All participating executives reported that they had been intimately involved in the process of selecting joint venture partners, and generally this involvement began in the initial stages of the partner search and evaluation process (even if it only involved one prospective partner). This contrasts with several prior studies which examined partner selection where there was a strong likelihood that some or all of the respondents had not been intimately involved, or had been involved only for a relatively small portion of the process.[3] In addition, data were collected only for the joint ventures that were actively pursued, rather than for hypothetical joint ventures.[4]

Because our respondents were typically senior executives, the following discussion of the partner selection process may reflect hierarchial bias. In general, the participants suggested that, for employees at the lower levels of the management hierarchy, the process of partner selection primarily emphasized more technical, functional-area skills (e.g., more "number crunching" and screening based upon purely technical criteria). In contrast, the selection decision process at more senior levels generally incorporated not only technically based skills and criteria, but also more subjectively based skills and criteria, such as the evaluation of the compatibility of individuals, cultures, and corporate strategies and objectives. Given this caveat, several conclusions may be stated regarding the process of partner selection at the more senior levels of the management hierarchy. These conclusions concern the following: the joint venture's perceived uniqueness, the identification and screening of prospects, and the participation of top management.

A Joint Venture's Perceived Uniqueness

There was a strong tendency by respondents, particularly those without significant prior experience in joint venture formation, to view their individual ventures as unique. This often translated into a perception that others' prior joint venture experience would have only limited applicability to their own circumstances. However, comments by joint venture "veterans," or those who had been involved personally with anywhere from four or five to several dozen joint ventures, as well as analysis of our 90 sample joint ventures, suggested that adamant assertions of the "uniqueness" of a particular joint venture may often be dysfunctional. Although each situation will, by definition, evidence unique elements, there did seem to be common elements to all joint ventures. This raises the prospect for experience curve benefits in some, if not all, aspects of the joint venture formation process. For this reason, veteran joint venture participants almost universally recommended that novice joint venturers seek experienced advisors when considering entry into joint ventures. This was especially stressed with regard to the partner selection process.

Identification and Screening of Prospects

James W. C. Tomlinson reported that the process of selecting partners had not been thoroughly implemented in most of the joint ventures he had examined.[5] He found that little or no screening had been done to compare alternative partners nor any in-depth investigation of the motives or capabilities of the prospective partners.

Tomlinson's findings were only particularly supported by our results. There were a number of instances in which partner identification seemed to occur primarily through chance: an unexpected introduction at a convention or trade show, a comment noticed while randomly scanning a newspaper or magazine, and even a nearly proverbial meeting resulting from executives having adjoining seats on an airplane flight. However, executives reported that partner prospects were predominantly identified via a specific search effort undertaken by the organization, although the search effort may have itself been triggered by a chance encounter. While the intensity and duration of the process varied substantially between firms, the vast majority of respondents noted that they had employed explicit criteria in the identification and screening of prospects and that they generally had been able to identify several organizations or individuals which seemed to satisfy the minimum requirements that the organization had established.

The tendency to devote greater attention to the identification and screening of prospects by firms sampled in this study, versus the situation reported by Tomlinson, may be partially explained by several factors, including the accessibility of information, the extent of international experience, and the nature of the investment.

Accessibility of information. The focus on joint ventures involving developed countries rather than less developed countries may have enhanced the volume of information that was readily accessible to the firms. Comments by respondents suggested that they generally had a superior level of knowledge of the joint ventures' target markets and the principal "players" therein than seemed to be the case with Tomlinson.[6] Therefore, the search process entailed lower levels of uncertainty and reduced search costs, thus reducing the real and perceived barriers to more thorough identification and screening efforts.

International experience. Overall, there has been a quantum increase in the cumulative level of experience in international trade and investment, including joint venture activity, since Tomlinson conducted his interviews in 1966 and especially since his sample joint ventures were formed.[7] This may have influenced the willingness and ability of this study's sample firms to undertake more extensive partner search efforts.

Nature of investment. The nature of the investments to be undertaken by the proposed joint ventures may also have influenced the thoroughness of the partner identification and evaluation process. The ventures examined by previous studies were oriented primarily toward local markets in less developed countries.[8] In contrast, 24 of the 90 joint ventures in this study expected to serve a global target market, and most of the remaining ventures expected to serve target markets that exceeded the national boundaries of a single developed country. Because of the difference in size of the target markets, the anticipated extent of competition, and the expected level of financial investment to be made in the joint ventures, the partner selection decision appeared to have assumed greater importance and resulted in a more thorough identification and evaluation process.

Participation of Top Management

Especially for the larger joint ventures and those accorded greater strategic importance, the top management of the company (e.g., chairman, chief executive officer, chief operating officer, president), generally had some level of participation in the partner selection process. Often, the very senior level executives did not assume a role as one of the key individuals who championed the joint venture. Nevertheless, their participation was viewed as critical to the successful formation and functioning of the joint venture. Involvement of top management helped communicate interfirm commitment to prospective partners. By demonstrating the extent to which the organization was committed to the proposed joint venture, top management involvement often helped convince prospective partners to undertake initial feasibility studies or to begin informal or formal negotiations. In addition, top management involvement provided intrafirm visability and legitimacy for the proposed joint venture, thereby helping to develop and sustain the level of commitment necessary to implement the partner selection process efficiently and effectively. Top management involvement often was critical in preventing or overcoming deadlocks or other disagreements which might erupt between the partners' lower echelon personnel who were involved in the joint venture formation process. Furthermore, top management involvement often had an important ceremonial role in publicizing the joint venture activities to external stakeholder groups, other business units of the company, and the general public.

KEY INDIVIDUALS AND THEIR ROLE IN JOINT VENTURE FORMATION

Executives suggested that generally from one to three key individuals, or sponsors, were critical to the partner selection decision and to the efforts to implement a joint venture agreement. These individuals typically became involved very early in the process, and they served as "champions" for joint venture formation. They tended to occupy line, versus staff, positions in the upper middle to upper levels of the organization's managerial hierarchy. When a company had more than one of these key individuals, they usually made identical or very similar responses to interview questions. In addition, they tended to become intimately involved in the joint venture process, frequently to the point where their careers and reputations within the organization were strongly influenced by the outcome. Because of this, and because of the limited amount of time that had passed between joint venture formation and the time they were interviewed, these key executives almost universally reported that their memory of the details of the process was especially vivid.

Because these key individuals functioned as the driving force for the joint ventures' formation, their continued involvement in the partner selection and joint venture formation process was essential. For this reason, respondents noted that the existence of more than one key individual in each partner organization generally enhanced prospects for successful partner selection and joint venture formation. When only one key individual existed in either of the partner firms, the loss of that individual frequently terminated joint venture efforts either immediately or within a relatively short period of time. However, when more than one key individual existed within a firm, loss of one of them may have created certain problems, but the process of forming and operating the joint venture generally was still able to proceed.

COMPARISON OF PARTNER SELECTION CRITERIA RESULTS

In Chapter 2, earlier studies addressing the issue of joint venture partner selection were reviewed. It was asserted that the results of these previous studies may, for a number of reasons, have questionable validity for this study's research focus. Therefore, one of our principal objectives was to identify the criteria used to select partners for joint ventures in developed countries. This section briefly reviews the dimensions of the partner selection criteria that were examined in this study, and it compares and contrasts these results with those obtained in previous studies of the joint venture partner selection process.

The usefulness of the results from several of the previous research efforts examining joint venture partner selection were hindered due to the lack of conceptual and statistical distinctness between selection criteria categories. Similarly, this study collected data on 27 partner selection criteria categories, many of which seemed to overlap conceptually or empirically. Therefore, as discussed in Chapter 5, data for the partner selection criteria categories were factor analyzed in an effort to identify the underlying dimensions of the selection criteria. Factor analysis produced nine orthogonal dimensions that seemed to embody statistical reliability. These nine dimensions were interpreted as follows:

1. Knowledge of local market, not technology
2. Similar firm with local government influence
3. Compatible partner
4. Low-cost production
5. Shared development
6. Sales and service experience
7. Strategically critical manufacturing capabilities
8. Opportunistic neighbor
9. Similar respected firm controlling inputs

Although there were several similarities between these dimensions of selection criteria and those reported in previous studies, there were also a number of differences.

It is useful to compare and contrast the partner selection criteria valences and the factor analysis results obtained in this study with the selection criteria results reported in the principal previous studies that examined the joint venture partner selection process. Table 40 provides a visual comparison of the results of these studies. In constructing this table, we attempted to use the pioneering study by Tomlinson as the conceptual basis for ordering categories.[9] Using Tomlinson's six general categories of partner selection criteria as the base (see leftmost column of Table 40), we endeavored to list the other studies' criteria in a manner facilitating comparison between studies. For instance, categories which seemed to overlap Tomlinson's "facilities" category (e.g., Adler and Hlavacek's "established marketing and distribution system"[10]) were listed in a horizontal relationship to this category. The conceptual indistinctness of Tomlinson's categories hindered these efforts, however, especially for the factor results for this study. In addition, several of the criteria did not seem to fit into any of Tomlinson's categories, or else they seemed to qualify for several of them, so these criteria categories were listed separately at the bottom of the table.

In general, the selection criteria categories from prior studies evidenced substantial overlap, although the extent of overlap was constrained by the limited number or range of the categories mentioned in several of the studies. The overlap appeared greatest for Tomlinson's "facilities," "resources," and "status" categories, which supports the perceived importance of those categories as selection criteria. However, the range of different criteria overlapping these three categories emphasized the importance of developing categories with greater conceptual and empirical distinctness.

In addition to the similarities to the criteria reported by these previous studies, there were also several differences which might be noted. These

Table 40

Comparison of Partner Selection Criteria from Current and Previous Studies

	TOMLINSON (1970)	RENFORTH (1974)	TOMLINSON & THOMPSON (1977)		HLAVACEK & THOMPSON (1976) / ADLER & HLAVACEK (1976)	GERINGER (1988)
			SEEK IN MEXICAN PARTNER	MEXICAN TO SEEK IN FOREIGN PARTNER		
FACILITIES		BUSINESS COMPATIBILITY			ESTABLISHED MARKETING AND DISTRIBUTION SYSTEM	STRATEGICALLY CRITICAL MANUFACTURING CAPABILITIES OPPORTUNISTIC NEIGHBOR SHARED DEVELOPMENT LOW COST PRODUCTION
RESOURCES	OBTAIN BEST MANAGEMENT LOCAL MANAGEMENT TALENT LOCAL FINANCING REINVEST EQUITY TRANSFER	FINANCIAL STATUS	ABILITY TO COMMUNICATE WITH MEXICANS	TECHNOLOGY AND EXPERIENCE IN ITS APPLICATION MANAGEMENT DEPTH FINANCIAL RESOURCES	TECHNOLOGY TO IMPROVE ON OR COMPLEMENT ONE'S OWN CURRENT TECHNOLOGY BASE SALESFORCE OF SUITABLE SIZE & CALIBER CALLING ON SPECIFIC CUSTOMERS KIND OF PERSONNEL NEEDED GIVEN MINIMUM FINANCIAL RESOURCE	SALES AND SERVICE EXPERIENCE KNOWLEDGE OF LOCAL MARKET, NOT TECHNOLOGY SIMILAR RESPECTED FIRM CONTROLLING INPUTS
STATUS	ABILITY TO NEGOTIATE WITH GOVERNMENT	FAVORABLE IMAGE CLOSE RELATIONS WITH GOVERNMENT INTERNATIONAL QUALITY STANDARDS		INTERNATIONAL VISIBILITY AND REPUTATION INTERNATIONAL EXPERIENCE		SIMILAR FIRM WITH LOCAL GOVERNMENT EXPERIENCE
IDENTITY						
PAST						
FORCED						
(ADDITIONAL CRITERIA)	SECRECY DIVERSIFIED PRODUCT MIX NON-PATERNALISTIC	COMMON GOALS COMPATIBLE ETHICS		COMMITMENT TO JOINT VENTURE	RELATIVE COMPANY SIZE	COMPATIBLE PARTNER

discrepancies primarily concerned the results of our study versus those reported by Tomlinson.[11] For instance, favorable prior association with the prospective partner (PSCPRIOR), which Tomlinson found to be the most important selection criterion for his sample, tended to be accorded a relatively low level of importance by our respondents. It evidenced a statistical mean of 1.49 for the unrecoded data, which ranked 18th out of the 27 categories examined. Although PSCPRIOR evidenced significant (> 0.30) loadings on three of the nine rotated selection criteria factors, none of these loadings had a value exceeding 0.44. These results suggest that favorable prior association was perceived by our respondents to be of secondary importance as a selection criterion, rather than of the highest importance as determined in Tomlinson's study.

Although the partner-related criterion of favorable prior association, or PSCPRIOR, did not seem to be as important in this study as in Tomlinson's, two other categories that were also defined as partner-related selection criteria did tend to be accorded a very high level of importance. The PSCCOMIT (strength of partner commitment to the joint venture) and PSCFREND (compatibility of partners' top management teams) categories evidenced higher average values than any of the other selection criteria categories. Furthermore, these two categories both had very high loadings (> 0.80) on selection criteria Factor 3. These results, and the manner in which Tomlinson defined his "past" category, suggest that the discrepancy in results between the two studies may partly be due to different means of defining variables and their scope.

Our results also differed from Tomlinson's regarding the relative importance of the local identity of the partner. Tomlinson reported that a partner's local identity was perceived to be the least important of the selection criteria categories. However, our results suggested that local identity (PSCLOCAL) tended to be accorded somewhat greater importance as a selection criterion. This category ranked 12th out of 27 categories for the unrecoded data, with a statistical mean of 2.08. In addition, it evidenced significant (> 0.30) loadings on two of the nine rotated selection criteria factors, including a relatively high 0.72 loading on Factor 1. Therefore, executives perceived that selection of a partner which might enhance the local or national identity of the joint venture was generally of greater importance in this study than it had been in Tomlinson's.

The relative importance of a third selection criteria category mentioned by Tomlinson, forced choice, was more difficult to ascertain from the results in the current study. The PSCREGUL (partner's ability to enhance compliance with government requirements or pressure) and, to a lesser extent, the PSCPATNT (partner's possession of needed licenses, patents, and know-how) categories seemed to overlap Tomlinson's "forced" category. The PSCPATNT category received higher average values from respondents than did PSCREGUL, but it also tended to have less overlap with the "forced" category, as defined by Tomlinson. Nevertheless, comments by participants and the relatively low values attributed to the PSCREGUL category suggested that a selection criterion of forced choice tended to be accorded substantially lower importance in this study than in Tomlinson's sample joint ventures. In large part, this result may reflect this study's emphasis on developed country markets, which were frequently perceived to embody a lower level of government mandates than was the case for less developed country markets.

There also tended to be a substantial difference conceptually, if not also empirically, between the criteria used by Renforth and those reported in this study.[12] Pretest interviews suggested that several of Renforth's criteria (e.g., "non-paternalistic," "equity transfer," "reinvest profits") were not directly applicable to most of the joint ventures in this study. Our results also suggested that Renforth's range of criteria was somewhat abbreviated, since it did not seem to include any significant references to what Tomlinson defined as "facilities." However, these discrepancies might merely reflect differences between the two studies in terms of the nature of the joint ventures and their target markets.

General Conclusions Regarding Comparison of Results with Prior Studies

The limited data provided by prior studies examining partner selection criteria hindered attempts to compare their results extensively to those obtained in this study. However, there seemed to be substantial overlap between the results for this study and those reported by Tomlinson; Renforth; Adler and Hlavacek; and Tomlinson and Thompson.[13] The overlap was greatest on the categories that Tomlinson termed "facilities," "resources," and "status." Although several differences were noted between the results of this study and previous ones, these differences could be explained by variations in sample composition due to sampling methods, the extent of industrialization of the target markets, and the industrial classifications of the sample joint ventures. The differences may also be partly explained by differences in variable definition, the qualifications of the individuals sampled, and differences caused by the passage of time. These and other factors may account for some or all of the discrepancies in the results, although the relative extent of their influence cannot be assessed accurately.

However, the results of this study highlight some of the conceptual and empirical limitations of the categories used in previous studies and the greater insights into the partner selection process that might be obtained through the development of more specific and distinct selection criteria categories.

Complementarity and Partner Selection

Several previous studies have stated or implied that complementarity is the basis of the partner selection decision.[14] These studies have typically claimed that firms seek partners with complementary skills, resources, or other traits. However, these authors have tended to be rather vague in regard to what constitutes complementarity. They have generally defined complementarity via reference to specific case examples, rather than providing an underlying conceptual model which could specify traits that would be "complementary" for a particular firm or joint venture. They provide little guidance as to whether complementarity entails similarity or dissimilarity between organizations on one or more dimensions.

In contrast, our results support the notion that complementarity is a useful concept in understanding joint venture partner selection. These data also suggest several insights into what constitutes complementarity and how firms might identify complementary partners.

Our data provide support for distinguishing between task-related and partner-related selection criteria. This distinction has usefulness in enhancing the understanding of the notion of complementarity. In general, firms seemed to have utilized, either implicitly or explicitly, a two-tiered screening process. First, they evaluated prospective partners for complementarity on task-related dimensions. Generally, if a prospective partner did not satisfy these task-related criteria, then either the prospect was eliminated from candidacy or the qualifying standards were modified. The latter was typically resorted to only if no satisfactory prospective partners emerged from the initial screening, or if a prospect with otherwise extraordinary capabilities or resources on one or more task-related dimensions was eliminated owing to some perceived deficiency.

If one or more prospects satisfied the screening requirements for complementarity on task-related dimensions, they generally were also screened for their ability to satisfy partner-related dimensions. This screening may have been undertaken simultaneously with screening for task-related dimensions, particularly for joint ventures where the organization had an extensive understanding of the industry and where the list of relevant candidates was relatively short. However, there typically was a lag effect between initiation of task-related screening and the initiation of partner-related screening efforts. Comments by executives suggested that this was largely a result of delegation of tasks within the organization and hierarchical traits of the decision process. As mentioned above, evaluation of prospective partners on task-related dimensions was typically undertaken by individuals within functional areas who were at lower echelons of the corporate hierarchy. Prospects that survived this initial appraisal of more technical, task-related dimensions then progressed to the more senior management levels, where the emphasis became oriented toward the partner-related dimensions of selection criteria.

It should be noted that these two types of screening were seldom approached in a strictly sequential manner, since the key individuals generally maintained involvement in both the task-related and partner-related screening processes. However, comments by participants typically suggested that satisfying the dictates of the task-related dimensions was a necessary, though not necessarily sufficient, prerequisite to the selection of an organization as a joint venture partner. On the other hand, while the ability to satisfy the dictates of partner-related dimensions was often the critical determinant for selection of a particular partner, there were numerous instances where firms stated that they compromised to some extent on partner-related dimensions in order to obtain partners able to satisfy the task-related requirements.

How was complementarity on task-related dimensions determined? At least in part, this evaluation seemed to have been made via the employment of the three task-related variables examined in this study: critical success factors, competitive position, and difficulty of internal development. As hypothesized in Chapter 3, and tested and discussed in Chapters 6 through 8, the valence attributed to a particular task-related section criteria dimension seems to be largely explained by management perceptions of the extent to which that dimension is critical to the venture's performance, the competitive position of the firm vis-a-vis that dimension, and the level of difficulty to be encountered in achieving or maintaining a viable competitive position on that dimension via internal efforts.

The determination of complementarity on partner-related dimensions appears to be a more complex endeavor than seemed to be the case for task-related dimensions. Partner-related partner selection criteria seem to have a much greater subjective component to them, which can increase variability in results and therefore frustrate efforts to test the hypotheses empirically. In addition, partner-related selection criteria tended to assume a subordinate position to the task-related selection criteria, thus further hindering hypothesis testing efforts. Nevertheless, our results permit several assertions regarding complementarity and partner-related dimensions of selection criteria.

Development of partner-related selection criteria tends to incorporate a greater level of subjectivity than is the case with task-related criteria, since less objective standards are generally available for comparison and evaluation. The greater reliance on more purely perceptual components can make this variable appear to be more prone to fluctuations and, therefore, more difficult to measure accurately. Nevertheless, complementarity on partner-related dimensions generally implied similarity between firms on a particular dimension, such as similar size or organizational culture. Although dissimilarity on a particular partner-related dimension may occasionally be perceived as a desirable characteristic in a partner, this very much seemed to be the exception rather than the rule, at least for the partner-related dimensions studied herein. However, it is interesting to note that firms frequently seemed willing, however begrudgingly, to accept a partner that was quite dissimilar on one or several partner-related dimensions. In part, this was due to their ability to complement a firm on other task-related or partner-related dimensions which were accorded greater strategic importance. Therefore, it appears that the difficulties associated with partner-related selection criteria entail not only evaluation of the absolute degree of complementarity of a particular dimension, but also the relative importance of that dimension vis-a-vis other partner-related as well as task-related dimensions.

Participants were asked what they might have done differently in selecting a partner, given the benefit of hindsight. In response, many executives remarked on the tendency, especially for those with limited prior joint venture experience, to have de-emphasized partner-related criteria relative to task-related criteria in the partner selection decision. However, the ongoing nature of negotiations within a joint venture and the continuing need to interact with a partner often resulted in a short honeymoon period followed by a rapid onset of interorganizational conflict, sometimes so severe that the joint venture was ultimately terminated despite a good "fit" in terms of task-related dimensions. An example of this tendency might be the observed correlation between the difficulty of development factor involving financial capability and the selection criteria factor involving compatibility of partners. This correlation was negative, suggesting that firms having difficulty accessing financial resources tended to de-emphasize selection of a compatible partner. While this may prove beneficial in the short term, one executive commented that "you can't buy happiness." Instead, he and other respondents cautioned against shortsighted efforts to de-emphasize the partner-related dimensions of selection criteria.

CONCLUSIONS REGARDING TASK-RELATED SELECTION CRITERIA

In addition to the above discussion, several additional conclusions may be stated regarding task-related selection criteria in particular. As noted, the data seemed to provide strong support for at least two of the three hypotheses involving task-related selection criteria categories. As hypothesized, the critical success factor and the difficulty of internal development variables generally evidenced a positive relationship with task-related selection criteria valences. On the other hand, although the competitive position variable tended to have a negative correlation with valences of task-related criteria, the data from this variable appeared to have been subject to confounding, particularly from the effects of the difficulty of internal development variable. Therefore, support for Hypothesis 2 may be questionable.

Overall, government influence via regulations or pressure, financing or other subsidies, and government purchases tended to be perceived as having relatively low levels of importance for the sample joint ventures' performance. Although this seemed to contrast with findings of prior studies, the discrepancy may be explained by the increased emphasis by sample joint ventures on developed versus less developed countries as target markets.

Market access, including capabilities in marketing, distribution, and post-sales service, tended to be viewed as important critical success factors, particularly within the context of a local or regional target market. However, it was frequently suggested that firms sought partners embodying not only marketing-related capabilities, but also a given minimum level of technology-related capability. In large part, this was probably due to the advanced technological features (relative to existing competition within the target market) expected to be incorporated in many of the joint ventures' products, which necessitated a certain amount of technological fluency in order to market and service the products effectively.

Despite much recent press regarding the erosion of U.S. technological leadership,[15] there was an overwhelming tendency for the U.S.-based firms to perceive themselves as the principal suppliers of technology to the joint ventures, with their partners typically being expected to provide the marketing-based know-how. The role of U.S.-based firms as suppliers of technology might help to explain the relatively low perceived importance of government-related influence, since possession of superior technology often enhanced an organization's leverage vis-a-vis the government. This conclusion, though tentative, seems to receive some support from the negative correlation observed between the critical success factor variable's factor of "experienced technical personnel" and the emphasis on government influence as a partner selection criterion.

Several interesting conclusions may be drawn regarding the relationship between access to financial resources and task-related selection criteria valences. First, the higher valences attributed to PSC$ vis-a-vis PSCGOVT$ suggests that firms tended to report substantially higher preferences for partners with access to nongovernmental sources of financing. In addition, and consistent with the findings of Adler and Hlavacek,[16] a number of respondents remarked that partners needed to have access to a given minimum level of financial resources. This minimum amount varied dramatically between joint ventures, but respondents frequently noted their avoidance of partners that were perceived to be unable or unwilling to generate a sufficient level of funding. The rationale for this bias is the desire to avoid partners that threaten to be "anchors," slowing venture growth and development due to an inability to provide their share of the joint venture's funding.

CONCLUSIONS REGARDING PARTNER-RELATED SELECTION CRITERIA

The results and discussion presented in this chapter, as well as the comments from the study's participants, suggest several additional conclusions regarding partner-related selection criteria. Partner-related criteria *do* appear to be an important element of most selection decisions, and they are typically the deciding factor in choosing among the partner prospects that passed the task-related criteria screening process. Two of the partner-related criteria categories, PSCCOMIT and PSCFREND, evidenced higher average values than any other task-related or partner-related criteria categories. In addition, partner selection criteria Factor 3 evidenced high loadings (> 0.30) only on partner-related selection criteria categories, and the highest loading category for partner selection criteria Factor 8 was another partner-related selection criteria category, PSCNEARU.

Although results suggested that partner-related criteria were important in the partner selection decision, responses also suggested that partner-related criteria tended to be viewed as secondary in importance to task-related criteria. In other words, executives' responses suggested that the primary consideration is to select a partner with task-related skills and resources but one that can enable the joint venture to be economically viable.

Data analysis and comments by participants suggest the need for further refinement of the partner-related criteria concept. As operationalized, the dimensions examined in this study did not seem to capture adequately the full scope of the partner-related dimensions. Further efforts seem to be necessary to determine what dimensions to measure and how to attempt their measurement adequately. However, despite the limitations of the categories used, several conclusions can be drawn regarding these and other dimensions of partner-related criteria. Some of these conclusions are addressed in Chapter 13; however, the following discussion addresses two of these topics: perceived task environment uncertainty and diversity of line functions.

Perceived Task Environment Uncertainty

Comparison of the data on perceived task environment uncertainty and partner-related selection criteria valences suggests that firms tend to place greater emphasis on selecting firms that are compatible on partner-related dimensions when the task environment uncertainty is perceived to emanate from overall environmental or market-related sources than when it is associated with manufacturing operations. It also appeared that firms perceiving higher levels of uncertainty on product design tended to seek similarly sized organizations as partners. Except for uncertainty emanating from governmental policies and procedures, firms tended to place greater emphasis on partner-related selection criteria when there was an increased level of perceived task environment uncertainty.

Diversity of Line Functions

Results suggest that as the joint ventures' expected number of line functions increased, firms tended to place greater emphasis on selecting partners that were in close geographical proximity to themselves, were similar in national or corporate culture, and had a compatible top management team. These results seem to be consistent with the previous discussions of partner-related selection criteria.

NOTES

1. James W. C. Tomlinson, *The Joint Venture Process in International Business: India and Pakistan* (Cambridge, Mass.: MIT Press, 1970); William E. Renforth, "A Comparative Study of Joint International Business Ventures with Family Firm or Non-Family Firm Partners: The Caribbean Community Experience," Ph.D. diss. Graduate School of Business, Indiana University, 1974; James W. C. Tomlinson and M. Thompson, "A Study of Canadian Joint Ventures in Mexico," working paper, College of Commerce and Business Administration, University of British Columbia, 1977; William E. Renforth and Sion Raveed, *A Comparative Study of Multinational Corporation Joint International Business Ventures with Family Firm or Non-Family Firm Partners* (New York: Arno Press, 1980); Jean-Louis Schaan, "Parent Control and Joint Venture Success: The Case of Mexico," Ph.D. diss. University of Western Ontario, 1983; Paul W. Beamish, "Joint Venture Performance in Developing Countries," Ph.D. diss., University of Western Ontario, 1984.

2. Tomlinson, *The Joint Venture Process*.

3. Tomlinson, *The Joint Venture Process*; Renforth, "A Comparative Study;" Lee Adler and James D. Hlavacek, *Joint Ventures for Product Innovation* (New York: American Management Association, 1976); James D. Hlavacek and Victor A. Thompson, "The Joint-Venture Approach to Technology Utilization," *IEEE Transactions on Engineering Management* (1976), pp. 35–41.

4. Renforth, "A Comparative Study."

5. Tomlinson, *The Joint Venture Process*.

6. Ibid.

7. Ibid. Some of Tomlinson's sample joint ventures were established before 1947, more than twenty years before his interviews.

8. Ibid.

9. Ibid.

10. Adler and Hlavacek, *Joint Ventures for Product Innovation*.

11. Tomlinson, *The Joint Venture Process*.

12. Renforth, "A Comparative Study."

13. Tomlinson, *The Joint Venture Process*; Renforth, "A Comparative Study"; Adler and Hlavacek, *Joint Ventures for Product Innovation*; and Tomlinson and Thompson, "A Study of Canadian Joint Ventures in Mexico."

14. Business International, *Pros and Cons of Joint Ventures Abroad* (New York:

Business International, 1964); Steffan Gullander, "Joint Ventures and Corporate Strategy," *Columbia Journal of World Business* (Spring 1976), pp. 104–14; Adler and Hlavacek, *Joint Ventures for Product Innovation*; James D. Hlavacek, Brian Dovey, and John Biondo, "Tie Small Business Technology to Marketing Power," *Harvard Business Review* (January-February, 1977), pp. 106–16; Edward B. Roberts, "New Ventures for Corporate Growth," *Harvard Business Review* (July-August, 1980), pp. 134–42.; Sanford V. Berg, Jerome Duncan, and Philip Friedman, *Joint Venture Strategies and Corporate Innovation* (Cambridge, Mass.: Oelgeschlager, Gunn & Hain, 1982); J. Peter Killing, "How to Make a Global Joint Venture Work," *Harvard Business Review* (May-June, 1982), pp. 120–27; Stefan H. Robock and Kenneth Simmonds, *International Business and Multinational Enterprises*, 3d ed. (Homewood, Ill.: Irwin, 1983); John D. Daniels, Earnest W. Ogram, Jr., and Lee H. Radebaugh, *International Business: Environments and Operations*, 3d ed. (Reading, Mass.: Addison-Wesley, 1983); Kathryn Rudie Harrigan, "Coalition Strategies: A Framework for Joint Ventures," working paper, Columbia University, 1984; Kathryn Rudie Harrigan, "Joint Ventures and Global Strategies," *Columbia Journal of World Business* 19, no. 2 (Summer, 1984), pp. 7–16; Seamus G. Connolly, "Joint Ventures with Third World Multinationals: A New Form of Entry into International Markets," *Columbia Journal of World Business* (Summer, 1984), pp. 18–22.

15. For example, see Jerome E. Schnee, "International Shifts in Innovative Activity: The Case of Pharmaceuticals," *Columbia Journal of World Business* (Spring, 1978), pp. 112–22.

16. Adler and Hlavacek, *Joint Ventures for Product Innovation*.

13

Implications

This chapter discusses the principal implications of our results and conclusions. These comments, many of a prescriptive nature, are primarily oriented toward managers, although public policy makers and academics may find the discussion to be interesting and useful.

This study involved the collection of data from over 100 executives who had been intimately involved in the formation and operation of at least one joint venture. Taken as a whole, the cumulative experience of these executives included involvement in more than 300 joint ventures over the past 40 years. Their generous contribution of time in discussing this wealth of experience provided an extensive overview of the joint venture partner selection process. However, the enormous volume of data makes it infeasible to relate all of the possible managerial implications resulting directly or indirectly from their comments. Instead, we will relate what seemed to be the most important prescriptions or considerations relevant to managers involved in, or contemplating, the formation of a joint venture. Although the focus was on two-party joint ventures in developed countries, comments from executives suggest much of our discussion may also apply to joint ventures with more than two partners, as well as to many joint ventures in less developed countries.

THE PROCESS OF SELECTING JOINT VENTURE PARTNERS

It was evident from responses of the participating executives that the specific partner selected for a joint venture is an important variable affecting the venture's operations. The specific partner chosen can influence the overall mix of available skills and resources, the operating policies and procedures, and the short- and long-term viability of the joint venture. Therefore, it is critical for prospective joint venturers to understand the process of partner selection and the means of influencing that process.

Identification and Screening of Partners

Finding and courting a partner for a joint venture can be an expensive process. Costs are not limited to negotiating and writing the legal and operating agreements. Substantial amounts of time and other resources frequently must be expended in identifying and screening prospective partners prior to formal negotiations. This is particularly imperative when a company's management has limited experience with the proposed venture's products or markets, although costs can be substantial even if managers already have a thorough knowledge of the venture's industry.

Despite its importance, managers may hesitate to devote a significant amount of corporate resources to the process of identifying and evaluating an extensive list of viable partner prospects. This is particularly true when a partner with the minimum technical requirements appears to have been found—through an introduction at a convention or trade show, a comment from a business associate or government official, or some other means. Often, partners appear to have been chosen for reasons not fully relevant to the organization's objectives and without a stringent comparison of alternatives. Many joint venture partners seem to have been selected almost by accident, or at least without full consideration of how they might influence the joint venture's operations. This may help account for the widespread perception that joint ventures tend to be fraught with problems and that they commonly fail within a relatively short period of time.

Research Aspects of Partner Identification

As with many other aspects of joint venture formation, identification of viable partner prospects is a research task. This is particularly true if the venture is to include local partners from an unfamiliar region. At a minimum, partners should be able to provide the additional capabilities that, in both the short and the longer term, are necessary to enable the venture to be competitive. This means a manager must analyze the venture's anticipated target market, as well as the businesses that prospective partners are currently in or likely to enter in the relatively near future, in order to identify possible synergies. However, unless a manager has a thorough knowledge of the venture's industry and the potential players, reliance on superficial scanning efforts is unlikely to result in an optimal partner selection decision. Particularly for fast-moving technologies, such as telecommunications, biotechnology, or robotics, managers should be cautious about making assumptions regarding other firms' capabilities. Reputations may be misleading, and many an executive has felt blindsided when he belatedly discovered that a partner did not have the skills necessary for the joint venture's success.

When identifying partners, there is no single approach that will be preferable in all situations. The evaluation must consider such factors as the peculiar characteristics of the industry, the firm's competitive position, and the venture's anticipated requirements for capital and other resources. Typically, among the first potential partners to be considered are the distributors, suppliers, and customers for the industry of the proposed venture. Yet, even these companies must be examined to see which ones are available for venturing and which might be preempted from participation due to prior agreements with competitors, sociopolitical biases, or other reasons.

Of course, extensive search and screening efforts are not always feasible. Sometimes, the nature of the proposed investment dictates a limited range of prospective partners. For instance, there may be only one firm with access to the technology or raw materials needed by the joint venture. In other cases, government fiat or regulations regarding foreign ownership may sharply limit the number of available partner prospects. However, even if one or a few viable partner prospects exist, screening these companies for suitability as joint venture colleagues is still a critical task. Unless a partner is perceived to be compatible over the long term, it may be desirable to pursue other non-joint venture alternatives, such as licensing, contractual relationships (e.g., supply contracts), or even full equity ownership. Conflicts between partners are best avoided if they are anticipated before the venture is established, so extreme care should be taken in selecting the other party, or parties. Prospects must be evaluated not only on the basis of complementarity of task-related capabilities, but also on organizational compatibility. The additional effort expended up front in selecting the "right" partner may repay itself many times over in avoided costs of misunderstandings, delays, and divorce.

If more than one firm seems to qualify as a viable partner prospect for a particular joint venture, then the firm must decide on an appropriate strategy for selecting which firm(s) to negotiate with. As discussed below, mutual trust and commitment between partners is essential to the formation of a viable joint venture. However, it is difficult to negotiate with more than one firm at a time and still foster the necessary trust and commitment. Therefore, management must decide whether they will try to screen and rank prospects and then contact them sequentially, or else to put out "feelers" to several or all of them. In the latter case, if more than one firm responds to the feelers, or if a preferred prospect fails to respond initially, the firm again must decide whether, and for how long, to pursue simultaneous negotiations with two or more prospects. These decisions should not be viewed lightly, since the effect on partner relations can be profound.

If a firm decides to negotiate with only one of the qualifying prospects, and if the prospects are viewed as nonhomogeneous in terms of the capabilities or resources they have to offer, then it may be necessary to conduct some form of matrix analysis of the prospects. The decision that was encountered by firms in such a situation can be envisioned via an X-by-Y type of matrix. One axis of this matrix lists the prospective partners and the other axis consists of the dimensions of selection criteria being employed. For such a mental matrix approach to work effectively, however, managers need to have a clear idea of the relative importance of alternative criteria, the trade-offs they are able and willing to make among these dimensions, and the likely impact of these trade-offs on subsequent joint venture performance.

The Role of Joint Venture Sponsors

In evaluating and selecting joint venture partners, there are people from each company who play a particularly critical role in the process. Examination of prior ventures reveals that there are usually from one to three key individuals, or sponsors, who are critical to the partner selection decision and to the efforts to implement a joint venture agreement successfully. Typically, these individuals become involved very early in the selection process and occupy line, rather than staff, positions in the upper middle to upper levels of the management hierarchy.

The joint venture sponsors serve as catalysts for the process of identifying, evaluating, and negotiating with prospective partners. Because they function as the driving force for the joint venture's formation, their continued involvement in the process is essential. For this reason, the existence of more than one sponsor in each partner company typically enhances the prospects for successful joint venture formation. When a company has only one primary sponsor, loss of that individual—due to transfer, turnover, or any other cause—frequently results either in termination of formation efforts or significant delays in the negotiation process while relationships are established with a new sponsor. However, when more than one sponsor exists, loss of one of them may create problems, but the process of forming and operating the joint venture is generally able to proceed with only minor delays.

Because of their central role in the formation process and the breadth of activities that must be addressed, certain types of managers seem to have been more effective as joint venture sponsors. In general, successful sponsors are characterized by broader, more generalized managerial training rather than by the more narrow technical specialties such as law, accounting, or other support activities. The preference for sponsors to evidence more generalized training emanates from the requirement for the sponsor to oversee and integrate a broad range of activities of the proposed joint venture, and to ensure that the proposed venture is likely to be economically viable. In addition to their general management orientation, at least one sponsor from each partner company should be fluent with the principal function(s) that the joint venture is expected to engage in, such as R&D, manufacturing, or marketing. Furthermore, to enhance decision making efforts and to communicate organizational commitment to partner prospects adequately, it is critical that sponsors evidence a level of hierarchial responsibility commensurate with the purported strategic importance of the venture. Without such hierarchical power, the organization seems to send a strong message to personnel that the venture lacks top management support, virtually ensuring that individuals will not commit themselves to it and thus harming prospects for successful performance.

When sponsors embody the above traits, their ability to evaluate and negotiate with prospective partners is significantly enhanced. Yet, despite this caveat, a surprising number of firms delegate responsibility for partner selection and negotiation to lower level line managers or to staff members, especially lawyers, who may be ill-equipped to function as full-fledged sponsors. As a result, the chosen employees are often unable to champion the venture effectively, further hindering formation efforts and prospects for successful long-term performance.

Involvement of Top Management Crucial

Especially for larger joint ventures and those accorded high strategic importance, top management of the company generally has some degree of direct participation in the partner selection process. These very senior level executives generally do not assume an active role as sponsors championing the venture. Nevertheless, their participation is often pivotal in successful joint venture formation and operation, due to their ability to communicate the extent of a company's commitment to prospective partners and to employees within their own firm. Top management involvement can help prevent or overcome deadlocks between the partners' operating-level personnel. Their participation also confers legitimacy to the proposed joint venture, helping develop and sustain the critical level of commitment necessary to complete partner selection and joint venture formation successfully, and to enhance the likelihood of satisfactory performance.

Location of the Partner Selection Decision

The final decision regarding partner selection is almost always made at the corporate headquarters level, and it usually involves a vote of the board of directors. However, except for very large joint ventures and those that are intimately linked with a company's core business activities, the *de facto* decisions regarding partner selection and venture formation are typically made by subsidiary or division level rather than corporate level management. Although the financial and market projections, and the overall strategic plans of the venture, may be reviewed at corporate headquarters, such review typically is of a summary nature. Instead, joint venture formation decisions are typically considered to be operating level and are thus delegated to the level of the hierarchy where responsibility rests for its operation. This fact further reinforces the importance of assigning extremely competent individuals to the joint venture task force, especially when those individuals are expected to function as the joint venture's sponsors.

CRITERIA FOR SELECTING PARTNERS

Defining a set of criteria for selecting the right partner would be roughly analogous to telling a person how to pick the right spouse—certainly a difficult, if not an impossible, proposition. Selection of a partner who will be compatible in the long term is a complex and individualistic endeavor. Each joint venture is unique in its own way, and each must be approached accordingly. Yet, there do seem to be common elements to many joint ventures. As a result, the experience of other managers may provide useful guidelines for selecting a joint venture partner. Nine considerations regarding the selection criteria to employ are discussed in the following paragraphs.

Complementary Technical Skills and Resources

The primary selection criterion is generally a partner's ability to provide the technical skills and resources that complement those of your company. If prospective partners cannot satisfy this criterion, formation of a joint venture should be a questionable proposition, at best. Therefore, technical complementarity should be viewed as a minimum qualification for selection of a partner.

Technical complementarity is determined by analyzing the key success factors—those few areas that strongly influence competitive position and performance—confronting the proposed venture. Once this has been done, managers should evaluate their company's current and anticipated future competitive position relative to these factors. Those areas in which deficiencies do exist can serve as the basis for assessing the technical complementarity of a partner. However, the analysis should identify more than just a financial deficiency—such resources may often be accessed via other options which will not entail the extensive managerial involvement of a partner. Although it may be initially appealing, a joint venture based solely on a partner's financial contributions is unlikely to foster long-term compatibility.

Technical complementarity can assume many forms. A common alliance consists of one parent supplying technology and the other furnishing marketing and financial capabilities. For example, an American medical equipment company wanted to expand sales of its product line in Europe. However, because of its small size and limited name recognition, the company was hesitant about increasing penetration of the European market on its own. Instead, it sought assistance from a joint venture partner. Strategic analysis of the proposed investment suggested that the partner must be a recognized player in the medical supplies industry and must have sufficient financial and marketing resources. The partner would also need to evidence the technological sophistication necessary to demonstrate the technical advantages of the U.S. firm's products to customers in Europe. Companies not satisfying this set of criteria were rejected as possible co-venturers.

Seeking a partner with complementary technical skills and resources can permit each partner to concentrate resources in those areas in which it possesses the greatest relative competence, while diversifying into attractive but unfamiliar business arenas. Rather than intensifying weaknesses, joint ventures can thus be a means of creating strengths.

Mutual Dependency: A Necessary Evil

Many managers have viewed dependency upon other organizations as undesirable and have avoided such situations whenever possible. However, in identifying suitable joint venture partner prospects, there should be some identifiable mutual need, with each partner supplying unique capabilities or resources critical to the venture's success. Proper matching should result in both partners perceiving that they have a vested interest in keeping the venture working, rather than resorting to some non-joint venture form of investment. By having one partner strong where the other is weak, and vice versa, mutual respect will be fostered and second-guessing and conflict can be mitigated.

Prior experience suggests that there should be a "middle level" of dependency between partners. If the level of dependency is too small, the joint venture is unlikely to survive difficult times. On the other hand, too much dependency may prove unstable because of fears of the consequences of loss of a partner. The latter case commonly occurs when small firms form joint ventures with much larger partners. A small firm may feel insecure, since it would not be able to exploit a market opportunity fully by itself, or only at a much slower rate and at a greater risk than in a shared endeavor. The smaller firm tends to be hungrier, and it may need revenues from the joint venture more than a larger partner. In addition, association with a prominent partner may influence the smaller concern's stock price. This is particularly worrisome if later termination of the venture is attributed to unsuccessful commercialization of the smaller firm's technology. While the larger firm may emerge relatively unscathed, joint venture termination may severely disable the small firm by causing customers, employees, and the financial and stock markets to question the firm's viability. The resulting damage to its reputation may cause a precipitous decline in its stock value, harm morale, and limit available strategic options.

Painful lessons regarding dependency between partners were experienced by many of the companies which, in the late 1970s and early 1980s, formed ventures with Asian firms as a means of rapidly accessing cheap labor or new markets. Frequently, American corporations contributed the initial technology and some of the financing, and they trained their partners in the intricacies of running the business. Once this had been accomplished, however, several of the ventures were dissolved and the partners later used technology obtained from the joint venture as a weapon against their former U.S. allies.

Several options are available to help ensure that joint venture partners will continue to perceive themselves as mutually dependent. One method of reinforcing mutual dependence is to establish some means of "exchanging hostages." For instance, it is often possible to insert conditions into a joint venture agreement whereby a unilateral decision to break up the corporate marriage prematurely will result in a substantial charge of some sort, "alimony" payments if you will, as well as covenants against engaging in competing activities within a specified time period. It may also be possible to guarantee cross purchases of specified volumes of products or services by the partners. This option can help reduce the potentially devastating impact of a breakup upon a more dependent firm by a guaranteeing access to critical raw materials or sales revenues during the painful readjustment period. By employing techniques such as these, the threat posed by dependency on a partner can be reduced substantially.

Avoiding "Anchors"

When contemplating a joint venture, it is necessary to determine whether the prospective partner can generate the level of financial resources necessary to maintain the venture's efforts. Managers frequently note their avoidance of potential anchors—partners likely to slow venture growth and development because of an inability or unwillingness to provide their share of the funding. As the vice president of a major manufacturing concern remarked, "Partners will almost always have differences of opinion regarding expansion. A small company may have fewer financial resources available for shouldering its portion of an expansion, or have to pay a higher financing rate than does the larger partner. This can not only cause operating problems, but may also result in some bruised egos, which can further intensify the difficulties."

A partner's inability to fulfill its financial commitments—whether due to small size, financial difficulties in its other operations, or the existence of different discount rates and time horizons—can create turmoil for the venture and its managers. Particularly in the early stages of a joint venture, when large negative cash flows are more likely to be encountered, the presence of an anchor can jeopardize an entire project. Commenting on his company's experiences, one senior executive said that, "The joint venture was functioning quite smoothly and was meeting or surpassing both companies' projections until the financial demands exceeded [the other company's] capabilities. . . . The resulting animosities ultimately caused the venture to be dissolved."

Although it is not always possible to identify potential anchors, several telltale signs may suggest the need for further inquiry. As one executive suggested, "You have to look at the partner's balance sheet and ask: 'Is it a financially solid company?' You have to look at their plans for growth and their profit orientation. Is there a difference in the strategic importance placed on the joint venture's activities? Is the partner likely to confront financial problems in one or more divisions? If so, what will be the effect upon other activities of the partner, especially the joint venture?"

A prospective partner's resource constraints can constitute a significant hurdle to the establishment of a successful joint venture. However, if proper precautions are observed, the presence of a partner with meager financial resources need not prevent joint venture formation or a premature buyout or termination. Especially when insufficient financial contributions are not due to financial insolvency, it may be possible to reduce noncompliance. For example, the agreement may include penalties if either partner attempts to back out of the relationship or otherwise sidestep its financial obligations. This agreement might also stipulate that the companies cannot engage in similar activities for a specified period of time. Furthermore, the agreement might be structured such that shareholdings or payouts are contingent upon the level of each partner's contributions, thus minimizing perceived inequities which might result from disparities in financial contributions. The use of these and similar mechanisms can reduce the undesirable effects of an anchor upon joint venture activities.

Relative Company Size: The Elephant and the Ant Complex

Relative company size is often of paramount concern when evaluating a prospective partner. Although exceptions are numerous, joint ventures often have the best chance of succeeding if both parents are comparable in sophistication and size, preferably large. When a small company decides to engage in a joint venture and chooses a similarly sized partner, the companies frequently magnify each other's weaknesses. This is less often the case between two large firms, which are likely to have similar values and control systems, similar tolerances for losses, and similar appetites for risk. Crises are less common in large firms, particularly in regard to short-term cash flow. Thus, larger companies typically offer greater "staying power," being able to commit a greater volume of resources over a longer time horizon.

Yet, sometimes ventures between firms of different sizes seem warranted. Size differences may yield synergies for the partners. A smaller company with innovative technology may venture with a large corporation which offers the financial and marketing clout necessary to commercialize that technology. Similarly, Nike, an innovative designer of athletic shoes, teamed up with Nissho Iwai, Japan's sixth-largest trading company. In 1978, Advanced Micro Devices, with $62 million in sales, formed a venture with Siemens, West Germany's largest electrical company, to produce a line of microcomputer systems and related products.

When partners evidence significant size discrepancies—dubbed "the elephant and the ant complex" by one executive— managers must be aware of the problems that may result. One frequently voiced concern is the possible domination of one company over the other, addressed earlier during the discussion of mutual need. A related problem is that the different operational environments and corporate cultures of the partners may appear incompatible. For instance, the typically bureaucratic environment of many large firms, with a relatively slow decision making apparatus and a voracious appetite for information gathering and analysis, sharply contrasts with the more entrepreneurial and quick-response orientation characteristic of many small firms. A small business, accustomed to reacting within short time frames, may feel paralyzed by the seemingly glacial pace at which the larger company operates. Yet, the small company's prodding and sense of urgency may make the larger partner nervous. The large company may interpret its smaller partner's Spartan environment and informality as indicative of a fly-by-night, shoestring operation that may not remain in business for long. Furthermore, the larger firm may perceive that most or all of the risk is being borne by itself—educating a sales force and customers about a new product's features; assuming responsibility for warehousing, distribution, and sometimes production; lending credibility to the product, along with enhancing the prestige and financial status of the smaller firm. In response to its partner's impatience, the larger firm may exercise even greater caution in its activities, further exacerbating the problem.

Differences in management style, decision making orientation, and perspective on time may effectively result in corporate culture shock, frustrating the management of each partner and hindering the development and maintenance of good rapport. Therefore, a joint venture between companies of widely disparate sizes often necessitates creation of a special environment in order to foster successful venture development. For instance, it might be possible to reduce the effects of partner size differences by giving the joint venture virtually a free hand in product development or other activities, minimizing administrative red tape and permitting quicker response time. This emphasis on autonomy might be particularly appropriate when a venture's environment is characterized by rapid change, and slow response might be akin to a kiss of death. The willingness of a partner to allow this autonomy might be a critical consideration in the partner selection decision.

Even if managers express a strong desire for working with partners with similar "systems" orientations, that need not dictate ventures between same-size corporation. On the contrary, the relevant measure often is not absolute corporate size, but the relative size of the respective business units. Therefore, managers may seek partners evidencing similar size at the business or division level. Another possibility for minimizing the effect of size differences is for a small firm to try to identify a large firm which is both hungry and has the marketing, financial, or technical muscle necessary for a successful venture. This may require greater diligence in identifying and contacting partners, however, since these attributes tend to be found in certain individuals or business units rather than in an organization as a whole. Yet, their presence helps ensure that the larger partner will be sufficiently aggressive to maintain respect from customers and competitors, and there is a greater likelihood that both partners will have similar perceptions of time as a vital component in the venture's success.

Strategic Complementarity: A Prerequisite for Long-Term Success

Although partner size is an important criterion for many companies, it is commonly asserted that relative size is not as important as complementarity among the partners' strategic objectives. Achieving a fit between companies' objectives for the joint venture is necessary for maintaining long-term commitment. From the onset of discussions, each partner must strive to understand clearly what the other participants desire from the union. As one seasoned veteran commented, "It is remarkable how many joint ventures are consummated where one or both partners do not clearly state their objectives. Under these circumstances, venture failure is almost inevitable."

Different objectives in forming a particular joint venture, including the timing and level of returns on their investments, frequently produces conflicts of interest between partners. For instance, one executive reflected upon a previous joint venture involving his company and an Asian firm. He noted that the venture evidenced a lack of strategic fit between the partners' objectives: his company sought rapid market access and a high rate of dividend repatriation so that its stock price would be maximized, enhancing an expansion strategy based on exchanges of stock. The partner, on the other hand, sought transfer of technology and long-term market development, rather than rapid financial returns. As a result of these differences, the joint venture performed poorly and was abandoned within a couple of years. The partner was reported to have used the acquired technological expertise to expand its own market position in Asia.

As partners' objectives diverge, there is an increasing risk of dissatisfaction and associated problems. This risk may be heightened when the venture's environment is characterized by a high level of uncertainty, since changes in a joint venture's operations are more likely under these circumstances. Unexpected events can cause problems because of the difficulty of formulating a mutually acceptable response to change. A power game can result, and the venture can collapse if the partners cannot reach an agreement on an appropriate course of action.

However, divergence of corporate objectives can lead to a venture's downfall even if performance is satisfactory. For example, Dow-Badische was formed in 1958 as a 50/50 joint venture between Dow Chemical and BASF of Germany, and it achieved good profitability over much of its life. Nevertheless, despite $300 million in annual sales, the venture was ultimately dissolved. BASF wanted to expand the venture, but Dow was reluctant to contribute additional capital since the venture's activities did not seem to fit within the firm's strategic focus. The gap between corporate objectives prompted BASF to buy out Dow's shares in 1978 and to transform the venture into a wholly owned U.S. subsidiary.

Although determining a prospective partner's objectives is often difficult, it is an essential task nevertheless. Failure to do so may significantly increase the prospect of later problems. The analysis needs to address not only the company's current situation and objectives, but also scenarios of its likely future position. The rationale for this is that joint ventures frequently encounter changes in their operating environments, and it is essential that companies anticipate how their partner is likely to be affected by, and respond to, these changes. Joint ventures tend to work only as long as each partner perceives that it is receiving benefits or is likely to benefit in the relatively near future. Because of differences in objectives, what is good for one company may be a disaster for the other party. Therefore, a compatible partner would ideally be one with similar values and objectives, in both a short- and a long-term sense. Such a situation will enhance the ability of managers to interpret one another's estimates, such as sales forecasts, development schedules, and cost estimates. This is particularly critical as the strategic stakes—the size of investment, the potential effect on corporate image, or the relationship to the organization's core technologies—increase in scale.

Evaluating Compatibility between Partners' Operating Policies

Another consideration during partner selection is the similarity of partners' operating policies. Executives related several instances in which differences between partners' policies had caused significant problems for joint ventures. For instance, one venture was nearly dissolved because inconsistencies between partners' accounting systems repeatedly produced disagreement regarding the timing of purchases, the allocation of costs, and so forth. Since the joint venture was only marginally profitable, the method of reconciling disagreements could determine whether the venture would appear on the parents' books as a profitable operation, an important consideration for the division-level management teams. Another executive reported that differences in vacation policies between his firm and his European partner created serious difficulties for their joint venture because the latter company shut down virtually all operations for a month each summer, whereas the U.S. firm allowed employees to schedule their own vacation time. As a result, the venture repeatedly encountered difficulties.

Partners should be clear about the types of policies they will be comfortable working with. For example, U.S. and Western European firms are typically accustomed to operating with lower debt-to-equity ratios than are firms in Japan. Such policies should be addressed thoroughly before the venture is formed. Differences in operating approaches often result from cultural biases, and managers may not be conscious of their existence. They may take for granted that there is a "right" way to do certain things. As one Japanese manager stated, "Many American executives attempt to force their Japanese partners to adopt American methods of operation, in disregard of the distribution structure and other financial and management methods which have prevailed in Japan for a long time. For this reason, many joint ventures in Japan ultimately fail." As these examples illustrate, the compatibility of partners' operating policies may need to be considered before forming a venture.

Being Aware of Potential Communication Barriers

Communication is another potential problem area. By nature, joint ventures tend to be fragile agreements, and communication problems make their operation even more difficult. Such problems may occur as a result of differences between national or ethnic cultures, including language, as well as differing corporate cultures. Cultural differences can impede the development of rapport and understanding between partners. The importance of a partner with an adequate English language capability should not be overlooked, nor one's firm's facility with the language of the partner. The simple ability to communicate with one's counterpart in the partner firm often makes a significant difference in a venture's prospects for success, and the absence of this ability has caused more than a few disasters.

Because of cultural or language differences, subtle nuances may be more difficult to communicate. This can require greater expenditures of time in negotiations, possibly delaying joint venture formation or major post-formation decisions. The use of buzzwords common to many industries tends to compound language problems. When buzzwords are used, misunderstandings can arise regarding each company's role in a joint venture. Especially in technology-oriented fields, commonly used terms may not have the same connotations for each partner. For example, specifications for the Boeing 767 jetliner called for fuselage panels to have a "mirror finish." Boeing's Japanese partners interpreted that specification too literally and engaged in excessive polishing efforts. As a result, labor costs for the initial panels were excessive, necessitating further discussions to resolve the misunderstanding. Because of the risk of misinterpretation, it may be advisable to attempt to substitute simple, "Dick-and-Jane"-type terminology for technical jargon during negotiations and follow-up discussions.

The existence of different cultural perspectives implies value systems that are not necessarily compatible; it cannot be assumed that promoting interests from one perspective will necessarily promote interests from another. However, managers should avoid the alternative assumption that different value systems will necessarily be incompatible. Values associated with different perspectives may be similar, even if only slightly, or they may be irrelevant to each other; it is not common for them to be in complete opposition.

Prior experience suggests that language and culture tend not to be insurmountable barriers, particularly for partners from industrialized nations, although they can be a significant handicap. Therefore, although cultural barriers are often considered when evaluating prospective partners, and especially when choosing between two otherwise equivalent partner prospects, they seldom function as the dominant selection criterion.

Compatible Management Teams Reduce Problems

It may be desirable to select a partner whose management team is compatible with one's own. Personal rapport between the principal decision makers is often an important factor in the selection decision, and the inability of management to "take to each other" has frequently been cited as the basis for rejecting a prospective partner or for terminating a venture. Close personal relationships, particularly among the senior operating-level managers, helps to nurture the level of understanding necessary for a successful joint venture relationship. Managerial compatibility can enhance the partners' ability to achieve consensus on critical policy decisions and to overcome the frequent roadblocks encountered during joint venture formation and operation.

Though building relationships between partners' managers takes time—a commodity many executives perceive to be in short supply when pursuing joint venture formation—it is an invaluable element of most successful ventures. This particularly characterizes joint ventures with Japanese firms, for whom establishment of close personal rapport is customarily a requirement before business negotiations can be concluded.

In many ways, it may seem unfortunate that joint ventures are so heavily dependent on personal rapport between a few individuals. Because of the informal nature of these relationships, including extensive utilization of unwritten "gentlemen's agreements," reliance upon executive rapport may lead to unnecessary disputes and conflicts of interests at a later date. To reduce prospects for such turmoil, an additional consideration when selecting a partner may be the likelihood of continuity among the critical personnel within a partner's management team. Such continuity can help minimize the incidence of misunderstandings between partners. In this regard, several managers commented that Japanese executives had expressed hesitancy about forming joint ventures with U.S. companies because the typically higher levels of management turnover in American firms hindered establishment and maintenance of close relations among the partners' managers.

Trust and Commitment: Essential Elements of Long-Term Relationships

Forming and operating a successful joint venture may not be synonymous with the maintenance of friendly and cordial relations between the partners' management teams. The perceived trustworthiness and commitment of a partner was a pivotal consideration in selecting many joint venture partners. Human chemistry is essential to the development and maintenance of trust and commitment, and interactions between managers helps provide the necessary foundation for their establishment. These interactions permit partners to understand more fully the people they will be working with, including their values, concerns, and needs, thus helping to assuage potential suspicions. One executive, noting the importance of mutual trust and commitment in the partner selection decision and the process for evaluating these traits, likened the process to a "mating dance." He envisioned the prospective partners as cautiously approaching each other, trying to "strut their stuff" and create favorable impressions, engaging in an often lengthy ritual of evaluating mutual attraction and compatibility before either would commit itself fully to the joint venture. Without full commitment by both parties, joint ventures tend to become short-term relationships, or "flings," often followed by divorce and parentless "children." For this reason, great emphasis is typically placed on selection of partners evidencing trustworthiness and commitment to the venture, particularly by the executives with more extensive joint venture experience.

The need for trust and commitment is especially critical if the joint venture involves activities closely related to one's firm's technological core. The technological core of many firms is the essence of their corporate strategies and competitive advantage. A manager may understandably react with some level of initial distrust regarding potential partners' motives. It is useful to recall the inherent fragility of joint ventures when choosing partners, since today's partners could become tomorrow's competitors. As one chief executive officer (CEO) noted, "You've got to be sure you're working with earnest and ethical people who aren't trying to undermine your company. Usually, a partner will have access to your trade secrets. He might attempt to complete a few projects, learn what you do, then exclude you from future deals."

Exposing your technological core to a partner who is unable to protect this knowledge adequately from technological theft or "bleed through" can threaten your company's competitiveness. As a result, an intuitive response may be to seek majority control, if not full ownership, of any venture, and then to hover over every decision the child might make—particularly if one does not trust a partner's intentions. Yet, such a response is unlikely to promote compatibility.

Many managers take the position that, given the likelihood of some misunderstanding between partners, the joint venture agreement should address every conceivable contingency. In contrast, managers experienced in joint ventures frequently emphasized the building of mutual trust and understanding, which make the formal written agreement more a symbol of commitment to cooperate than an actual working document. As one CEO commented, partners generally "don't start looking at the specifics of the venture agreement until the relationship starts breaking down and you're contemplating getting out."

Regardless of the protections written into the joint venture agreement, no legal document is fail-safe. "You can write all sorts of legal contracts and other formal agreements, but the partners must trust each other and be committed to the venture in order for it to work," noted one executive. "A partner may be able to muster a virtual battalion of lawyers, making it very expensive for you to take a grievance to court, much less to win it." Therefore, one must be comfortable that the partner will honor the spirit, not just the letter, of the agreement. Often, particularly in ventures involving the Japanese, demands to develop extensive formal contracts dealing with every conceivable dispute will be viewed as evidence of mistrust. Managers are to be reminded that a joint venture relationship is delicate at best and complicated at worst. Without fundamental trust and commitment by each party, there is little hope for a working partnership.

In developing the criteria for selecting partners, it is essential that managers consider inclusion of partner-related dimensions of criteria. Although performance data were not rigorously gathered, because many of the joint ventures had not yet begun operations or they had been in operation for only a short while, comments suggested that long-term compatibility of the partners was critical for long-term joint venture success. The implication is that managers should select a partner that offers strong prospects for the development of an effective long-term working relationship. Although satisfying the perceived task-related requirements of the joint venture is a *necessary* element of the joint venture partner selection decision, it is *not* sufficient. Rather, what we have termed "partner-related" criteria are also essential elements of successful partner selection decisions.

Despite their importance, partner-related criteria have tended to be de-emphasized in many partner selection decisions. It is especially prevalent among first-time joint venturers. Most often, the criteria associated with perceived long-term compatibility of the partners receive abbreviated attention. However, de-emphasis of criteria related to long-term compatibility of partners in favor of criteria oriented toward short-term contributions of partners can, and generally does, result in long-term problems. Therefore, managers attempting to establish joint ventures with some degree of longevity are strongly advised to consider inclusion of partner-related criteria in their partner selection decision. (In some instances, a firm may consciously *not* want the joint venture to be long-lived. Managers in such situations may nevertheless appreciate the value of including partner-related criteria in their partner selection decision, although the emphasis may not be on selection of a compatible partner.)

THE ONGOING NATURE OF JOINT VENTURE NEGOTIATIONS

Managers should recognize that joint ventures are usually characterized by ongoing negotiations, even after the initial stages of discussions have been concluded and the joint venture has been formally established. This is true regardless of the absolute sharing of the venture's equity. A minority partner consistently finding itself outvoted on important issues is less likely to perceive that its strategic objectives are being attained, particularly if they are experiencing sub-par returns from their participation. As a result, the probability that problems will arise is increased, and prospects for joint venture longevity will be slim. Thus, regardless of whether the equity is split equally or if one partner has a majority share, consensus is still desirable on major decisions.

It is inevitable that unanticipated changes in the internal and external environment will occur. Under such circumstances, strict reliance on the initially negotiated contract may produce less than satisfactory performance for one or both of the partners, threatening the venture's long-term viability unless modifications are implemented. While not all aspects of a joint venture agreement may be subject to renegotiation, the principal impetus for reopening discussions on some or all parts of the joint venture agreement is concern over potential inequities or domination. This is particularly the case if there is also disparity in the relative sizes of partners, where the much smaller firm may feel victimized by disparate outcomes. Since a balanced agreement is essential to the maintenance of trust, circumstances that produce perceived imbalances typically result in partner outcry and pressure for modifications to the agreement. To the extent that partners perceive incompatibilities between themselves and their venture mates and an inability to rectify the situation, what begins as a relatively minor annoyance may mushroom into a significant, and possibly fatal, source of friction.

One means of minimizing problems within a joint venture is to maintain continuity among the key personnel. Because of their ongoing relationship with their peers in the partner organization, they are a critical element in the maintenance of mutual trust. Personnel changes, especially among the venture's sponsors, can threaten the personal chemistry that has been built up between the partners and may necessitate further negotiations to reestablish this human balance. Although several firms have consciously exploited this tendency as a means of reopening negotiations, be forewarned that such a strategy may also entail significant risks.

Avoid a Zero-Sum Game Mentality

In the end, the partner selection decision is generally based on nonquantifiable human judgment, especially the judgment of those individuals who serve as the venture's sponsors. In this regard, managers should refrain from a tendency to approach negotiations as a zero-sum game. Because of the presumed long-term nature of the relationship and the need for fostering mutual trust and commitment, attempting to "beat" the partner in the negotiation stage will generally prove dysfunctional in the long run. As one food industry executive stated, "The content of any proposed agreement should be reasonable for all parties. If you believe it's reasonable, don't hesitate to lobby strongly for it. However, it's useless to pursue an unreasonable agreement. Even if you're able to convince the partner to initially agree to it, he'll eventually feel cheated and the agreement will ultimately fail."

For some, the idea of cooperating with a partner appears to stand in direct opposition to a corporate value system holding self-sufficiency and aggressive competition as central ideals. Yet, regardless of the size or type of business, the joint venture must be founded and operated in the spirit of compromise and cooperation. A parent unwilling to recognize this principle should pursue other, non-joint venture options, or it will find itself confronting constant difficulties. An inequitable agreement, unless remedied, can result in deadlocks or dissolution, causing the partners to suffer foregone opportunities, lost capital and other resources, and compromised proprietary information, as well as an enormous amount of stress and emotional anguish.

CONCLUDING REMARKS

Joint ventures marrying corporate partners can be a valuable option for many firms and projects, and it may be a less harrowing option than going it alone. But caution is necessary when selecting partners. It is easy for companies to get married, yet if the courting ritual is not conducted in a thorough manner, divorce is likely. The result—long and acrimonious legal battles, parentless children, and possibly serious scars—may place a company in a worse position that it was before.

Success or failure of a developed country joint venture depends not only on a venture's underlying strategic rationale, but also on how well the partner companies can work together, despite differences in management styles, strategies, resources, and culture. The effect of such corporate chemistry is difficult to predict and control, but it is a critical consideration since joint venture agreements usually provide each partner with an ongoing role in the venture's management. Compatibility of partners, beyond mere technical complementarity, is an important prerequisite for successful corporate marriage. This is particularly important in partner selection because of the influence this decision can have on joint venture operating policies and performance.

When identifying suitable partner prospects, analysis of past joint ventures suggests that no single approach promises to provide optimal results in every situation. Rather, the method will be contingent upon the nature of the proposed investment. However, in developing selection criteria, it is essential that a partner offers strong prospects for developing an effective long-term working relationship. Partners have a tendency to crystallize into personalities, of which some types may not be conducive to the venture's long-term viability. Although satisfying the joint venture's technical requirements is a necessary element of the partner selection decision, it alone is generally not sufficient. It should also be apparent that the partners, linked together, will form a complete business, both in terms of technical capabilities and their ability to interact successfully.

Management of a joint venture may differ from typical business activities because it may involve a mixture of, and sometimes clashes between, different cultures, thought patterns, and attitudes toward competition. There is a strong tendency for managers, particularly those without significant prior joint venture experience, to view their prospective ventures as unique. This often translates into a perception that the joint venture experience of others has only limited applicability to their own circumstances. However, adamant assertions of the uniqueness of a particular joint venture may often be overstated. Although each situation will evidence some unique elements, there do seem to be common elements in some, if not all, aspects of the joint venture formation process. For this reason, the process of locating suitable joint venture partners should, when possible, be carried out with the assistance of experienced advisors who are thoroughly familiar with the law and business practices of the target industry and market.

Because of the presumed long-term nature of most joint ventures and the costs associated with premature dissolution, relatively high financial and human costs tend to be associated with the selection of partners for successful joint ventures. Firms must be willing to incur substantial search costs, including those associated with developing criteria and evaluating partners, as well as the extensive resource expenditures typically involved in the negotiation stage. In addition, the process must be approached with considerable patience and realistic expectations. If a company is unwilling to accept these preconditions, it should probably consider other investment options. It should not try to minimize resource expenditures by cutting corners on the quantity and quality of effort expended on the partner selection and evaluation process.

14

Evaluation of Research Method and Future Research

This chapter briefly examines the major strengths and potential limitations of the research method employed in this study. The discussion addresses the issues of bias in sample composition, measurement inadequacies, interviewer bias, coding inaccuracies, recoding of data, use of factor analytic techniques, construct validity, statistical conclusion validity, and interpretation of results. The chapter concludes with several suggestions for future research on the issue of selecting partners for joint ventures.

EVALUATION OF RESEARCH METHOD

Bias in Sample Composition

Despite extensive efforts to the contrary, the composition of our sample may have introduced bias which could limit the generalizability of the results. The sources of potential bias include size and nature of ownership, date of formation, geographical scope, multiple listings for corporations, and response rate. To the extent that these factors introduced significant bias into the research sample, the external validity of the results and conclusions could become suspect. Therefore, the following subsections address each of these potential sources of bias individually.

Size and nature of ownership. The sampling frame may have been biased toward the inclusion of larger and publicly held firms since the activities of these types of organizations are more likely to be reported. However, the extent of this bias was not expected to be significant, since five different sources were used to identify proposed or actual joint ventures.

Date of formation. The sample may have been biased as a result of the temporal restriction on the dates of joint venture formation. Since only joint ventures pursued or formed between January 1, 1979, and February 1, 1985, were included in this sample, this may have resulted in a bias attributable to unique factors operational during this time period, such as economic or political cycles. However, this possible temporal bias may have been somewhat mitigated by the fact that selection criteria may have been developed one or more years prior to the date of formation, thereby increasing the range of years during which the selection criteria may have been developed.

Geographical scope. Random selection of joint ventures from a convenience sample of five geographical clusters may have resulted in some sample bias due to the exclusion of certain geographical areas. To the extent that there were differences between clusters in terms of industrial composition, management styles, and economic conditions, *inter alia*, the exclusion of certain geographical areas may have biased the data that were obtained. Although the possible extent of this bias is unknown, the percentage of sampling frame joint ventures included in the sampled clusters (53.7 percent), the diversity of geographical areas covered, and the use of random sampling within the geographical clusters were expected to have limited the extent of possible bias caused by the geographical scope of the sample.

Multiple listings for corporations. Sample bias may have been introduced because the sampling frame consisted of individual joint ventures rather than individual corporations which had engaged in qualifying joint ventures because a number of organizations had been involved in more than one qualifying joint venture. In addition, several of the corporations participating in this study had more than one of their joint ventures included in the sample. Therefore, this could have produced some bias in the sample results.

However, since the *de facto* joint venture partner selection decision tended to be made at the business level or below, rather than at the corporate level, and since different business units tended to use different approaches and different people in the partner selection process, this potential bias was reduced. In addition, even when a single business unit had participated in more than one joint venture, the perceived uniqueness of each venture meant that respondents reported different criteria and different perceptions of the relative importance of the underlying variables. Therefore, the potential bias caused by multiple listings was perceived to be relatively inconsequential.

Response rate. Less than full participation of the contacted firms which qualified for the study may have introduced bias into the sample data. However, because of the high level of participation, 82.6 percent, and the rationales given for nonparticipation, this potential bias was not expected to be significant.

Measurement Inadequacies

The measures that were employed to collect data may have been inadequate, thereby threatening the statistical conclusion validity of the study's results. The potential limitations of the measures, including the collection of perceptual data, the lack of multiple measures, the measurement scale limitations, the lack of multiple respondents, the potential for intentional deception, and an *ex post* rationalization in responses, are discussed in the following subsections.

Collection of perceptual data. The *ex post* collection of perceptual data may have produced deficient research data, thereby hindering the ability to draw valid conclusions. The nature of the study not only prevented the researcher from instituting experimental controls, but it also raised the prospect of memory decay.

As discussed in Chapter 3, the nature of the research topic dictated an *ex post* research design. However, extensive efforts were undertaken to minimize the potential measurement inadequacies associated with this design, thereby enhancing statistical conclusion validity. For instance, to minimize memory decay, the sample was limited temporally to joint ventures pursued or formed between January 1, 1979, and March 1, 1985. In addition, distribution of the questionnaire prior to interviews and careful sequencing of interview questions helped to minimize memory decay by providing contextual clues and by encouraging reference to printed or human sources for confirmation of data accuracy. Furthermore, because of the significance of the partner selection process to the organizations and to the individuals' careers, respondents reported that the details of the process were still clearly etched in their memories.

Lack of multiple measures. Because the questionnaire did not directly employ multiple measures of the research variable categories, the statistical reliability of the data might be suspect. However, the potential limitations might have been mitigated somewhat because many of the questionnaire responses were rechecked during the interviews, when the researcher asked specific questions regarding the most or least important categories of a variable, as well as the relative importance of one category versus another. Although these checks were conducted only on a subset of the questionnaire categories, due to limited interview time, the responses supported the statistical reliability and the construct validity of the questionnaire-based results. In addition, results of the factor analysis suggested that the overlap of several of the variable categories (e.g., PSCLOWC and PSCLOWP) often approximated the use of multiple measures.

Measurement scale limitations. The use of five-point Likert-type scales produced ordinal data rather than interval-approximating data such as might have been gathered via Thurstone-type scales. Although the data collected via the later scales might have better facilitated the use of certain statistical techniques in data analysis, their absence was not perceived to be a significant drawback. In fact, pretest results and comments by participants suggested that Thurstone-type scales would have been too time consuming and too complex to have been feasibly employed, given the range of variable categories examined and the limited amount of senior executive time available for data collection.

Another possible limitation associated with the measurement scales concerned the use of fixed alternative questions on the questionnaires. These types of questions may introduce bias by forcing respondents to choose from a given set of alternatives or by making the respondent think of alternatives that might not otherwise have occurred to him or her. This potential problem was mitigated somewhat by the use of NA, or not applicable, responses, which permitted the respondents to ignore those categories that may not have been operationalized during the partner selection process. In addition, respondents were also asked during the interviews if they had any difficulties or additional comments regarding the questionnaires and, for instance, if they had employed any additional criteria besides those listed on the questionnaire. Therefore, the potential problems resulting from the use of fixed alternative response categories was believed to have been mitigated at least somewhat.

Lack of multiple respondents. Because this study did not employ multiple respondents per joint venture, the reliability of the data may be suspect. However, the use of multiple respondents was virtually precluded as an option for most of the joint ventures due to the limited number of key individuals who would have been able to provide the requisite data, the limited amount of senior executive time able to be allocated to the study by individual firms, and the extensive level of personnel changes which had occurred since the time of joint venture formation, which often meant that additional respondents were inaccessible due to location (e.g., stationed overseas) or because they were no longer with the firm and their current whereabouts were unknown.

Potential for intentional deception. The validity of the results may be suspect owing to intentional deception on the part of respondents. However, extensive efforts to establish rapport with the participants, as well as guaranteed confidentiality of the data and the presumably noncritical nature of the topic, suggests that intentional deception on a significant scale would be unlikely due to lack of incentive. Furthermore, random deceptive responses would be expected to cancel themselves out due to the use of random sampling in selecting joint ventures for the study.

Ex post rationalization in responses. A potential problem confronting studies such as this is the prospect of participants intentionally or unintentionally biasing responses via *ex post* rationalizations or over-intellectualization. This problem was expected to be mitigated by several methodological characteristics of the study, including grouping individual questions on a variable-by-variable basis, encouraging respondents to refer to additional data sources (e.g., company files or other managers) for confirmation of responses, undertaking extensive efforts to establish trust and rapport, and addressing variable topics chronologically during the interviews.

Interviewer Bias

The use of a semistructured interview format may have introduced interviewer bias because of the way in which topics were ordered and questions were phrased. However, since the statistical analysis was based upon questionnaire data, which ensured identical ordering and phrasing of questions for each respondent, the effect of interviewer bias was expected to be negligible. Furthermore, the use of interview coding forms with topics arranged in chronological order enabled the interview format to be quite comparable between respondents, thus reducing the potential effect of interviewer bias upon the data obtained in the interviews.

Coding Inaccuracies

Potential inaccuracies in data coding and entry can influence the reliability and validity of the research results. However, this study incorporated several checks against coding inaccuracies. First, questionnaire data (except the diversity of line functions variable) were obtained via integer-based Likert-type scales which did not require any transformation prior to computer entry. All data entry was conducted via a double-entry system, whereby two separate data files were created using the same input data. After entry, the two files were checked for any differences that had resulted from inaccuracies in the data entry phase, and any discrepancies between the files were checked and corrected. In addition, the use of the FREQUENCIES routine on SPSS-X allowed for further visual checks for data inaccuracies.

Inaccuracies in note taking of interviews were minimized by careful sequencing of topics, the use of interview coding forms, and review of notes immediately after completion of interviews.

Recoding of Data

The use of recoded data, whereby NA responses were converted into integer data, may have reduced the validity or reliability of the results obtained therefrom. However, comments of respondents suggested that the NA responses tended to have logical integer values, thus reducing concerns about the recoding scheme. Furthermore, the recoded data were almost exclusively utilized as a check for the statistical reliability of the results obtained from the unrecoded data. The similarity of the results typically

obtained from the recoded and the unrecoded data samples suggested that
the effect of recoding on data reliability tended to be inconsequential.

Use of Factor Analytic Techniques

The results of the factor analysis of the sample data may be misleading
because ordinal-level data were used for statistical techniques which technically require interval- or ratio-level data. However, except for the extent
of shared control variable, the data satisfied the basic requirements for factor
analysis, including normality of distributions, linearity, and homoscedasticity. In addition, the ordinal-level data, obtained via Likert-type scales,
seemed to approximate interval-level data. Therefore, the exploratory use
of factor techniques for analyzing the sample data seemed warranted. The
robustness of the results that were obtained, despite the use of different
specifications of methods and different samples, and the conservative manner in which the factors were interpreted, suggested that the employment
of factor analytic techniques on the sample data was justified.

Construct Validity

The extent of intercorrelation between categories and/or factors of the
research variables constituted a potential threat to the study's construct
validity. The presence of moderate intercorrelations suggested the existence
of potential substitute variables, thereby threatening to confound efforts to
describe accurately or explain the phenomenon under study. However, the
extensive use of partial correlation analysis on the research variables helped
to mitigate this threat to construct validity. Efforts to correct for intercorrelation via the use of partial correlation appeared to enhance the validity
of the study's results significantly, particularly for the three task-related
variables. The researcher's confidence regarding construct validity was further bolstered by the consistency of individual participants' responses between the questionnaire and the interview discussion.

Statistical Conclusion Validity

The statistical conclusion validity of the study's results was potentially
suspect for several reasons. One possible drawback was the absence of
multiple independent samples for the statistical analysis, a situation characteristic of the vast majority of empirical research on macro policy issues.
The nature of the research topic virtually dictated an inability to access
either multiple samples or a single sample sufficiently large to permit statistical analysis on both principal and holdout samples. Therefore, the threat
to statistical conclusion validity on this count was virtually unavoidable.
Nevertheless, several efforts were undertaken to reduce this threat. First,

use of multiple appropriate statistical tests and statistics helped to ensure the correctness of the results by avoiding the chance occurrence of significant outcomes. Because the results thus obtained tended to evidence stability across different methods of analysis, the validity of the statistical conclusions appeared to have been enhanced.

Interpretation of Results

Most of the results presented in Chapters 5 through 11 were based on data obtained from the mail questionnaire. One of the problems typically associated with mail questionnaires is the potential for misinterpretation of the data and inaccurate conclusions. The likelihood of such problems in this study was significantly reduced by the utilization of interviews with all the individuals who completed the questionnaires. The interviews provided mini-case histories and anecdotal evidence that highlighted the subtle nuances of the research data. Therefore, the simultaneous use of interviews and questionnaires for data collection significantly reduced the likelihood of misinterpretation of the research results.

SUGGESTIONS FOR FUTURE RESEARCH

The results of this study strongly support the assertion that the partner selection process as a whole, and partner selection criteria in particular, represents an important topic within the joint venture literature. Because it has previously received such scant attention, the topic of partner selection offers a number of fruitful areas for future research. This section addresses several promising avenues for research efforts, including the process of partner selection, partner selection criteria, sample composition, and joint venture performance. The section concludes with several suggestions regarding research methodology.

Process of Partner Selection

Largely because of the lack of significant amounts of prior research on the topic, at the present time there are no well-developed theoretical or empirical models of the joint venture partner selection process. Those studies that have attempted to examine the process, including this one, generally have had to piece together *ex post* data from a number of different joint ventures in a effort to gain insights into the process phenomena associated with partner selection.

A potentially interesting study would be for a researcher to use a longitudinal field study design to examine one or, better yet, several proposed joint ventures from their initial feasibility study through their formation. In doing this, it would be of potentially great value to examine the process from the perspective of each of the partners. This should enhance understanding not only of the process by which partners are identified, evaluated, and selected, but also of the concept of complementarity. In addition to refinement of the concept of task-related selection criteria, such a study could greatly enhance the level of knowledge regarding partner-related criteria, including what dimensions comprise the latter, the relationship between task-related and partner-related selection criteria dimensions, the manner in which the operationalization of selection criteria may change over time, and the way in which firms determine the trade-offs they are willing or able to make between alternative criteria dimensions, especially when choosing between nonhomogeneous prospects. Furthermore, the conceptual and statistical overlap of the competitive position and difficulty of internal development variables, as operationalized herein, suggests that refinement of those variables may be in order. A longitudinal study could be a particularly suitable methodology for accomplishing that end, due to its potentially greater ability to capture the dynamic, as well as the static, element of an organization's relative competitive position.

One of the more difficult challenges of this suggestion would be gaining access to the joint venture firm(s) at a sufficiently early stage of the formation process. The strategic sensitivity of the negotiations, and the need to quickly overcome suspicions and mistrust between partners, may limit the number of firms willing to permit an outside researcher to participate in even an observer role. However, the relatively large number of joint ventures being pursued of late suggests that finding one or more suitable joint ventures would not be an insurmountable task.

Partner Selection Criteria

The data presented herein give a much fuller meaning to the concept of complementarity as a basis for partner selection. They help to highlight under what circumstances or for what dimension complementarity will be viewed as similarity or dissimilarity on a particular criteria dimension. In this regard, the distinction between task-related and partner-related selection criteria categories seems to have some usefulness as a conceptual tool for enhancing understanding of the partner selection process. In particular, the critical success factor, competitive position, and difficulty of internal development variables seemed to be valuable in understanding the assignment of valences to task-related criteria categories. They provide the foundations for developing a simple, yet robust, framework for this aspect of partner selection, and they appear to be consistent with the existing literature in business strategy. In addition, comments by Charles W. Hofer and Dan Schendel[1] regarding the relative ease of evaluating potential critical success factors suggests that the relationship obtained between the critical success factor, competitive position, and difficulty of internal development variables and task-related partner selection criteria may have some predictive potential, further enhancing its value as a conceptual and diagnostic tool.[2] Both the task-related and the partner-related concepts need further refinement, especially in light of the intercorrelation observed among the research variables. Nevertheless, the data from this study suggest this might be a fruitful area for future study.

Although the data appear to be more tentative than was the case for the task-related dimensions, the concept of partner-related variables also seems to have some merit for future study. It is apparent that more effort needs to be directed at defining the appropriate scope for, and dimensions of, the concept. In addition, particularly for perceived task environment uncertainty, the variables examined in association with the partner-related criteria seem to have some usefulness in enhancing understanding of the partner selection process. However, especially for the extent of shared control variable, the operationalization of these variables needs to be refined vis-a-vis the exploratory mode used in this study.

The list of selection criteria prepared in this study needs to be supplemented with the addition of such criteria as the prospective partner's long-term financial viability and the partner's corporate and/or business level strategic goals and objectives. In addition, the criterion of size needs to be enhanced to distinguish between relative and absolute size and to determine what measure of size to employ (e.g., assets, revenues), as well as corporate versus business level size.

In examining the selection criteria employed by firms, it would be valuable to examine the potential for obtaining meaningful rank orderings of the principal criteria categories. This may be difficult, since firms may make trade-offs between criteria, particularly in an uncertain environment with partner prospects that differ significantly. In addition to rankings, it would be interesting to see whether, under what conditions, and for what criteria firms establish maximum or minimum "threshold" requirements. This latter notion might also permit more systematic examination not only of what traits were sought in a partner, but also what traits were avoided and why.

Finally, the usefulness of a joint venture partner selection model would be increased immensely if a researcher could identify independent variables that evidence a strong and predictable relationship with selection criteria valences and which could be measured using objective measures, rather than relying on such subjective data as management perceptions. To the extent that this quest is successful, the potential predictive power of a resulting model should be significantly enhanced. On the basis of our results, we believe that the task-related dimensions of selection criteria examined in this study provide a valuable base for future efforts to develop such a predictive model.

Sample Composition

This study focused on bilateral joint ventures with at least one U.S.-based partner and one or more developed country as its target market. It would be interesting to compare and contrast the results from this study with the results of similar studies using different samples. This suggests the segmentation of the population of joint ventures to identify, for instance, joint ventures with more than two partners, joint ventures with one or more less developed countries as the target market, or joint ventures involving only certain types of industries. Another promising means of segmenting would be to examine only non-U.S.-based firms. In all of these cases, it would be insightful to compare the results with the results obtained in this study. What differences or similarities exist based on sample composition, and what principal variable(s) seem to account for the differences or lack thereof? Answers to these questions would spur the development of a much more sophisticated model of the joint venture partner selection process.

Joint Venture Performance

From the standpoint of both practitioner and theorist, it would be useful to examine the link between the overall partner selection process, including partner selection criteria and joint venture performance. Unless a longitudinal analysis is employed, however, the researcher will have to trade off recency of the selection process (and, thus, less risk from memory decay) against the time span of operations for which performance will be evaluated. It might be desirable to obtain each partner's evaluation of performance and to use several different performance measures in order to enhance the level of understanding and insight available from a study such as this.

METHODOLOGY

Contacting Firms

If the research objective is to understand partner selection from a strategic perspective, it is generally best to initiate the contacts at the top level of the corporation or business unit. Senior level managers are more likely to know to whom to forward a letter or whom to telephone, and managers tend to be substantially more responsive to a research inquiry when it is forwarded from their superiors rather than their subordinates.

It may be advisable to send a letter briefly describing the proposed study and then follow up soon thereafter with a phone call. This permits the executive to determine where to forward the request, and it ensures that the letter will get prompt attention in anticipation of a follow-up call.

Reliance on written communication can result in very slow response, but exclusive use of phone calls can also impede response due to uncertainty (and possible suspicion) regarding the true identity and objectives of the researcher. Many of the executives seemed to be somewhat gun-shy regarding reporters and other purported "researchers," and a preliminary letter helps to assuage their fears and contribute to the development of trust.

Persistence appeared to be the key to a satisfactory participation rate. Frequently, six or more calls and transfers were necessary before the appropriate manager was identified and contact was able to be established. In addition, when one individual expresses an unwillingness to participate in a study, it might be possible to circumvent the potential roadblock by contacting other members of the organization. In several instances, calls were forwarded to the corporate counsel's office, where the legal staff consistently declined corporate involvement in the study. However, in all but one of these cases, it was possible to reinitiate the process by contacting another of the senior executives and having them refer the project's letter to the appropriate line manager.

Data Collection Instruments

Executives repeatedly asserted that they probably would not have participated in this study if it had only entailed completion of a long (or even a short) questionnaire without the personal contact of an interview. There were also suggestions that many of the anonymously sent questionnaires that are completed and returned may not be filled out by the appropriate individuals. Therefore, it may be desirable, to the extent resources will permit, to avoid exclusive reliance on mail questionnaires as a data source. The typically low response rates, the questionable validity of the respondents, and the potential difficulties encountered in interpreting the results can each seriously undermine the usefulness of the data and the conclusions that result from an exclusively mail-questionnaire-based data collection methodology.

NOTES

1. Charles W. Hofer and Dan Schendel, *Strategy Formulation: Analytical Concepts* (St. Paul, Minn.: West Publishing, 1978).

2. The prospects for effective employment of the task-related criteria concept may be enhanced further through employment of complementary analytical techniques such as value chain analysis. For example, see Michael E. Porter, *Competitive Advantage* (New York: Free Press, 1985).

APPENDIX A

Questionnaire for Participants

DIRECTIONS FOR PROJECT PARTICIPANTS: This questionnaire is intended to complement the material covered in interviews. Designed for easy completion, it should only take a few minutes to complete. Your cooperation is appreciated.

Name of Your Company: _____

Name of Joint Venture Partner: _____

Name of Joint Venture: _____

Nation of JV incorporation: _____

Share of JV equity originally held by your firm:___< 50% ___50% ___> 50%

Principal JV products/services: _____

_____

Anticipated Geographic Target Market Focus of JV, at the time it was

formed: _____

At the time it was formed, how much influence was each of the following factors expected to have on the venture's performance? (If a factor was not relevant, mark NA)

		minimal influence			strong influence		
a.	Government pressures, regulatory requirements, etc. . . .	0	1	2	3	4	NA
b.	Access to financial resources	0	1	2	3	4	NA
c.	Government subsidies, tax credits, & other inducements.	0	1	2	3	4	NA
d.	Experienced managerial personnel	0	1	2	3	4	NA
e.	Technically skilled employees	0	1	2	3	4	NA
f.	Location of joint venture facilities	0	1	2	3	4	NA
g.	Low per-unit costs	0	1	2	3	4	NA
h.	Patents, licences, or other proprietary knowledge . . .	0	1	2	3	4	NA
i.	Trademarks or reputation of parent firms	0	1	2	3	4	NA

j. Rapid market entry . . . . 0 1 2 3 4   NA
k. Low price to customers . . . . 0 1 2 3 4   NA
l. Full line of products or services . . . . 0 1 2 3 4   NA
m. Sales to government . . . . 0 1 2 3 4   NA
n. Perceived local or national identity of venture . . . . 0 1 2 3 4   NA
o. Marketing or distribution systems . . . . 0 1 2 3 4   NA
p. Post-sales customer service network . . . . 0 1 2 3 4   NA

When the venture was formed, how much uncertainty was associated with each of
the following? (If a factor was not relevant, mark NA)   no   great
                                                           uncertainty   uncertainty
a. Product design . . . . 0 1 2 3 4   NA
b. Production skills and equipment . . . . 0 1 2 3 4   NA
c. Sourcing and costs of raw materials & components . . . 0 1 2 3 4   NA
d. Marketing and distribution policies . . . . 0 1 2 3 4   NA
e. Pricing of products . . . . 0 1 2 3 4   NA
f. Overall changes in the venture's operating environment. 0 1 2 3 4   NA
g. Level of demand for the venture's products/services . . 0 1 2 3 4   NA
h. Government regulations or nationalistic pressures . . . 0 1 2 3 4   NA

At the time the venture was being formed, how strong was your firm's
competitive position relative to your principal rivals along the following
dimensions? (If a factor was not relevant, mark NA)   minimal   strong
                                                            influence   influence
a. Government pressures, regulatory requirements, etc. . . 0 1 2 3 4   NA
b. Access to financial resources . . . . 0 1 2 3 4   NA
c. Government subsidies, tax credits, & other inducements. 0 1 2 3 4   NA
d. Experienced managerial personnel . . . . 0 1 2 3 4   NA
e. Technically skilled employees . . . . 0 1 2 3 4   NA
f. Location of joint venture facilities . . . . 0 1 2 3 4   NA
g. Low per-unit costs . . . . 0 1 2 3 4   NA
h. Patents, licences, or other proprietary knowledge . . . 0 1 2 3 4   NA
i. Trademarks or reputation of parent firms . . . . 0 1 2 3 4   NA
j. Rapid market entry . . . . 0 1 2 3 4   NA
k. Low price to customers . . . . 0 1 2 3 4   NA
l. Full line of products or services . . . . 0 1 2 3 4   NA
m. Sales to government . . . . 0 1 2 3 4   NA
n. Perceived local or national identity of venture . . . . 0 1 2 3 4   NA
o. Marketing or distribution systems . . . . 0 1 2 3 4   NA
p. Post-sales customer service network . . . . 0 1 2 3 4   NA

At the time it was formed, which of the following activities were expected to
be engaged in by the joint venture? (Please check all categories that apply.)

____ 1. Mining or other extractive activities

____ 2. Basic, non-applied research

____ 3. Applied research and development

____ 4. Manufacturing of components, or raw materials refining or processing

____ 5. Assembly of finished goods

____ 6. Marketing

____ 7. Distribution

____ 8. Post-sales service

As evaluated at the time the venture was formed, how difficult would it have
been to achieve a viable competitive position on the following factors solely
through internal efforts of your firm? (If a factor was not relevant, mark NA)

		minimal influence		strong influence		
a.	Government pressures, regulatory requirements, etc.	0	1	2	3 4	NA
b.	Access to financial resources	0	1	2	3 4	NA
c.	Government subsidies, tax credits, & other inducements.	0	1	2	3 4	NA
d.	Experienced managerial personnel	0	1	2	3 4	NA
e.	Technically skilled employees	0	1	2	3 4	NA
f.	Location of joint venture facilities	0	1	2	3 4	NA
g.	Low per-unit costs	0	1	2	3 4	NA
h.	Patents, licences, or other proprietary knowledge	0	1	2	3 4	NA
i.	Trademarks or reputation of parent firms	0	1	2	3 4	NA
j.	Rapid market entry	0	1	2	3 4	NA
k.	Low price to customers	0	1	2	3 4	NA
l.	Full line of products or services	0	1	2	3 4	NA
m.	Sales to government	0	1	2	3 4	NA
n.	Perceived local or national identity of venture	0	1	2	3 4	NA
o.	Marketing or distribution systems	0	1	2	3 4	NA
p.	Post-sales customer service network	0	1	2	3 4	NA

In forming this joint venture, how much importance did your company place on
selecting a partner with the following skills or characteristics?

		not important		very important		
a.	Enables venture to qualify for subsidies or credits	0	1	2	3 4	NA
b.	Can provide low cost labor to the venture	0	1	2	3 4	NA
c.	Helps comply with government requirements/pressure	0	1	2	3 4	NA
d.	Has access to raw materials or components	0	1	2	3 4	NA
e.	Will provide financing/capital to venture	0	1	2	3 4	NA
f.	Can supply technically-skilled personnel	0	1	2	3 4	NA
g.	Can supply general managers to the venture	0	1	2	3 4	NA
h.	Is close to your firm, geographically	0	1	2	3 4	NA
i.	Possesses needed licences, patents, know-how, etc.	0	1	2	3 4	NA
j.	Controls favorable location (e.g., for manufacturing)	0	1	2	3 4	NA
k.	Possesses needed manufacturing or R&D facilities	0	1	2	3 4	NA
l.	Has access to marketing or distribution systems	0	1	2	3 4	NA
m.	Has access to post-sales service network	0	1	2	3 4	NA
n.	Has valuable trademark or reputation	0	1	2	3 4	NA
o.	Enhances perceived local or national identity	0	1	2	3 4	NA

When you were selecting a partner, what assignment of responsibility for the
following activities did your company seek?(If factor was not relevant, mark
NA)

		you control		share control		partner controls		
a.	Design of product or service	2	1	0	1	2	NA
b.	Sourcing of raw materials or components	2	1	0	1	2	NA
c.	Determining manufacturing technology & set-up	2	1	0	1	2	NA
d.	Hiring and firing joint venture managers	2	1	0	1	2	NA
e.	Setting prices and sales targets	2	1	0	1	2	NA
f.	Overseeing costs and quality control	2	1	0	1	2	NA
g.	Authorizing major capital expenditures for venture	2	1	0	1	2	NA
h.	Determining marketing & distribution policies	2	1	0	1	2	NA
i.	Day-to-day management of the joint venture	2	1	0	1	2	NA

In forming this joint venture, how much importance did your company place on
selecting a partner with the following skills or characteristics?

		not important			very important		
a.	Seems to have a strong commitment to the venture . . .	0	1	2	3	4	NA
b.	Top management of both firms are compatible	0	1	2	3	4	NA
c.	Will enable the venture to produce at lowest cost . . .	0	1	2	3	4	NA
d.	Permits faster entry into the target market	0	1	2	3	4	NA
e.	Has knowledge of target market's economy & customs . .	0	1	2	3	4	NA
f.	Can enhance the venture's export opportunities	0	1	2	3	4	NA
g.	Provides better access for your company's products . .	0	1	2	3	4	NA
h.	Has similar national or corporate culture	0	1	2	3	4	NA
i.	Is similar in size or corporate structure	0	1	2	3	4	NA
j.	Has had satisfactory prior association with your firm .	0	1	2	3	4	NA
k.	Enhances venture's ability to make sales to government.	0	1	2	3	4	NA
l.	Has related products, helps fill JV's product line . .	0	1	2	3	4	NA

**** Thank you. Please use the back of this page for any additional ****
**** comments. Mail completed questionnaire to address below.   ****

Statistical Methods Employed in Analysis

VARIABLE LABELS

To facilitate analysis and interpretation of data, a system of consistent variable labels was employed when coding the data. For each variable, a one- to three- character prefix was used for each of the corresponding variable categories. For instance, each of the 27 partner selection criteria categories had a prefix of "PSC." The use of consistent variable labels thus enhanced identification and interpretation of the output from the statistical analyses. The prefixes used for each variable are listed below:

PREFIX	VARIABLE
PSC	Partner selection criteria
CSF	Critical success factor
CP	Competitive position
DD	Difficulty of internal development
UN	Perceived task environment uncertainty
F	Diversity of line functions
SC	Extent of shared control

To facilitate ease of interpretation even further, a system of common labels was used with the above prefixes to identify individual variable categories. These common labels followed their respective prefixes to identify the specific variable category being referred to. For instance, the label "EES" referred to "technically skilled employees." Therefore, PSCEES referred to the partner selection criteria category of "the importance of selecting a partner with technically skilled employees," whereas CSFEES referred to the critical success factor category of "the importance to the joint venture's performance of having technically skilled employees." Corresponding variable labels and definitions were applicable for CPEES and DDEES.

Tables listing the variable labels and associated definitions for each variable category are included in Chapters 5 through 11.

STATISTICAL TECHNIQUES UTILIZED IN DATA ANALYSIS

All statistical analysis was conducted using Version 2 of the SPSS-X statistical package.[1] The general procedures that were employed included frequencies, cross tabulations (bivariate correlations), partial correlations, and factor analysis.

Descriptive Statistics

Descriptive statistics for the research variable categories, including statistical means, standard deviations, and frequencies, were calculated using the FREQUENCIES procedure in SPSS-X. Except for instances in which responses were recoded, only integer values of 0 to 4 were included in the statistical computations; "not applicable," or NA, responses were coded as missing values and were thereby excluded from these calculations.

The following descriptive statistics were calculated for each of the variable categories by the FREQUENCIES procedure: mean, standard error of the mean, median, mode, standard deviation, variance, skewness, standard error of the skewness statistic, kurtosis, standard error of the kurtosis statistic, range, minimum and maximum observed values, and frequency. Histograms were also plotted. However, due to the large number of variables and corresponding statistics, only the mean, standard deviation, and frequency are generally reported in Chapters 5 through 11. The other statistics and plots were examined for each variable in order to screen for unusual characteristics or noncompliance with the requirements for other statistical techniques. Significant deviations are addressed, where appropriate, in Chapters 5 through 11.

Bivariate Correlations

Testing of the research hypotheses required the computation of bivariate correlations between the appropriate variable categories. These correlations were calculated using the CROSSTABS procedure in SPSS-X. Except for the instances in which responses were recoded, only integer values of 0 to 4 were included in the statistical calculations; "not applicable," or NA, responses were coded as missing values and were thus excluded from the correlational computations.

The CROSSTABS procedure is capable of providing a broad range of descriptive statistics and measures of association. The data for all of the variables were ordinal, except for the nominally measured diversity of line functions variable. Therefore, the appropriate measure of association available from the CROSSTABS procedure included Kendall's tau-a, tau-b, and tau-c statistics; Goodman and Kruskal's gamma; and Somer's d. The relatively large number of tie values likely to occur in the correlation analyses meant the tau-a statistic was not appropriate. Of the remaining statistics, tau-b, gamma, and Somer's d are all commonly used and accepted measures of association for ordinal data, and all are similar in their derivation. However, the analysis was going to include the exploratory use of factor analytic techniques, which technically require interval-level data as input. In many respects, the Kendall tau-b statistic is an ordinal variable analog of the Pearson r-square statistic used widely with tests involving interval-level data.[2] Therefore, the tau-b statistic was chosen as the preferred measure of association for testing this study's research hypotheses, and it is the statistic used in Chapters 5 through 11 when reporting the statistical significance of the one-tailed tests of the correlations.

Partial Correlations

The presence of moderate intercorrelation between task-related and/or partner-related variable categories had the potential for confounding efforts to use bivariate correlations effectively to test the research hypotheses associated with the individual variables, thus constituting a threat to construct validity. To the extent that moderate intercorrelation existed, it would be difficult for the researcher to discern the relationship between a particular pair of variables because of the possible effects of other moderately correlated variables.

This potentially troublesome situation arose in the current study. As suggested by J. P. Guilford,[3] a rough guide for assessing the magnitude of a correlation might be as follows:

< .20	Slight; almost negligible relationship
.20–.40	Low correlation; definite but small relationship
.40–.70	Moderate correlation; substantial relationship
.70–.90	High correlation; marked relationship

> .90   Very high correlation; very
                                                              dependable relationship

Using the above as a rough guideline, it was apparent from a correlation matrix of the research data that a substantial number of moderate intercorrelations occurred between categories of the task-related and between the partner-related research variables. For categories of an individual variable, the potential problems of moderate intercorrelations between the categories were eased by factor analysis, which enhanced convergent and discriminant validity by identifying the orthogonal dimensions underlying the individual variables' categories.

However, because of the existence of moderate intercorrelations between categories of different task-related and partner-related variables, enhancement of construct validity necessitated examination of the partial correlation coefficients for these categories. The use of partial correlation coefficients enabled us to test the research hypotheses because it permitted the relationship between individual task-related or partner-related categories and the relevant partner selection criteria categories to be determined when correcting for the effects of other moderately correlated task-related or partner-related categories.

The partial correlation coefficients were obtained via the PARTIAL CORR procedure in SPSS-X. However, it was not possible to obtain partial correlation coefficients based on the Kendall tau-b statistic used in the bivariate correlations. Instead it was necessary to use partial correlation coefficients based on the Pearson r statistic. Although the use of the Pearson r-based partial correlation coefficients would potentially introduce some differences into the results that were obtained, owing to method variance, this effect was unavoidable if the use of partial correlation analysis was desired.

Factor Analysis

Because of the limited prior literature involving the research variables and because of the potential conceptual and statistical overlap of the variable categories that were used, factor analysis was performed on several of the variables. Factor analysis is a statistical technique used to identify a relatively small number of factors that can be used to represent relationships among sets of many interrelated variables. Factor analysis enhances the convergent validity of the results, helping to identify the underlying, not directly observable, constructs that may characterize a set of variables or variable categories.

A potential limitation to the employment of factor analytical techniques on this study's data was that these techniques technically require interval- or ratio-level data as input, whereas the data obtained from the questionnaire were only ordinal or nominal level. However, although the Likert-type response categories used to measure the variables were technically ordinal, we appraised them as sufficiently approximating interval-level data to warrant exploratory use of factor analysis on the data produced by them. The decision to make such an appraisal, and thus to use interval-approximating ordinal level data as input for factor analysis, has been previously supported by the work of several eminent researchers.[4] Given that certain assumptions are satisfied regarding the statistical characteristics of the data, these authors have maintained that such applications may often be legitimately undertaken when conducting statistical analyses. The principal caveat is that the researcher may need to exercise a degree of caution when interpreting the results.

As mentioned, the data used for input should embody certain characteristics in order for the exploratory use of factor analytic methods to be justified. These characteristics, including normality of distributions, linearity of relationships, and homoscedasticity, appeared to have been satisfactorily met by the data obtained from the sample firms for each of the variables except the extent of shared control. Therefore, employment of factor analysis was deemed to be justified for these variables. The data for the extent of shared control variable deviated significantly from the above requirement; therefore, no factor analysis was conducted on this variable.

Factor analysis was performed using the FACTOR procedure in SPSS-X. Cases with missing values (i.e., NA responses) on one or more of the categories of the variable being analyzed were deleted in a list-wise manner, which is the default value of SPSS-X. List-wise treatment of missing values, although reducing the sample size available for the factor analysis, tends to produce more consistency in results than any of the other available options, such as pair-wise treatment of missing values.

Factors were extracted via the principal components analysis technique, which transforms a set of correlated variables into a set of uncorrelated variables, or principal components. The principal components are linear combinations of the observed variables.

Varimax rotation of initial factors, using Kaiser normalization in rotating, was employed to obtain uncorrelated orthogonal factors as final output. The varimax method of factor rotation is designed to minimize the number of variables loading highly on each factor, thus enhancing the interpretability of the factors that are obtained. The orthogonality of the factors thus obtained enhances the discriminant validity of the results.

To enhance confidence in the outcomes that were obtained, efforts were undertaken to evaluate the effect of variations in the method of factor rotation. For each of the variables that were factor analyzed via the varimax method of rotation, oblique rotations of the factors were also attempted. In contrast to the factors resulting from varimax rotation, the axes resulting from oblique rotations may not be maintained at right angles to each other.

Therefore, there can be correlations among the factors obtained from oblique factor rotations. These oblique factors are often capable of yielding substantively meaningful factors, thereby enhancing factor interpretation and researcher confidence in results obtained via the varimax method of rotation. Oblique rotation of factors was successful only for the data on the competitive position, difficulty of internal development, and perceived task environment uncertainty variables. However, the factor results obtained for these three variables suggested that variations in the choice of the factor rotation method had only minor influences on the outcomes obtained for the research data. This finding enhanced the researcher's confidence in the statistical reliability and validity of the conclusions obtained by the list-wise, Kaiser, and varimax options previously discussed.

Only rotated factors with eigenvalues greater than 1.0 were interpreted in Chapters 5 through 11. The eigenvalues, the total percentage of variance explained by each factor, and the cumulative percentage of variance explained by the rotated factors, are reported for each successful factor rotation. In interpreting the individual rotated factors, only the variable categories with factor loadings of 0.30 or greater were viewed as important, consistent with the work of Jae-On Kim and Charles W. Mueller.[5]

For bivariate correlations of variable factors, the factor scores were preserved via the SAVE subcommand of the FACTOR procedure SPSS-X. Because the factors were obtained via the principal components method of extraction, the factor scores that were obtained and saved were exact, rather than estimated, values. These saved factor scores were thus able to function as unique "new" variables which could then be used as input for additional computations, such as the CROSSTABS procedure.

RECODED SAMPLE

Because of the relatively large number of NA, or not applicable, responses on several of the variable categories, the resulting sample sizes were inadequate for performing certain statistical tests. However, based on comments made in the interviews and on analysis of the questionnaire, it was apparent that the NA responses could be recoded to meaningful integer values without significant distortion of the data. This recoding permitted certain statistical tests, especially factor analyses, to be conducted with greater confidence, and the results provided a basis for evaluating the statistical reliability from the original, unrecoded data sample.

In recoding variable categories, it was important to identify correctly to which integer an NA response corresponded. The following subsections discuss the values to which each NA response was recoded.

Partner Selection Criteria

An NA response on a partner selection criteria category was recoded to a "0" value for the recoded sample. The rationale for this recoding is as follows: A response suggesting that a particular criterion was not applicable is approximately the same as stating that the particular criterion had no importance in the selection decision, or a value of zero.

Critical Success Factor

An NA response on a critical success factor category was recoded to a "0" value for the recoded sample. The rationale for this recoding is as follows: A response suggesting that a particular critical success factor category was not applicable is approximately the same as stating that the particular critical success factor category had no importance, or a value of zero.

Competitive Position

An NA response on a competitive position category was recoded as a "2" for the recoded sample. The rationale for this recoding is as follows: A response suggesting that a firm's competitive position on a particular dimension was not applicable may be interpreted as stating that the firm's competitive position on that criterion was approximately the same (neither worse, nor better) as its competitors, or a value of two.

Difficulty of Internal Development

An NA response on a difficulty of internal development category was recoded as a "0" for the recoded sample. The rationale for this recoding is as follows: If a particular category is not applicable for a firm, then management would anticipate minimal difficulty in intraorganizational efforts to attain a viable competitive position on that dimension. Thus, a value of zero seems appropriate when recoding an NA response on this variable.

Perceived Task Environment Uncertainty

An NA response on a perceived task environment uncertainty category was recoded as a "0" for the recoding sample. The rationale for this recoding is as follows: If a particular dimension of potential task environment uncertainty is not applicable for a firm, then there is minimal perceived uncertainty on that dimension, and it should be recoded as a zero.

Diversity of Line Functions

There were no NA responses for this variable, so no recoding was necessary.

Extent of Shared Control

An NA response on an extent of shared control category was recoded as a "2" for the recoded sample. The rationale for this recoding is as follows: If a particular activity is not applicable for the joint venture, then neither partner controls it. Therefore, it would be coded as a two, to signify shared control over the activity.

NOTES

1. See Marija J. Norusis, *SPSS-X Advanced Statistics Guide* (New York: McGraw-Hill, 1985); Marija J. Norusis, *SPSS-X Introductory Statistics Guide* (New York: McGraw-Hill, 1985), and *SPSS-X User's Guide*, 2nd edition (New York: McGraw-Hill, 1986).

2. David K. Hildebrand, James D. Laing, and Howard Rosenthal, *Analysis of Ordinal Data* (Beverly Hills, Calif.: Sage, 1977), p. 16.

3. J. P. Guilford, *Fundamental Statistics in Psychology and Education* (New York: McGraw-Hill, 1956).

4. For example, see Jum C. Nunnally, *Psychometric Theory*, 2nd edition (New York: McGraw-Hill, 1978).

5. Jae-On Kim and Charles W. Mueller, *Introduction to Factor Analysis* (Beverly Hills, Calif.: Sage, 1978).

Bibliography

Adams, Walter. "Comment." *Journal of Economic Issues* (June, 1975): 341–42.

Adler, Lee, and James D. Hlavacek. *Joint Ventures for Product Innovation*. New York: American Management Association, 1976.

Aharoni, Yair. *The Foreign Investment Decision Process*. Boston: Harvard University Press, 1966.

Aiken, Michael, and Jerald Hage. "Organizational Interdependence and Intra-Organizational Structure." *American Sociological Review* (December, 1968): 912–30.

Alchian, A.A., and H. Demsetz. "Production, Information Costs, and Economic Organization." *American Economic Review* (December, 1972): 777–95.

Aldrich, Howard. *Organizations and Environments*. Englewood Cliffs, N.J.: Prentice-Hall, 1979.

Aldrich, Howard, and Diane Herker. "Boundary Spanning Roles and Organization and Structure." *Academy of Management Review* (April, 1977): 217–30.

Allison, Graham T. *Essence of Decision*. Boston: Little, Brown, 1971.

Alwin, Duane F. "Making Errors in Surveys." *Sociological Methods and Research*. November, 1977: 131–50.

Anderson, Carl R., and Frank T. Paine. "Managerial Perceptions and Strategic Behavior." *Academy of Management Journal* (December, 1975): 811–23.

Andrews, Kenneth. *The Concept of Corporate Strategy*. Homewood, Ill.: Richard D. Irwin, 1971.

"Are Foreign Partners Good for U.S. Companies?" *Business Week* (May 28, 1984): 58–60.

Arrow, Kenneth J. *The Limits of Organization*. New York: Norton, 1974.

Bachman, Jules. "Joint Ventures and the Antitrust Laws." *New York University Law Review*. 40 (1965): 651–71.

———. "Joint Ventures in the Light of Recent Antitrust Developments: Joint Ventures in the Chemical Industry." *Antitrust Bulletin* 10 (January-April, 1965):7–23.

Ballon, R. J., ed. *Joint Ventures and Japan*. Tokyo: Sophia University, 1967.

Beamish, Paul W. "The Characteristics of Joint Ventures in Developed and Developing Countries." *Columbia Journal of World Business* (Fall, 1985): 13–19.

———. "Joint Venture Performance in Developing Countries." Ph.D. diss. University of Western Ontario, October, 1984.

———. *Multinational Joint Ventures in Developing Countries*. London: Croom Helm, 1988.

Beamish, Paul W., and Henry W. Lane, "Need Commitment and the Performance of Joint Ventures in Developing Countries." Working Paper, University of Western Ontario, July, 1982.

Bennis, Warren G. *Changing Organizations*. New York: McGraw-Hill, 1966.

Berg, Sanford V., and Philip Friedman. "Corporate Courtship and Successful Joint Ventures." *California Management Review* (Spring, 1980): 35–51.

Berg, Sanford V., Jerome Duncan, and Philip Friedman. *Joint Venture Strategies and Corporate Innovation*. Cambridge, Mass.: Oelgeschalager, Gunn & Hain, 1982.

Berghoff, John C. "Antitrust Aspects of Joint Ventures." *Antitrust Bulletin* 9, no. 2 (March-April, 1964): 231–54.

Bergman, Michael. "The Corporate Joint Venture under the Antitrust Laws." *New York University Law Review* 37 (1962): 711.

Berlew, F. Kingston. "The Joint Venture—A Way into Foreign Markets." *Harvard Business Review* (July-August, 1984): 48–54.

Bernstein, Lewis. "Joint Ventures in the Light of Recent Antitrust Developments: Anti-Competitive Joint Ventures." *Antitrust Bulletin* 10 (January-April, 1965): 25–29.

Beyer, Janice M. "Ideologies, Values, and Decision Making in Organizations." In *Handbook of Organizational Design*, edited by Paul C. Nystrom and William H. Starbuck vol. 2, (New York: Oxford University Press, 1981), pp. 166–202.

Birnbaum, Philip H. "The Choice of Strategic Alternatives under Increasing Regulation in High Technology Companies." *Academy of Management Journal* 27, no. 3 (1984): 489–510.

Bivens, K. K., and E. B. Lovell. *Joint Ventures with Foreign Partners*. New York: National Industrial Conference Board, 1966.

Blalock, Hubert M., Jr. *Social Statistics*. 2d ed., rev. New York: McGraw-Hill, 1979.

Boulding, Kenneth. "General Systems Theory—The Skeleton of a Science." *Management Science* 2 (1956): 197–208.

Bower, Joseph L. *Managing the Resource Allocation Process*. Boston: Division of Research, Harvard Business School, 1970.

Boyle, Stanley. "An Estimate of the Number and Size Distribution of Domestic Joint Subsidiaries." *Antitrust Law and Economic Review* (Spring, 1968): 81–92.

———. "The Joint Subsidiary: An Economic Appraisal." *Antitrust Bulletin* (May-June, 1960): 303–18.

Brodley, Joseph F. "Joint Ventures and the Justice Department's Antitrust Guide for International Operations." *Antitrust Bulletin* 24 (Summer, 1979): 337–56.

———. "Joint-Venture Marriages." *Across the Board* (January, 1984): 18–22.

———. "The Legal Status of Joint Ventures under the Antitrust Laws: A Summary Assessment." *Antitrust Bulletin* 21, no. 3 (Fall, 1976): 453–83.

Burns, Thomas, and Gerald M. Stalker. *The Management of Innovation*. London: Tavistock, 1961.

Burton, F. N., and F. H. Saelens. "Partner Choice and Linkage Characteristics of International Joint Ventures in Japan: An Exploratory Analysis of the Inorganic Chemicals Sector." *Management International Review* 22, no. 2 (1982): 20–29.

Business International. *European Business Strategies in the United States: Meeting the Challenges of the World's Largest Market*. Geneva: Business International S.A., 1971.

———. *Ownership Policies at Work Abroad*. New York: Business International, 1965.

———. *Pros and Cons of Joint Ventures Abroad*. New York: Business International, 1964.

———. *Recent Opportunities in Establishing Joint Ventures*. New York: Business International, 1972.

Caves, Richard E. "Uncertainty, Market Structure and Performance: Galbraith as Conventional Wisdom." In *Industrial Organization and Economic Development*, edited by J. W. Markham and G. F. Papanek (Boston: Houghton Mifflin, 1970), pp. 283–302.

Cheung, Steven. "Transaction Costs, Risk Aversion, and the Choice of Contractual Arrangements." *Journal of Law and Economics* (April, 1969): 23–42.

Child, John. "Managerial and Organizational Factors Associated with Company Performance." *Journal of Management Studies* 11, pt. 1 (1974): 175–89.

———. "Organizational Structure, Environment and Performance: The Role of Strategic Choice." *Sociology* (January, 1972): 1–22.

Clapp, Andrew D., ed. *The Yearbook on Corporate Mergers, Joint Ventures and Corporate Policy*. Boston: Cambridge Corporation, annual, 1979 to 1984.

Coase, R. H. "The Nature of the Firm." *Economica* (1937): 386–405.

Cohen, M. D., J. G. March, and J. P. Olson, "A Garbage Can Model of Organizational Choice." *Administrative Science Quarterly* 17 (1972): 1–25.

Comstock, D., and W. Scott. "Technology and the Structure of Subunits." *Administrative Science Quarterly* 22 (1977): 177–202.

Connolly, Seamus G. "Joint Ventures with Third World Multinationals: A New Form of Entry into International Markets." *Columbia Journal of World Business* (Summer, 1984): 18–22.

Curhan, Joan P., William H. Davidson, and Rajan Suri. *Tracing the Multinationals*. Cambridge, Mass: Ballinger, 1977.

Cyert, R. M., and J. G. March. *A Behavioral Theory of the Firm*. Englewood Cliffs, N.J.: Prentice-Hall, 1963.

Daft, Richard L. *Organization Theory and Design*. St. Paul, Minn.: West Publishing, 1983.

Daft, Richard L., and Karl E. Weick. "Toward a Model of Organizations as Interpretive Systems." *Academy of Management Review* (1984): 284–95.

Daniel, W. W. "Nonresponse in Sociological Surveys: A Review of Some Methods for Handling the Problem." *Sociological Methods and Research* (February, 1975): 291–307.

Daniels, John D. *Recent Foreign Direct Manufacturing Investment in the United States*. New York: Praeger, 1971.

Daniels, John D., Ernest W. Ogram, Jr., and Lee H. Radebaugh. *International*

Business: Environments and Operations. 3d ed. Reading, Mass: Addison-Wesley, 1983.

Davidson, William H. "Participation Policies." In *Global Strategic Management*, edited by William H. Davidson (New York: John Wiley, 1982), pp. 23–84.

Day, George S. *Strategic Market Planning: The Pursuit of Competitive Advantage.* St. Paul, Minn.: West Publishing, 1984.

de Houghton, Charles. *Cross-Channel Collaboration.* London: PEP, 1966.

Dillman, Don A. *Mail and Telephone Surveys.* New York: John Wiley, 1978.

Directory of Corporate Affiliations 1985. Wilmette, Ill.: National Register Publishing Co., 1985.

Dixon, Paul Rand. "Joint Ventures: What Is Their Impact on Competition?" *Antitrust Bulletin* 7, no. 3 (May-June, 1962): 397–410.

Downey, H. Kirk, Don Hellriegel, and John W. Slocum, Jr. "Environmental Uncertainty: The Construct and Its Application." *Administrative Science Quarterly* (December, 1975): 613–29.

Dun and Bradstreet, Inc. *Million Dollar Directory 1984.* Parsippany, N.J.: Dun and Bradstreet, 1984.

Duncan, Jerome L., Jr. "The Causes and Effects of Domestic Joint Venture Activity." Ph.D. diss., University of Florida, 1980.

Duncan, Robert B. "Characteristics of Organizational Environments and Perceived Environmental Uncertainty." *Administrative Science Quarterly* (1972): 313–27.

———. "Modifications in Decision Structure in Adapting to the Environment: Some Implications for Organizational Learning." *Decision Sciences* 5, no. 4 (1974): 122–42.

———. "Multiple Decision-Making Structures in Adapting to Environmental Uncertainty: The Impact on Organizational Effectiveness." *Human Relations* (1975): 273–91.

Edwards, W. "Behavioral Decision Theory." *Annual Review of Psychology* (1961): 473–98.

Emery, F. E., and Eric Trist. "The Causal Texture of Organizational Environments." *Human Relations* 18 (1965): 21–31.

Emory, C. William. *Business Research Methods.* Homewood, Ill.: Irwin, 1980.

Export-Import Bank of Japan. *International Cooperation for Plant Construction Overseas.* Tokyo: EXIM Bank of Japan, 1983.

Flick, Sol E. "The Human Side of Overseas Joint Ventures." *Management Review* (January, 1972): 29–42.

Fowler, Floyd J., Jr. *Survey Research Methods.* Beverly Hills, Calif.: Sage, 1984.

Franko, Lawrence G. "The Art of Choosing an American Joint Venture Partner." In *The Multinational Company in Europe: Some Key Problems,* edited by Michael Z. Brooke and H. Lee Remmers (London: Longman Group Ltd., 1972), pp. 65–76.

———. *The European Multinationals.* London: Harper & Row, 1976.

———. *Joint Venture Survival in Multinational Corporations.* New York: Praeger, 1971.

———. "Strategy Choice and Multinational Corporate Tolerance for Joint Ventures with Foreign Partners." Ph.D. diss., Harvard University, 1969.

Friedmann, Wolfgang G., and George Kalmanoff. *Joint International Business Ventures.* New York: Columbia University Press, 1961.

Fusfield, Daniel R. "Joint Subsidiaries in the Iron and Steel Industry." *American Economic Review* (May, 1958): 578–87.

Galbraith, Jay. *Designing Complex Organizations*. Reading, Mass.: Addison-Wesley, 1973.

Guilford, J. P. *Fundamental Statistics in Psychology and Education*. New York: McGraw-Hill, 1956.

Guion, Robert M. "Choosing Members for Organization." In *Handbook of Organizational Design*, edited by Paul C. Nystrom and William H. Starbuck, vol. 2 (New York: Oxford University Press, 1981), pp. 358–81.

Gullander, Steffan. "Joint Ventures and Corporate Strategy." *Columbia Journal of World Business* (Spring, 1976): 104–14.

———. "Joint Ventures in Europe—Determinants of Entry." *International Studies of Management and Organization*. (Spring-Summer 1976): 85–111.

Hall, R. Duane. *The International Joint Venture*. New York: Praeger, 1984.

Hambrick, Donald C. "Operationalizing the Concept of Business-Level Strategy in Research." *Academy of Management Review* 5, no. 4 (1980): 567–75.

Harrigan, Kathryn Rudie. "Coalition Strategies: A Framework for Joint Ventures." Working paper, Columbia University, 1984a.

———. "Integrating Parent and Child: Successful Joint Ventures." Working paper, Columbia University, 1984b.

———. "Joint Ventures and Global Strategies." *Columbia Journal of World Business* 19, no. 2 (Summer, 1984c): 7–16.

———. "Multinational Corporate Strategy: Editor's Introduction." *Columbia Journal of World Business* 19, no. 2 (Summer, 1984d): 2–6.

———. *Strategies for Joint Ventures*. Lexington, Mass: Lexington Books, 1985.

———. Strategies for Vertical Integration. Lexington, Mass: Lexington Books, 1983.

Hays, William L. *Statistics*. 3d ed. New York: Holt, Rinehart & Winston, 1981.

Hildebrand, David K., James D. Laing, and Howard Rosenthal. *Analysis of Ordinal Data*. Beverly Hills, Calif.: Sage, 1977.

Hills, Stephen M. "The Search for Joint Venture Partners." In *Academy of Management Proceedings*, edited by Jeffrey C. Susbauer. San Francisco: Academy of Management (1978), pp. 277–81.

Hlavacek, James D., and Victor A. Thompson. "The Joint-Venture Approach to Technology Utilization." *IEEE Transactions on Engineering Management* (1976): 35–41.

Hlavacek, James D., Brian Dovey, and John Biondo. "Tie Small Business Technology to Marketing Power." *Harvard Business Review* (January-February, 1977): 106–16.

Hochmuth, Milton S. "The Effect of Structure on Strategy: The Government Sponsored Multinational Joint Venture." Ph.D. diss., Harvard University, 1972.

Hofer, Charles W., and Dan Schendel. *Strategy Formulation: Analytical Concepts*. St. Paul, Minn.: West Publishing, 1978.

Holton, Richard H. "Making International Joint Ventures Work." In *The Management of Headquarters-Subsidiary Relationships in Multinational Corporations*, edited by Lars Otterbeck (Hampshire, England: Gower, 1981), pp. 255–67.

Hood, Neil, and Stephen Young. *The Economics of Multinational Enterprise*. New York: Longman, 1979.

Hrebiniak, Lawrence G. *Complex Organizations*. St. Paul, Minn.: West Publishing, 1978.

Ito, Jack K., and Richard B. Peterson. "Effects of Task Difficulty and Interunit Interdependence on Information Processing Systems." *Academy of Management Journal* (March, 1986): 139–48.

Jackson, John H., and Cyril P. Morgan. *Organization Theory: A Macro Perspective for Management*. Englewood Cliffs, N.J.: Prentice-Hall, 1978.

Janger, Allen R. *Organization of International Joint Ventures*. New York: The Conference Board, 1980.

Javidan, Mansour. "The Impact of Environmental Uncertainty on Long-Range Planning Practices of the U.S. Savings and Loan Industry." *Strategic Management Journal* 5 (1984): 381–92.

Katz, D., and R. L. Kahn. *The Social Psychology of Organizations*. New York: John Wiley, 1966.

Kent, David H., and Don Hellriegel. "Coalitional Stability: A Comparative and Longitudinal Study of Two Joint Ventures." Working Paper, Texas A&M University, 1985.

Kerlinger, Fred N. *Foundations of Behavioral Research*. 2d ed. New York: Holt, Rinehart & Winston, 1973.

Killing, J. Peter. "How to Make a Global Joint Venture Work." *Harvard Business Review* (May-June, 1982): 120–127.

———. *Strategies for Joint Venture Success*. New York: Praeger, 1983.

Kim, Jae-On, and Charles W. Mueller. *Introduction to Factor Analysis*. Beverly Hills, Calif.: Sage, 1978.

Kobayashi, Yotaro. *Expectations and Counter-Expectations in Joint Ventures in Japan*. Bulletin no. 52. Tokyo: Sophia University Socio-Economic Institute, 1973.

Kobrin, Stephen J. *Managing Political Risk Assessment*. Berkeley, Calif.: University of California Press, 1982.

Landes, William M. "Harm to Competition: Cartels, Mergers and Joint Ventures." *Antitrust Bulletin* (Summer, 1983): 625–35.

La Palombara, Joseph, and Stephen Blank. *Multinational Corporations and National Elites: A Study in Tensions*. New York: The Conference Board, 1977.

Lasserre, Philippe. "Selecting a Foreign Partner for Technology Transfer." *Long Range Planning*. (December, 1984): 43–49.

Lasserre, Philippe, and Max Boisot. "The Transfer of Technology from European to ASEAN Enterprises: Strategies and Practices in the Chemical and Pharmaceutical Sectors." Working paper, Euro-Asia Center, INSEAD, Fontainebleau, France, 1980.

Lawrence, Paul, and Jay W. Lorsch. *Organization and Environment*. Boston: Graduate School of Business Administration, Harvard University, 1967.

Leff, Nathaniel H. "Strategic Planning in an Uncertain World." *Journal of Business Strategy* (Spring, 1984): 78–80.

Leidecker, Joel K., and Albert V. Bruno. "Identifying and Using Critical Success Factors." *Long Range Planning* 17, no. 1 (1984): 23–32.

Lewis, Edward E. *Methods of Statistical Analysis in Economics and Business*. 2d ed. Boston: Houghton Mifflin, 1963.

McCaskey, Michael B. "Tolerance for Ambiguity and the Perception of Uncertainty in Organization Design." In *The Management of Organization Design: Research and Methodology,* edited by Ralph H. Kilman, Louis R. Pondy, and Dennis P. Selvin (New York: North-Holland, 1976), pp. 59–85.

"Making Joint Ventures Work." *Chemical Week* (August 17, 1983): 30–36.

March, James, and Herbert Simon. *Organizations.* New York: Wiley, 1958.

March, James G., and Johan P. Olsen. *Ambiguity and Choice in Organizations.* (Bergen, Norway: Universitesforlaget, 1976).

Mead, Walter J. "The Competitive Significance of Joint Ventures." *Antitrust Bulletin* 12 (Fall, 1967): 819–49.

Mergers and Acquisitions. Philadelphia: Information for Industry, quarterly, 1979–1986.

Michael, Donald N. *On Learning to Plan—And Planning to Learn.* San Francisco: Jossey-Bass, 1973.

Miles, Raymond E., and J. Pfeffer. "Organization and Environment: Concepts and Issues." *Industrial Relations* 13 (1974): 244–64.

Miles, Raymond E., and Charles C. Snow. *Organizational Strategy, Structure, and Process.* New York: McGraw-Hill, 1978.

Miller, R. *Innovations, Organization, and Environment.* Sherbrooke, England: University of Sherbrooke Press, 1971.

Mitchell, Terence R. "An Evaluation of the Validity of Correlational Research Conducted in Organizations." *Academy of Management Review* 10, no. 2 (1985): 192–205.

Mohr, L. "Organization Technology and Organization Structure." *Administrative Science Quarterly* 16 (1971): 444–59.

Moxon, Richard W., and J. Michael Geringer. "Multinational Ventures in the Commercial Aircraft Industry." *Columbia Journal of World Business* 20, no. 2 (Summer, 1985): 55–62.

Nachmias, David, and Chava Nachmias. *Research Methods in the Social Sciences.* New York: St. Martin's Press, 1976.

Newman, William. "Shaping the Master Strategy of Your Firm." *California Management Review* (Spring, 1967): 77–88.

Nishikawa, Koichiro. "Examples and Evaluation of International Cooperation in the Construction of Overseas Machinery and Plants." In *International Cooperation for Plant Construction Overseas.* Tokyo: Export-Import Bank of Japan, 1983, pp. 37–46.

Norusis, Marija J. *SPSS-X Advanced Statistics Guide.* New York: McGraw-Hill, 1985.

———. *SPSS-X Introductory Statistics Guide.* New York: McGraw-Hill, 1983.

Nunnally, Jum C. *Psychometric Theory.* 2d ed. New York: McGraw-Hill, 1978.

Osborn, Richard N., and James G. Hunt. "Environment and Organizational Effectiveness." *Administrative Science Quarterly* 19 (1974): 231–46.

Overton, P., R. Schneck, and C. Hazlett. "An Empirical Study of the Technology of Nursing Subunits." *Administrative Science Quarterly* 22 (1977): 203–19.

Pate, J. L. "Joint Venture Activity, 1960–1968." *Economic Review,* (Federal Reserve Bank of Cleveland, 1969): 16–23.

Pearce, John A., II, and Richard B. Robinson, Jr. *Strategic Management: Strategy Formulation and Implementation.* Homewood, Ill.: Irwin, 1982.

Pennings, Johannes M. "The Relevance of the Structural-Contingency Model for

Organizational Effectiveness." *Administrative Science Quarterly* 20 (1975): 393–410.

Peterson, Richard B., and Justin Y. Shimada. "Sources of Management Problems in Japanese-American Joint Ventures." *Academy of Management Review* (October, 1978): 796–804.

Pfeffer, Jeffrey. "Merger as a Response to Organizational Interdependence." *Administrative Science Quarterly* 17 (1972): 383–94.

———. "Patterns of Joint Venture Activity: Implications for Antitrust Research." *Antitrust Bulletin* (Summer 1976): 315–94.

Pfeffer, Jeffrey, and Phillip Nowack. "Joint Ventures and Interorganizational Interdependence." *Administrative Science Quarterly* (September, 1976): 398–418.

Pfeffer, Jeffrey, and G. R. Salancik. *The External Control of Organizations.* New York: Harper and Row, 1978.

Porter, Joseph H., and Robert J. Hamm. *Statistics: Applications for the Behavioral Sciences.* Monterey, Calif.: Brooks/Cole Publishing Co., 1986.

Porter, Michael E. *Competitive Advantage.* New York: Free Press, 1985.

———. *Competitive Strategy.* New York: Free Press, 1980.

Porter, Michael E., and Mark B. Fuller. "Coalitions and Global Strategy." In *Competition in Global Industries,* edited by Michael E. Porter (Boston: Harvard Business School Press, 1986), pp. 315–43.

Predicasts F&S Index of Corporate Change. Cleveland: Predicasts, Inc., 1979 through 1985. Annual.

Radway, Robert J. *Joint Ventures in Mexico.* New York: American Management Association, 1984.

Rafii, Farshad. "Joint Ventures and the Transfer of Technology: The Case of Iran." In *Technology Crossing Borders,* edited by Robert Stobaugh and Louis T. Wells, Jr. (Boston: Harvard Business School Press, 1984), pp. 203–37.

Rand Corporation. *A Million Random Digits with 100,000 Normal Deviates.* New York: Free Press of Glencoe, 1955.

Raveed, S. R., and W. Renforth. "State Enterprise–Multinational Corporation Joint Ventures: How Well Do They Meet Both Partners' Needs?" *Management International Review* 23, no. 1 (1983): 47–57.

Rees, D. G. *Essential Statistics.* New York: Chapman & Hall, 1985.

Renforth, William E. "A Comparative Study of Joint International Business Ventures with Family Firm or Non-Family Firm Partners: The Caribbean Community Experience." Ph.D. diss., Graduate School of Business, Indiana University, 1974.

Renforth, William E., and Sion Raveed. *A Comparative Study of Multinational Corporation Joint International Business Ventures with Family Firm or Non-Family Firm Partners.* New York: Arno Press, 1980.

Reynolds, John I. *Indian-American Joint Ventures: Business Policy Relationships.* Washington, D.C.: University Press of America, 1979.

Roberts, Edwards B. "New Ventures for Corporate Growth" *Harvard Business Review* (July-August, 1980): 134–42.

Robock, Stefan H., and Kenneth Simmonds. *International Business and Multinational Enterprises.* 3d ed. Homewood, Ill.: Irwin, 1983.

Robock, Stefan H., Kenneth Simmonds, and Jack Zwick. *International Business and Multinational Enterprises.* Homewood, Ill.: Irwin, 1977.

Rockart, John F. "The Changing Role of the Information Systems Executive: A Critical Success Factors Perspective." *Sloan Management Review* (Fall, 1982): 3–13.

Rowe, Frederick M. "Antitrust Aspects of European Acquisitions and Joint Ventures in the United States." *Law Policy in International Business* 12, no. 2 (1980): 335–68.

Schaan, Jean-Louis. "Parent Control and Joint Venture Success: The Case of Mexico." Ph.D. diss., University of Western Ontario, 1983.

Schnee, Jerome E. "International Shifts in Innovative Activity: The Case of Pharmaceuticals." *Columbia Journal of World Business* (Spring, 1978): 112–22.

Schwartz, David S. "Comments on Market-Structure and Interfirm Integration." *Journal of Economic Issues* (June, 1975): 337–40.

Shaw, Marvin E., and Jack M. Wright. *Scales for the Measurement of Attitudes.* New York: McGraw-Hill, 1967.

Shortell, Stephen M. "The Rose of Environment in a Configurational Theory of Organizations." *Human Relations* 30 (1977): 275–302.

Siegel, Sidney. *Nonparametric Statistics for the Behavioral Sciences.* New York: McGraw-Hill, 1956.

Simiar, F. "Major Causes of Joint-Venture Failures in the Middle East: The Case of Iran." *Management International Review* 23, no. 1 (1983): 56–68.

Simon, Herbert A. *Administrative Behavior.* 2d ed. New York: Macmillan, 1957.

SPSS-X User's Guide. 2d ed. New York: McGraw-Hill, 1986.

Standard & Poor's Register of Corporations, Directors and Executives. New York: Standard & Poor's 1985.

Starbuck, W. H. "Organizational Growth and Development." In *Handbook of Organizations,* edited by J. G. March (Chicago: Rand McNally, 1965), pp. 451–533.

Steiner, George A. "Strategic Factors in Business Success." (Los Angeles: Graduate School of Business Administration, University of California, Los Angeles, 1968).

Stopford, John M., and Louis T. Wells, Jr. *Managing the Multinational Enterprise.* New York: Basic Books, 1972.

Sudman, Seymour, and Norman M. Bradburn. *Asking Questions.* San Francisco: Jossey-Bass, 1983.

Sullivan, Jeremiah, and Richard B. Peterson. "Factors Associated with Trust in Japanese-American Joint Ventures." *Management International Review* 22, no. 2 (1982): 30–40.

Sullivan, Jeremiah, et al. "The Relationship between Conflict Resolution Approaches and Trust—A Cross-Cultural Study." *Academy of Management Journal* (December, 1981): 803–15.

Suzuki, Yoshio. "Significance of International Cooperation on Overseas Plant Construction Projects." In *International Cooperation for Plant Construction Overseas* (Tokyo: Export-Import Bank of Japan, 1983), pp. 11–21.

Terreberry, Shirley. "The Evolution of Organizational Environments." *Administrative Science Quarterly* 13 (1968): 590–613.

Thompson, James D. *Organizations in Action.* New York: McGraw-Hill, 1967.

Tomlinson, James W. C. *The Joint Venture Process in International Business: India and Pakistan.* Cambridge, Mass.: MIT Press, 1970.

Tomlinson, James W. C., and S. M. Hills. "Potential Opportunities for Canadian Joint Ventures in Venezuela and Columbia." Working paper, College of Commerce and Business Administration, University of British Columbia, 1978.

Tomlinson, James W. C., and M. Thompson. "A Study of Canadian Joint Ventures in Mexico." Working paper. College of Commerce and Business Administration, University of British Columbia, 1977.

Tosi, Henry, Ramon Aldag, and Ronald Storey. "On the Measurement of the Environment: An Assessment of the Lawrence and Lorsch Environmental Uncertainty Subscale." *Administrative Science Quarterly* (1973): 27–36.

Tung, Rosalie L. "Dimensions of Organizational Environments: An Exploratory Study of Their Impact on Organizational Structure." *Academy of Management Journal* 22 (1979): 672–93.

Tushman, Michael L "Technical Communication in Research and Development Laboratories: The Impact of Project Work Characteristics." *Academy of Management Review* 21, no. 4 (1978): 242–48.

Tushman, Michael L., and David A. Nadler. "Information Processing as an Integrating Concept in Organizational Design." *Academy of Management Review* (July, 1978): 613–24.

U.S. Department of Commerce, International Trade Administration. *Foreign Direct Investment in the United States: 1974–1980 Transactions.* Washington: Government Printing Office, 1982.

———. *Foreign Direct Investment in the United States: 1981 Transactions,* 1983.

———. *Foreign Direct Investment in the United States: 1983 Transactions,* 1984.

———. *Foreign Direct Investment in the United States: 1984 Transactions,* 1985.

Van de Ven, A., A Delbecq, and R. Koenig. "Determinants of Coordination Modes within Organizations." *American Sociological Review* 41 (1976): 322–38.

Vepa, Ram K. *Joint Ventures.* New Delhi: Manohar Publications, 1980.

Vernon, Raymond. *Storm over the Multinationals.* Cambridge, Mass.: Harvard University Press, 1977.

von Bertalanffy, Ludwig. "General Systems Theory—A Critical Review." *General Systems* 7 (1962): 1–20.

Wall Street Journal Index. New York: Dow Jones & Co., annual, 1979 to 1985.

Walmsley, John. *Handbook of International Joint Ventures.* London: Graham and Trotman, 1982.

Weber M. "Bureaucracy." In *From Max Weber,* edited by H. Gerth and C. Mills. New York: Oxford University Press, 1947.

Webster's Deluxe Unabridged Dictionary. 2d ed. New York: Simon & Schuster, 1983.

Weick, Karl E. "Enactment Processes in Organizations." In *New Dimensions in Organizational Behavior,* edited by Barry M. Staw and Gerald R. Salancik. Chicago: St. Clair Press, 1977.

———. *The Social Psychology of Organizing.* 2d ed. Menlo Park, Calif.: Addison-Wesley, 1979.

West, Malcolm W., Jr. "Thinking Ahead." *Harvard Business Review* (July-August, 1959): 31–32.

Weston, J. Fred, and Eugene F. Brigham. *Essentials of Managerial Finance.* 4th ed. Hinsdale, Ill.: Dryden Press, 1977.

Williams, Frederick. *Reasoning with Statistics*. 3d ed. New York: Holt, Rinehart & Winston, 1979.

Williamson, Oliver E. "A Dynamic Theory of Interfirm Behavior." *Quarterly Journal of Economics* (November, 1965): 579–607.

———. *Markets and Hierarchies: Analysis and Antitrust Implications*. New York: Free Press, 1975.

Wilson, John W. "Market Structure and Interfirm Integration in the Petroleum Industry." *Journal of Economic Issues* (June, 1975): 319–35.

Woodward, Joan. *Industrial Organization: Theory and Practice*. London: Oxford University Press, 1965.

World Bank. *World Development Report 1984*. New York: Oxford University Press, 1984.

Wright, Richard W. "Joint Venture Problems in Japan." *Columbia Journal of World Business* (Spring, 1979): 25–31.

Wright, Richard W., and Russel, Colin. "Joint Ventures in Developing Countries— Realities and Responses." *Columbia Journal of World Business* (Summer, 1975): 74–80.

Young, G. Richard, and Standish Bradford, Jr. *Joint Ventures: Planning and Action*. New York: Financial Executives Research Foundation, 1977.

Yuchtman, E., and S. E. Seashore. "A System Resource Approach to Organizational Effectiveness." *American Sociological Review* 32 (1967): 891–903.

Zaltman, G., R. Duncan, and J. Holbek. *Innovation and Organizations*. New York: Wiley, 1973.

Index

About the Author

J. MICHAEL GERINGER is Assistant Professor of Policy in the School of Business Administration at the University of Western Ontario. He has lectured and written extensively on the subject of joint ventures and other forms of strategic alliances.